CHASING THE MONGOOSE

By Danny Suster

DEDICATION

Dedicated to Lanny Fried, may he rest in peace, whose prodding, inspiration, and belief in me are what I needed to proceed. He was the little brother I never had until I did.

PROLOGUE

I continue to experience changes that emanate from the incongruous feelings and behaviors I've had over the years. In the expert's opinion, it'll take a year for me to experience full recovery and get back to my old self. This is a false assurance. These lingering, unforeseen emotional outbursts weren't part of my makeup prior to this illness.

I'm perplexed. My emotional state is unbalanced. Two years have passed since the surgery. Demonstrating simultaneous outbursts of sadness and joy, I'm unable to contain the emotions triggered by specific stimuli. Place a happy scene before me I choke back tears that suddenly arise as if weeping is the appropriate reflex response. A giggle of discomfort tries to break through but to no avail. The tritest scene elicits a reaction. I fail when attempting to initiate flight from the emotion. The eruption is unavoidable. Gagging in defiance, I thank Hashem for the passing sensation.

Why do I sadly cry when a happy scene transpires? Positive outcomes are the driving force, the foundation, and the gift of life endowed in a cherished stroke of chance. It's the universal spark igniting purpose and direction. Can a near-death experience alter our basic emotional well-being? Are feelings always going to align with the loss that was or the gains that might have been? Is this a consequence of traumatic stress? But wait, this is not supposed to be my life. Aren't I a miracle baby? A moral person? Or was I chasing love in all the wrong ways?

TABLE OF CONTENTS

CHAPTER 1
MISFORTUNE OF A PRISONER

I have a 7:00 am mail callout. It's about a one-hundred-yard walk from the unit to the designated open-air location. Lagging behind the others who have the same goal in mind, swollen legs will not let me keep up with their pace.

The early morning sun is intense, and the short walk is a long trek. I pause several times to gather the strength to continue. Arriving, we learn there's a wait to get situated. Under a tree, I try to avoid the hot morning sun.

Ground seating is the only available resting spot. Not feeling well, exhausted with no other shade found, I lean against a parked car in the surrounding lot.

Within moments, I'm admonished by a uniformed guard with the orders, "Move and stand under the tree." He is relentless, and my obvious anguish has no impact.

Forty minutes go by. A van pulls up, and a uniformed lady signals to approach. Taking a step, attempting to lead with my left leg, I collapse, falling forward; there is no sensation. Panicked, the unfamiliar accompanying fellows offer aid, attempting to lift an uncooperating body into a standing position.

Assuring them, "I'm okay. The leg fell asleep. Just give me a moment for the feeling to return."

The guard does not relate to the situation in any manner or form.

Supported by these mates, I'm lifted into a standing position. The walk back is even more strenuous. Falling backward and banging the back of my head on the asphalt while smashing the right knee beneath my pants, the burning, bleeding skin scrapes the cloth with each step. I slowly limp along.

The beating sun is hotter, the salty sweat showering my eyes. To propel me forward, I focus on the destination, which is only yards away. The morning community meetings begin at 8 a.m., but it is now 8:45 a.m.

A passing counselor, seeing me limp along in spite of the broadcast anguish, instructs, "Visit the infirmary after the completion of the morning session."

Little do I know or realize that today's agenda will not proceed without me. These morning meetings are held in the partitioned visiting room and have an average attendance, including counselors totaling approximately seventy. Attendance is mandatory unless officially excused.

Head hung low, shoulders sloped, cloudy eyes unfocused, I open the outer door and pass through a vestibule to find faces awaiting my grand entrance. The director questions the delayed arrival. Explaining what happened, I'm prompted to the other end of the gathering, where a stand and microphone are situated.

Protesting, "I'm injured and unable to do so," a chair is brought to me in which drops a drained, aching body.

Subjected to accusations, "You are a selfish community member who does not care about the welfare of others; censure or expulsion will restore harmony to the program."

Given the physical injury endured and my current state of mind, protesting the inappropriate timing of this inquisition goes unheeded.

With the morning agenda set, I'm forced to go with the flow. Have you guessed where I am? I reside on the lower bunk in a drugfree barracks housing on any given night more than eighty men.

CHAPTER 2.
INQUISITION

I snore when I sleep. The sounds emanating from this horn, I'm told, "Could cause the walls of Jericho to tumble down."

Of course, not cognizant of the nightly symphony, I feel guilty and vulnerable just the same. Hostility makes me self-conscious and anxious. I'm viewed as a disturbance to be shunned and rejected. In fact, in the darkness, men aggressively shake the frame of the bed during all hours of the night to disrupt the disturbance. Slumber shattered; confusion nets a fear response. Frightened, I turn to my side in a fetal position. Acceptance here is the key to survival. Considered selfish both for untreated sleep apnea and the infirmary physician's unresponsiveness, I stand accused! The act of not caring for others is justifiably addressed by the attendees with the same degree of disregard for which I stand accused. So what if I collapsed moments earlier? The authorities must confront this intolerable behavior and, if necessary, exorcize it to save the larger body for the sake of the common good.

Sitting slumped in that chair, the charges are read to me by whom, up until that moment, I considered a little brother but given his tattoo-covered muscular physique, he could flatten anyone twice his weight. The intimate discussions we comfortably shared are suddenly forgotten. Betrayal of a friend endears him to be cheered on by those who have known him for a long time. They are further advanced in the program and well-versed in how to implement its philosophy to one's advantage. A microphone is placed in my hand for all to hear a response to the charge.

The spokesperson representing the plaintiffs speaks into a microphone,

"Suster, you have demonstrated total disregard for our community. You refuse to eradicate your disturbing behavior and are hostile when we point out your lack of caring for others. The other morning, once again, I told you to rectify the problem, or I'll see to it that you're removed from the program. Your response: smirks and belligerence. This defiance shows us that you are not prepared to correct your 'self-talk' and eliminate your criminal thinking errors. What do you have to say to us about your attitude?"

The words barely break through the fog that blankets any cognizance. I'm falsely accused emotes in a barely discernible monotone.

"I've completed and submitted sick call forms to the infirmary on two separate occasions when standing at the entrance waiting for the nurse for up to forty-five minutes. As you're aware, this must occur at 6:15 a.m., and its acceptance for scheduling an appointment with a doctor is up to the discretion of the nurse on duty. It's stated on these requests that I need a test for sleep apnea. Furthermore, I stood at the infirmary entrance yesterday morning, waiting thirty minutes for the nurse, only to give up and leave. I can't help that my legs died and couldn't support me anymore. If you care and want to help me resolve the situation, you'd wait there in the early morning and fetch me when the nurse arrives. Instead, things got hostile, and here we are."

"Suster, I'm asking you once again. Why don't you show responsibility instead of demonstrating a lack of caring for others? We offer to sell you a relatively new sleep apnea unit that is no longer needed by another inmate. Acceptance would show us that you care

5

about our sleepless nights. This selfish criminal thinking error indicates that you're not ready to rectify your criminal ways, and you'll return to criminal behavior upon release."

"Acceptance of this offer is illegal. The equipment you are offering is the property of the government and, unless officially authorized, would constitute possession of contraband, resulting in a transfer to a high-security prison. Furthermore, I have not been diagnosed with sleep apnea and the need for a CPAP machine. That's your conclusion, but it's still not medically indicated. Let me ask, would you employ a breathing machine that's used its sterility compromised?"

The program director interjects, "Federal law protects a person's health privacy. We won't discuss health conditions."

I can't help but think about the illegality of their solution but do not press the point. Their righteousness is phony and self-serving, yet I stand accused. Where's the director's input? Behavior and attitude are the object lesson of the day, and I'm the reference material. There's an impatient murmur in the audience to end the interrogation with me acquiescing. We go back and forth over refusing to cop a guilty plea. Defiance becomes the issue. I'm fighting against the program's attempt to break and reprogram. I am still not feeling well. The resistance dissipates.

Agreeing to be open and acknowledge my inner struggles with criminal thinking, "I will work on my behavior."

Self-recognition indicates the program is breaking through behavioral patterns. This admission will always result in a counselor's reprieve when confronting attitude and coping issues. The session ends.

Returning to bed for the remainder of the morning, I skip lunch. Waiting on the chow line requires overwhelming exertion to perform the simplest tasks. I have no appetite. The food is repulsive.

Barely reaching the urinal in time, mission complete, I wonder, "Do I have the strength to visit the commissary?"

This is the biweekly assigned time to purchase necessities. An hour window remains for me to shop, and no designee is permitted to help. Struggling to return to the dormitory, laying down with legs swollen to more than twice their normal size, covered in pinpoint red dots, I'm cold. The purchase remains unpacked alongside my bed.

Wearing a sweatshirt over layered clothing, I start to tremble and the tremors will not stop. I refrain from visiting the infirmary because of all the previous times I approached the nurses, only to be treated superficially and dismissed. Two white-collar physician acquaintances housed in the unit respond to the complaints and insist on examining my legs.

Consulting together, they insist, "You appear to have edema indicative of a heart problem. You must immediately force yourself to see the nurses."

The counselor who that morning told me to get examined by the nurse comes to mind. I hobble to the infirmary, moving in slow motion. Seeing me, one nurse objects, claiming her hours for the day are about to end, but I interject,

"An officer sent me, and I'm very sick. Call the director and confirm that I collapsed earlier in the day, and you must receive me per her instructions. Her response, "my daughter has a doctor's appointment and needs me."

Instead of accepting the obvious since all prisoners lie, she calls to obtain confirmation and only then acquiesces.

On the examining gurney, shivering out of control, I'm pulling the sweatshirt collar up, attempting to capture exhaled breath for warmth. Temperature and blood pressure are gauged, and there's a low-grade fever of 100.9 F. The two nurses examine my legs and quietly confer with one another. Calling the medical director, who is at the main facility a five-minute walking distance away, to ask if he could join them, I hear raised voices over the phone. It's apparent he refuses to make the effort. Clearly stressed, they call him again, argue, and angrily disconnect.

One nurse says to the other, "I'm not losing my license over this."

Agreeing to override the doctor's sole authority, they summon an Emergency Medical Services ambulance. Wondering what will happen next while lying prone, I'm immobilized.

The paramedics arrive and whisk me away. "Where are you taking me?"

It's comforting to know that I'm removed from the Bureau of Prisons Health Services personnel, where I fear for my life.

"You're being taken to the new South Baptist Medical Center satellite emergency room that's technologically equipped to diagnose your health status."

Hearing these words indicates the condition is severe. The E.R. smells like a brand-new car not yet occupied. There are countless empty bays. Wheeled down the hall to an isolated cubicle, the nurse immediately presents forms to sign permitting all procedures and specifically blood transfusions when needed.

Blood drawn afterward, I'm told, "You must have an immediate blood transfusion. Hemoglobin is at 4.1, and you're in immediate danger of stroke and/or heart attack. How's that?"

Words barely audible, the nurse leans forward to hear me. "You're oxygen-starved."

"Is that why I've had no appetite?"

"Probably," is the response.

The nurse runs off. The urgency displayed has me thinking I might die at any moment. I'm scared. The attending physician says, "We're rushing you to the main hospital. We aren't equipped to provide the care you need."

Wheeled to another ambulance with IV tubes attached and a portable heart monitor resting on my chest, I'm told, "You're also in kidney failure." The information sinks in. I cry out.

"My family is unaware, and I might never see them again. They don't even know where I am. I'm not allowed to contact anyone since this constitutes a security risk."

There is no one to hear me.

Overcome with thoughts of imminent death and the tragic aftermath, I anticipate the wife's and children's pain and sorrow. If you haven't lost a loved one, you can't fathom the depth of suffering these thoughts generate. Passing through the moment believing Hashem will protect your family, faith provides enduring strength.

The moment is surreal. I anticipate a wake-up offering great relief, but there's none. I'm continuously surrounded by doctors, nurses, and technicians who   rapidly move about.

At Baptist Hospital, a member of the assigned medical team states, "You must undergo emergency open heart surgery. There's a delay until early morning as oxygen levels must be increased with constantly administered blood transfusions to minimize danger. Also, kidney failure adds to the complexity of the surgery. Since you can't pass urine, a nurse will soon arrive and insert a catheter through your penis."

Seeing the forms to sign acknowledging that I'll be heavily sedated, which could lead to death, I can't stop thinking about my family. I'm overwhelmed with worry. There's no one to counsel me. No hugs or assurances that everything will be okay are forthcoming. I'm the loneliest person in the world.

The nurse is holding the catheter, which looks like a ten-inch wire in length. She tells me, "This will hurt a little."

I'm about to jump out of my skin. The pain is sudden in the most sensitive organ. I scream out, "Are you fucking crazy?"

I can't help but moan. The catheter, attached via a tube to a plastic bag, collects the urine. I'm taken to cardiac ultrasound diagnostics and undergo other radiological procedures where the equipment could have come right out of a sci-fi movie.

Back in the room, the anesthesiologist tells me, "The surgery will last approximately six hours, and you'll undergo deep sedation. Upon awakening, you'll be disoriented for a time. In recovery/ICU, you'll find a tube inserted in your throat, and as uncomfortable as it may be, you must endure this for about one hour. You'll be intubated!"

The heart surgeon informs me, "We will saw an opening in

your thoracic cavity. A mitral valve replacement and an aorta bypass are planned. There's a fungus growing on the valve, which must be removed surgically."

Assuring me he knows what to do, "You will come out of this okay."

No time is wasted on small talk. Can't stop thinking that I want my wife and kids' hugs and comfort. I'm so alone. Stunned to see so many tubes inserted, I'm finally sedated. This long, arduous day ends.

ECG electrodes are taped to my upper body, and a heart monitor is set alongside the bed. I'm instructed that an additional portable monitor reporting data directly to the nurse's station must always be worn. Beeping sounds fill the air as the monitors report bodily functions. There's a constant urge to urinate, but soreness has me afraid. Continence took over. Red tinctured liquid finally appears in the bag. The orderlies arrive, lift me out of bed, place me on a gurney, and I'm rolled to an elevator. Prone on the operating table, I'm joking about the countless big-screen monitors mounted above that will map every move: "This must be what the space shuttle command deck is like."

The anesthesiologist places a mask over my airways, stating, "Count backward from one hundred." Within moments, I'm gone.....

Straining to open my eyes, disoriented with no sense of time or place, there's a pipe wedged, causing excruciating discomfort. Desperately wanting it removed, a reflex reaction combats the choking sensation. In a windowless room, absent eyeglasses, I see the nurse's station as a blur through the entranceway. Huge mittens encase my hands. Struggling to raise them and failing to gain the nurse's attention, I'm paralyzed. The commands go nowhere. I won't survive the pipe's intrusion; I'm trying to thrash talk, but there's no physical response. Throat dryness grinds away with each torturous breath. All I want is relief. Vitals need to stabilize before this occurs. The mittens prevent pulling at the invading connections as if I could move my arms. Frozen body glued down to the bed, I try to fight against this. The surgeon enters the room. He proclaims,

"The operation was successful, and for now, you'll remain in recovery. We completed all the planned procedures."

The pipe is removed. It felt dry and stuck; the pull irritating my throat. Wanting soothing liquid, the nurse says, "For now, ice is all that'll wet your lips." From the corner of my eye to the left, I see a prison correctional officer in uniform, charged with preventing escape, sitting in a recliner. Clever use of labor. Not going anywhere. The Bureau of Prisons is preventing a rescue attempt in case some outsider knows where they are keeping me. The family certainly is preoccupied with thoughts like, "Something tragic has befallen Dad. He always telephones, if only for a minute, to let us know he's okay."

Repeatedly asking the uniform guard to contact the family, he responds, "It's not allowed per BOP rules."

In kidney failure, the doctors fail to determine the cause. I'm informed that once vitals stabilize, there will be dialysis on alternate days. The bladder drainage bag collects urine infused with blood, a sign of diseased organs. The physicians are concerned that if dialysis is ongoing, there's a chance this will lead to permanent kidney failure and a lifetime of treatment. The nightmare escalates. I'm given morphine with the saline drip and soon drift off to sleep.

Upon awakening, my fingers are still frozen in place, just like the rest of me. Intermittently, there are projections of rabbits running across the walls and ceiling. "Is this an intentional aspect of recovery or a hallucination?" I'm so confused! The nurse feeds me Jell-O, but I'm still not allowed any liquids. The correction officer outside my door is a fixture. Ashamed to ask about the rabbits, I continuously call out to the nurses. "Please let me call my family." Fearing being dead and buried before my family learns of my fate adds stress. Incarceration is the mission; prisoner well-being is irrelevant, no matter the circumstance. Empathizing with their pain over the imagined loss, the hell with me. I'm getting what I deserve, but what about them?

Time passes slowly. I drift in and out of sleep. When conscious, ants and cockroaches crawl on the blanket and throughout the room. Disgusted and wanting to run away but unable to move, I debate, "Are these hallucinations? It's so real." Unable to physically react, the doubts force a confused silence. Thoughts run rampant. Can vermin inundate an ICU unit? The morphine eases physical discomfort, but over time, the delusions strengthen.

Accompanying other patients in this cardio unit are 3D-printed versions of visitors portrayed in black and white. They appear dressed as clergy, coming and going to visit the sick. I'm convinced this is a business-inspired plot launched by the hospital to sell patients the benefit of open-heart surgery.

It's their last hope, even when medically unnecessary. It's big business, and the hospital is recruiting customers. This place is not what it appears to be. I'm going to expose what they are. Time has stopped, yet obsessed with thoughts, the disquiet is unsettling.

Anxiety and derangement are relentless. I am moved to another section of the floor and placed under the supervision of a physician assistant.

He's charged with allaying my paranoia. I promise him that I'll transfer funds to his bank account if he gets me forbidden craved food and only then will I behave. "A Whopper would do wonders."

Convinced that a Russian plot is behind the management of care, I attempt to grasp the bed railing, then turn, flip my legs over the side, stand up, and escape.

Wearing a hospital gown with my backside totally exposed, I scheme to reach the intersection at street level, find a taxi, and go home. Rabbits and cockroaches are everywhere. Struggling to move, the alarm goes off. The aide implores me to stop before I rip out the catheters and self-inflicted harm occurs. We strike a deal, but the food never comes, only sleep.

Orly and the kids come to visit. Aleph Institute, an organization aiding Jewish prisoners, located me.

With barely any recollection of it happening, they eventually told me, "Dad, you were delirious, and if I shared the words you said, you wouldn't believe the nonsense we heard."

A pink heart-shaped pillow tells me the visit was not an illusion.

A kidney biopsy is performed. Warned of discomfort beforehand, but it's laughed off, given what I've already endured.

The cause of kidney failure is still undetermined, and the concern is a lifetime of dialysis. When a hook-up occurs, tears and sobs flow, bringing on deep sleep. I'm wiped out afterward.

The effects of the anesthesia must have diminished; the delusions are less intense. Still glued down to the bed, unable to slightly move a limb, to pass the time I focus on past choices, trying to comprehend my decisions and the events that led to this moment.

CHAPTER 3.
UNCERTAINTY

The beginning could have gone a bit smoother. This introduction to the world has made me forever grateful that I've been awarded the gift of life. Born on May 1, 1952, prematurely weighing in at just under two and a half pounds, I am about to bring changes to the family dynamic. When held, I fit into the palm of an adult hand. To visualize this, just imagine a small packaged whole chicken displayed in the supermarket meat section. Spending the first three months in an incubator at Kings County Hospital, a public facility located in Brooklyn, doesn't provide comfort to Mom, who suddenly begins bleeding and undergoes a cesarean section. We miss the initial moments of bonding. The separation doesn't allow for touch, smell, or breastfeeding. After spending ten weeks in the hospital incubator, I'm released. Back then, survival, given this birth weight, was a miracle.

Although I'm lucky to be alive, Mom doesn't quite feel the same way. Throughout childhood, I heard variations of disappointment voiced in how the birth turned out for her. It made walking difficult. Her feet and ankles betrayed her sense of balance soon thereafter. Mom was convinced it was a result of cause and effect. She made sure to let me know. She didn't plan to have a third child. The siblings are respectively seventeen and ten years older than me, both male.

Socializing with new acquaintances, sometimes in my presence, Mom shares how she foolishly tried home remedies to abort me. The words intend no harm, but given a child's tendency to be literal, they're received as rejection, evoking suppressed anger

16

and surreptitious defiance.

"Not wanted, no matter, I'm here."

Mom is resigned to bearing a third child. She prays daily that it'll be the daughter she yearns for. Convinced this will be the inevitable outcome, her mindset is that I'll carry her mother's name, Sarah Denah. During the delivery, anesthetized and soon thereafter semiconscious, her visiting family at the bedside refers to me as Sarah Denah. Often retold by Mom, accompanied by laughter, I try to distance myself from the hearing range. Separated, not meeting me until a brief time later, she's surprised that I'm a boy. Disappointed and struggling to digest the fact no one pays heed to the birth certificate issued, recording the wrong name, Danny is officially Dave! It's not corrected. Is this an innocent oversight or a sign of indifference and disappointment?

Mom is the youngest surviving sibling of twelve, and her family pranks her at times because she's very energetic and funny. Wanting to be center stage in their presence, she seeks attention. The only one to have a three-child household; everyone else has two kids. At my birth, Mom was thirty-six years old, and Pop was forty-eight. All my first cousins and my brothers are a generation older. The age differential doesn't allow for full integration. It's as if I'm there in the background, like a shadow. Older cousins offer minimal attention, and I'm treated like a cute artifact that doesn't belong. Compounding the alienation, all members of the family are Cuban immigrants, and being a gringo I'm not spoken to in Spanish. Never learning the language enhances estrangement. At family gatherings, remaining detached and distant, younger second cousins converse in Spanish. At events, Latin music is prevalent. To emphasize, my family doesn't neglect my basic needs. They're just not provided with the physical and emotional warmth a child requires. I feel I don't belong. Interacting with immediate family members, I fight for attention. Energetic, I have no outlets. Their responses demonstrate impatience, and I'm readily dismissed. Searching for reasons to assure and love myself, I feel entitled. I didn't ask to be here! To my detriment, behavioral patterns are being established by how I'm treated, but I'm just a little boy.

The household is under financial stress. A year before Mom's pregnancy, Pop entered a partnership with two fellow shoe factory employees acquainted through union membership. Their goal was to own and manage a manufacturing plant. Pop and Mom operated their own small factory back in Cuba, producing shoes up until 1948 when they emigrated. Soon thereafter, our economy was hit with a recession. Within 90 days after the start of this venture, the family's life savings were gone. I witnessed Mom throughout the years when Pop was alive, angrily blaming him for not accepting her cautious warnings that his partners were inept swindlers. She maligned him until his passing day for ending up a common laborer in a shoe factory.

Mother is obsessed with her middle son, Bernard, who is ten years older than I. As he matures and their relationship intensifies, Pop's involvement with his wife wanes. Pop shares minimal communication with Bernard in reaction to the mother-son mutual dependency.

Bernard enters adulthood, and Pop's health slowly fails. He assumes the role of secondary male decision-maker in the household. Pop doesn't have the willpower to object. Mom renders him irrelevant by consulting with her son on all important decisions.

Pop is my love source. He's a quiet, gentle, unassuming,

physically frail man who appears older than his age.

When demanding attention, he never lets me feel that I'm a disturbance. Talking incessantly, he listens. The primary response is in Yiddish, but I speak to him in English. Mom never hugs, but he does when called upon. Saturday mornings are our favorite bathing time, and if asked, he lets me join him in the tub. It's so soothing to lie in the warm water, the two of us naked, my head resting on his chest with closed eyes. Mom, afterward, toweling me down is not so gentle. Before fabric softener was available, clothesline-dried towels were rough. Pop soothes me. Mom irritates me!

Confined to the crib, passing hours alone, there's no playpen available to situate near where the family congregates. I engage in a strange habit that's soothing. Instead of sucking a thumb or having a blankie like other infants, I stroke a soft rag held between my thumb and index finger, accompanied by guttural sucking and humming sounds emanating from my throat.

Mesmerized, spending hours at it, time, or place doesn't matter. Getting older, I'm self-conscious around people. Even though embarrassed, the ritual continues. I hope they are not paying attention.

When self-engaged, I stare out into space, giving little, if any, notice to my surroundings. These moments are so very calming. When in a social setting or school without access to the "Mosh," the upper open-button portion of the shirt worn is a substitute. Flannel material is in fashion and a favorite. All shirts eventually have sewn-on patches in those spots since the rubbing creates holes. I'm so ashamed of donning these shirts around other kids. We refer to the rag as the "Mosh." The habit ends around the time I turn ten.

My wardrobe consists of hand-me-downs, always oversized and eventually patched. Play activity often tears holes in them. The knees are the most vulnerable. For holiday gift giving, instead of toys, the aunts purchase basic clothing. I'm so disappointed at not receiving toys like other kids. Physically awkward, I'm forced to wear orthopedic shoes with metal or leather arch supports to relieve my flat feet. I plead for a pair of sneakers, but Mom consistently refuses. Running is cumbersome. I'm always the slowest kid around. The first pair of Keds high tops arrive at the age of twelve. To compound awkwardness, I'm a chubby kid who finds comfort in indulging in the weekly home-baked cake Mom prepares before the Sabbath.

At Pop's factory job, he both designs and assembles shoes. Income is, in part, predicated on production. He often brings layered leather soles home that he needs to glue together. Each week, he sits at the kitchen table, pulls out his pay stub, and reconciles it against a ledger. Mom insists he does so to make sure he isn't short-changed. Leaving home at 5:30 a.m. and returning at 6 p.m., Monday through Friday, earns, on average, one hundred dollars during a productive week. Mom manages all the money. She efficiently handles the household budget to the smallest detail. We don't own a home or a car but have a hot meal every evening.

The best memories of Pop start after we move into our third rental. I'm five years old. It's a second-floor railroad flat situated in a private home. It provides me with a first bedroom, enabling the crib to go. Depending on the apartment layout, the sleeping location was either a common area or a living room. Saturdays are family visiting days for Mom when she breaks away from the daily monotonous routine of a mother and housewife. She travels by bus to her sisters, who also reside in Brooklyn. Aunt Paula, the eldest of the three siblings, is usually the primary hostess, but Mom varies the location from time to time. Aunt Paula isn't very nice to me, and the most frequent visits are my least favorite. At Aunt Freda's, Uncle Wolf provides a cigar box loaded with used pens and pencils, allowing me to forget the mosh. When at Aunt Paula's, the mosh is prominent.

My parents are of Central European origin. After the First World War, they immigrated to Cuba and eventually met. Yankel, my dad, was a bachelor tenant living in my grandparents' villa. It was a custom to accept Jewish emigres when children were married off, creating vacancies. She would often tell us that she was smitten from the moment she laid eyes on him. Her orthodox religious father objected to the marriage. They eloped. Pop was twelve years her senior. Mom was seventeen years old when she married.

Yiddish is the primary language spoken at home, and Spanish kicks in when the maternal family gathers. Their hearts remain in Cuba, and language sustains the connection. Born in Cuba, and being ten and three years older than me respectively, my brothers speak the three languages to which they were exposed. When I was a bit older, I challenged Mom about this exclusion.

Her response, "Upon arrival to this country, Leon and Bernard, wherever they went, were called Spics, a racist term for Latinos. I'm protecting you."

The answer is self-serving and manipulative. It makes no sense. When it comes to me, minimal effort is too much.

On those Saturdays when Pop is convinced to let me stay home with him, I'm the happiest little boy. Physically and verbally bouncing all over the place in constant motion, bubbly as can be, we take long walks together. Pestering to take me to the railroad yards, when he agrees, the adventure brings on butterfly sensations. Another favorite nearby location is Betsy Head Park. It's inundated with baseball fields where we watch young men play for hours on end. This was when the game became my favorite spectator sport. When the television broadcasts wrestling with Bruno Sammartino, I sit cuddling next to Pop on the sofa. When alone together, Pop, using his worn work pencil upon request, draws pictures of birds. The renditions are so exact and delicate. During these intimate moments together, I can't love him enough.

Self-reliance and creativity are the impressions that stand out from these early childhood years. Not offered much interaction or stimulation, left alone to find activities to engage with, and always wanting to be outdoors, the urban jungle alongside our home keeps me busy. Being away keeps Mom happy. Hunting insects in the pavement cracks and watching their behavior when caught is fun. Syrup-filled wax candies are the ant's favorite. The concrete running alongside our home's perimeter fence leaves space, exposing damp soil. Using my fingers, the soil under my nails doesn't deter me. Finding a worm, at first, I'm afraid to touch it with a popsicle stick, my tool. Seeing if it will interact or avoid the ants, I observe, but nothing happens. The worm hunt is the best!

I enter the backyard, climb over the adjacent wood fence, and surreptitiously explore yard to yard until an adult discovers the activity and chases me off. The goal is to move quickly and see how many backyards I can cross until caught. Tearing up knees on protruding nails that become chronically infected requires medical attention, another burden handed to Mom. Godfather Bernie, after a day at the hospital, comes to attend. She complains. I feel guilty, like I'm imposing.

Mom discourages neighborhood kid visits. This means hosting children and providing refreshments. Asking, "Can I invite friends over?"

Corresponding body language says it all. To illustrate the lack of attention afforded, our newlywed sister-in-law taught me the proper way to hold eating utensils when at the dinner table. It's a struggle. I'm six years old. In the first grade, I'm a slow reader. The teacher complains that remedial work is necessary, informing Mom, who addresses this to the best of her ability. Forbidding after-school play, she forces me to sit with her and read aloud. This structured time I perceive as punishment. Not sitting still, wanting freedom of movement, I relinquish. I know that my release will soon happen. English is her fourth spoken language, which includes Polish, Yiddish, and Spanish. We struggle, but Mom prevails.

Pressuring Mom, she has Bernard subscribe to Children's Digest. I eagerly await the postman's drop-off of the rolled-up issue. It will, for a moment, distract me from my lonely routines. My godparents visit bringing along a stack of books, and with their encouragement, I become a vociferous reader. Discovering an escape from mundane activity, reading is the choice. Nurturance and encouragement to happily tackle challenges of interest are all I want.

There is one family outing that I repeatedly shared with my parents. On summer weekends, we ride the bus and subway, heading for the Brighton Beach shoreline. For a little boy, the walk to the bus stop while lugging beach chairs as big as me is arduous. No complaints. I'm allowed to play in the sun. Pent-up energy ready to burst out of its shell, non-stop talking, I'm unable to contain the anticipation of what lies ahead. I'm having an unbridled day at the seashore to share with Pop.

"Play at the water's edge, but don't enter the ocean without an adult holding on." Mom makes it clear. She never accompanies me.

Voicing frustration, Pop is the aquatic's partner. I insist we wade out until the ocean reaches our shoulders. To keep our heads above the waterline, we jump over the waves. Frightened by the bottomless sensation of not feeling the ground beneath my feet, I hold on to Pop for dear life. He allows it. Becoming accustomed to the water and dunking within feet of Pop, he lets go, and treading water is real. Realizing this, I swim underwater towards him. Salt stinging my open eyes reveals adventurous possibilities. Courage drives me to swim between his spread legs until there's no air. His presence is my anchor. This quickly becomes a favorite game. Diving for seashells challenges me to push onward, reaching beyond my limits. Afterward, I wash and stack the findings in a plastic bucket to take back home at the end of the day. Constructed sand walls, no matter how tall and thick, are always erased by the afternoon's rising tide. The waves show no mercy. Resistance is a losing battle I will never win. Acceptance is eagerly stomping on the mounds to assist in a quick demise while I'm filled with happy moments that are at odds with home life.

I'm a sickly child. Suffering from chronic allergies and seasonal hay fever renders breathing difficult. My sinuses are forever clogged, nostrils dripping with secretion, and sneezing fits come in waves, yet I'm a non-stop ball of energy. At the back of the school bus, King of the Mountain is the morning conquest. Always on the move during snow days, it's impossible to contain me. Even with my fragile health status, nagging continues incessantly until surrender releases me to the outdoors. Climbing up snow mounds, rolling in the snow, and fighting over who's the conqueror results in contracting pneumonia each winter for over five years before I reach the age of ten. After a play session, I'm soaked to the bone from slush and ice and red-faced like a tomato. I return home, and before I take off my slush-packed rubber boots, Mom admonishes me for my wild behavior.

A burden, Mom continuously complains that she has no choice but to deal with my illnesses. Regularly at the doctor's office and convalescing at home for extended periods, she efficiently attends to me but shows little warmth. Pediatric allergy shots occur bi-weekly. Mom follows her beliefs regarding what it takes for her family to consider her a caring mother. Initially, I resisted. The lack of sincerity troubled me, and I felt unloved. Afterward, I acquiesced. Appearances are so important! Her phoniness makes me not like her.

I have the simplest toys. When I turned three, my godparents gifted me a tricycle and a little red wagon with which I ventured everywhere. The toy box consisted of a cardboard carton mustered up at the local grocer. I loaded it with toy soldiers, my favorite, a spinning top, yoyo, string for a cat's cradle, pick-up sticks, crayons and coloring book, soda bottle tops to play skelly, jacks, a deck of cards, marbles, and Spalding rubber balls. Receiving the first board game at the age of seven as a Hanukkah gift, Candy Land, I played alone, assuming the roles of multiple players, making do, passing the hours. Discovering DC comic books at the corner candy store, I would pester Pop to give me a quarter to buy and collect them. It's that or baseball cards.

In pre-kindergarten, I'm enrolled in the Hebrew Education Society's summer day camp. Mom doesn't want me to spend long, supervised days around her. Bernard is a counselor there and resents my presence. Assigned to a group of older kids, Mom makes it clear that he's responsible for me. It's the first day of attendance.

Having never been away from home, I break down sobbing, "I want my brother. I want to go home."

Arriving to see what's up, rather than offering comfort, I'm berated as an imposition and called a "Nudnik." Wanting the apple of Mom's eye to love and approve of me, seeking his attention and acceptance, I'm dismissed as a pain in the ass. A consoling female counselor intervenes.

At the local public school, when mischievously seeking attention, I don't comply with the kindergarten teachers' rules of behavior. Her disciplinary response to civilize me condemns me to the darkened classroom clothes closet. A toothpick anchored sweet potato class project housed in jars of water is my company. Their exposed root systems demand attention. I'm released. Instead of being humbled, I point out how well the roots are growing from the buds. To egg on the disruptive classmate's reaction, I challenged the disciplinarian standing before us. When I hand Mom a note from the teacher, now informed, she picks up her heavy orthopedic shoe and hits me with the heel. Running into the bedroom closet, she is right behind me, all the while swinging her arms and screaming in Yiddish about the shame I cause.

Defiantly, I shout back, "Hit me, hit me again, I don't care. It doesn't hurt. This is who I am."

Repeatedly knowing that fatigue will overcome her rage before she inflicts damage makes resistance unbreakable.

A new family moves into an old friend's house around the corner on Amboy Street, and I become street friends with a boy who's the same age. Invited to his basement playroom and gym, there are eleven foster and adopted children, ranging from toddlers to adults, residing in the house. This becomes an oasis where I'm wholeheartedly received. Offering to share their food, I decline. I only eat kosher food like I've been taught. The thought of doing otherwise makes me feel guilty for disobeying. Boxing lessons, gloves and all, and a pool table are our activities. The color of skin means nothing to a little boy, but it could be affecting Mom.

It's November. I'm in the second grade. A devoutly religious uncle arrives from Cuba and boards with us for a week. His grandson attends an Orthodox religious yeshiva in Crown Heights, Brooklyn. He lives in the dorm as a homeless student; his parents and two siblings are back in Cuba. Out of nowhere, Mom fabricates a racist story conveyed in Yiddish that "shvartza" kids in the school hallway had pressed a knife against my stomach. To protect me, she's enrolling me in the Lubavitch Yeshiva. The world flips on its head. Familiarity is ripped away.

I cry to sleep, thinking, "I'm being manipulated against my wishes that don't count anyway."

For religious studies, I'm placed in a first-grade level class. I have no training in the Hebrew language alphabet. All students conduct prayers in Hebrew. I'm pressured to address this shortcoming while sitting disinterestedly in class. During religious studies, while playing with jawbreaker candies, one inadvertently gets stuck up a nostril. Attempting to remove it pushes the ball further.

Distressed, I shout out to the Rabbi, "Help, I have a jawbreaker stuck in my nose."

Hearing this, the class goes wild. Punished, I'm forced to stand up in front of the class, situated between his back and the blackboard, face forward with hands raised straight up over my head while remaining in place. Each time fatigue takes over, he swings back, hitting me with a pointer. The nasal drip slowly melts the candy. In short order, it falls out.

Loving the attention from riveted classmates, I shout out, "Thank you, Rabbi, you helped get the jawbreaker out of my nose."

In response and to discourage this kind of outburst, he places me over his knee and spanks away.

School bus pick-up is around 6:20 a.m., and I return at 6 p.m., Sundays included. Friday, school days end at noon in respect to the Sabbath that starts at sunset. On this day, Mom provides a quarter and sends me off to the local movie theater. It's a mile hike from home. Instructing me not to return before 5 p.m., the weekly ritual keeps me out of her hair while she cleans the apartment and prepares a special dinner in honor of the Sabbath. Mom's priority is to keep me away from home for as many hours as possible. We're not a religiously orthodox home but rather a family that follows tradition over edicts. Attending an Orthodox school, whose teachings aren't adhered to at home, creates contradictions as I question and challenge the values taught at school. Reflexively, I dismiss authority. The structure is undermined, and the lack of attention at home only compounds doubt about which values to adopt. Confusion reigns. I'm in conflict.

Reading skills rank me at a higher level than my classmates, but arithmetic is difficult. It's hard to focus when straying mentally. Bernard, under Mom's control, establishes the expected academic standard. He's going to be a doctor. She forces Bernard against his wishes to tutor. Sitting next to him at the dinner table, terrified of the repercussions when not catching on quickly, he stabs me with the front end of a fork, breaking skin. I struggle to comprehend. Apprehension and fear only make it worse. His impatience and hostility intensify the panic. During my infancy, Mom often forced him to change my soiled cloth diaper. He harbors resentment not at Mom, who assigned the task, but at me, the interloper. He can't refuse Mom's requests. Facing his anger, which I take as rejection, I can't manage the possibility of failure. My self-esteem is already on shaky ground. It causes me to avoid challenges. Wanting a big brother, I am always in the way.

Sunday, upon returning from school this eight-year-old is sharing the dinner table with his visiting older brother and family. Someone asks, "Why don't you question Pop's absence? How don't you notice?"

From their somber tones, I surmise the worst and bawling breakdown until Leon explains his whereabouts.

"Pop had a heart attack, and we took him to the hospital, where he's taken care of. He smokes unfiltered Pall Mall cigarettes. His medical history includes both high blood pressure and high cholesterol. Let's hope he'll be okay."

With that announcement, life never feels the same. Living in constant fear that I could lose Pop at any moment, I have frequent nightmares that awaken terror hidden in the night darkness. Dreams of monstrous bears stealing children's parents away and causing them harm seem ever so real. Shaking under the blanket and wetting the bed, there is no one to turn to for comfort. I'm ashamed. Mom's solution is to place a plastic cover between the mattress and the sheet. Pops recovers and returns home. The nightmares are less frequent.

I like to hide under my bed or in a dark closet. The tight

space envelops me in privacy so I can feel apart from Mom and Bernard. I'm an appendage. I want to escape. I'm angry with them for making me feel this way. Hiding in the closet, I rummage through Pops' outer garment pockets, searching for forbidden-to-touch coins. Finding a quarter, trembling, I take it, knowing it's wrong. I tell myself, "You're a good boy, but they don't treat you nicely, so I'm going to take Pop's money. He loves me, won't punish me, and I deserve it."

I quickly hide the money.

Now an incessant reader, books provide my solace and haven. After being introduced to the public library, I find myself visiting, lingering, and reluctant to return home, spending hours at a table perusing the card catalogs. Looking up at the tall stacks, I explore the shelves organized by subject category. Bernard introduced me to the librarian and arranged for a library card in my name. When I put the card away, I feel important; it's my first personal possession. Other than watching silent cartoons on Saturday mornings, reading is my main distraction, with coloring books and crayons coming in second.

Around the time I turn ten, we relocate to Luna Park co-ops located in Coney Island. Our eligibility and acceptance are based on a household income assessment. This is a state-subsidized cooperative earmarked for working-class, middle-income families. Even with our meager family income, Mom saves up the two-thousand-dollars deposit required. It's Sunday. Mom and Bernard are completing the required paperwork at the management office. I discover Joel and Jeffery, who are my next-door neighbors back home on Newport Street. They await their parents. They're going to move to Luna Park housing. I'll have immediate friends in this new, unfamiliar place. We'll reside two blocks from the beach and Nathan's Famous. Mom has Bernard select the new location. The alternative under consideration was in nondescript Williamsburg. This is the first high-rise exposure I've ever experienced. Residing on the seventh floor, it takes weeks to get accustomed to the height. The walk to the elevator on the open-air fenced shared terrace has me pressing against the wall and shimmying along. Seeing this brings Bernard immense joy. His teasing is relentless.

Climbing the monkey bars and playing around as ten-year-olds do, Eric, a new classmate, shows up. He starts picking on Jeffery, Joel's older brother by two years. Jeffery is mentally challenged, and this is realized when he speaks. His physical movements are awkward and not smooth. Eric starts to target and victimize Jeffery, and I tell him to stop. Ignored, emotions begin to seethe. Joel, the younger brother, watches, remaining passive. Coming to the victim's defense, fighting ensues. The cruelty stops, but I walk away sporting a blackeye. Physically defeated, I won for Jeffery's torment ends. Eric and I strike up a friendship. He turns me on to naked Playboy photos kept in his dad's night table drawer.

Entering the fourth-grade class at the local public school, although secular learning at the yeshiva is limited to three hours a day, I'm ahead of the math curriculum. Bernard's cruelty achieved the desired results. I'm so proud and happy running home to share the news. The school day ends at 2:15 p.m. This schedule is good for only two weeks. Once again, a lie is perpetrated to return me to the long days of religious schooling. The yeshiva previously attended refuses to send academic records to a public institution. Their position is that a Jewish child must have a Jewish education. I don't believe this. Again, I'm manipulated by Mom. How accommodating Mom must feel. Her disregard for what I want says it all! It's all about her.

For just a moment, I gained community, friends, team sport participation, and belonging. In the blink of an eye, I'm an outsider who resides in a housing development containing hundreds of kids who attend the same school. Friends happen at school. Team sports are prolific on Saturday mornings. Kids choose sides, and I'm left out to watch, considered an unknown entity. No one knows what I have to offer and bring to the game. Orthodox religion makes Sabbath sports participation prohibitive. Yeshiva classmates live in the community. If I'm seen playing on the Sabbath when they're headed to the synagogue, the Rabbi who also teaches at the school will be informed. I'll be shamed. Torn between religious orthodoxy and secular needs, I'm angry, frustrated, and scared of reprisal if the edicts are disobeyed. This concern seals my ostracization from secular peers. I keep moving in a direction not of my choosing. The loneliness intensifies. Longing to participate, I'm resigned to spectator status. I'm on the inside looking out. I'm not happy!!!

Each morning, with a bus pass in hand, riding public transportation to the yeshiva, the bus stop is alongside Nathan's Famous, which is one block from the boardwalk. Catching the same scheduled bus regularly, I befriended the bus driver. He allows me to hug the white line while standing alongside him as he drives and picks up passengers. Eating up the attention, carrying on incessantly about baseball or whatever comes to mind, I talk off his ear. He taught me a geography word game to keep us engaged. Here's an adult, albeit a stranger, accepting a little boy's outreach. Every morning, I look forward to seeing him. I'm very in need of connecting with someone. I'm more comfortable around adults than kids, so it's easy to connect with them. It makes sense, given the quality of family visits I'm exposed to.

The yeshiva raises charitable funds by giving each student a can with a slot on top. Jewish tradition requires donations before the Sabbath. The "pushka" is placed at home for family members' contributions. Taught that giving charity to the poor is one of Hashem's commandments; God blesses givers. The Rabbi offers prizes to participating students at a ten percent value of the money collected. I determined the amount by valuing the items on the rewards list.

Industrious, wanting to make a mark, on Friday and Sunday afternoons, thanks to early dismissal, I ride the subway, walk down the carriage's aisles, can in hand, and solicit the sitting passengers asking, "Would you donate to the Yeshiva of Brighton Beach?"

Fearlessly, I pass through the subway cars of the moving train. In those days, the doors between cars weren't locked. The sound of the grinding wheels against the metal rails and the resulting odor released by the friction entice me. Sparks fly, wheels screech, and the bends are sharp. To minimize my being thrown about, I loosen my legs at the knees and ride the train, imagining I'm on a surfboard. Sometimes, a wheelchair-relegated man with no legs is escorted down the aisle seeking charity as well. After a while, the can is heavy, and I return home.

The Rabbi, impressed after a successful Sunday, is informed that there is no longer any interest in the prize list. I'll continue the effort if he gives me ten percent of the proceeds. It's a fair trade. Mutual greed prevails, and this becomes an ongoing after-school enterprise. Mom says, "You're a born businessman," encouraging me to continue this eleven-year-old's questionably appropriate activity.

Rebellion in the classroom challenges the Rabbi's discipline.

Surreptitiously gaining the attention of students who sit nearby, engaged with tic tac toe or passing notes, egging on misbehavior, spitballs fly freely. I'm an enigma that the teachers view as a lost cause. Learning basic ancient civil Jewish law in Aramaic, as scribed in the Talmud, we're exposed to contract disputes, property rights, and critical thinking. Students who memorize the language written on both sides of a page, called a "blot," and recite this in front of the class receive praise, recognition, and a one-dollar bill from the school principal. To disprove the prevailing view, with Pop's tutoring, I present orally to the astonishment of everyone.

Bathing in the glory of the moment, I feel angry and defiant, the unspoken declaration: "I can do this, but I chose not to. It's not who I am or what I want." With Pop's help, for a moment, I overcome the fear of failure.

Riding the subway, I observe passengers with ears glued to transistor radios, learning that JFK has been shot. He's my hero. People sobbing, I end the afternoon pursuit and urgently head home. For days frozen to the television screen, trying to reconcile the taking of this wonderful man's life, I'm comprehending death for the first time. I'm just a boy watching our nation grieve. John Jr. is riveting. I'm drawn to this now fatherless boy.

Bored, I start a postage stamp and coin hobby. Having no funds, I soak stamps off mail received and pester family members to open their change purses so I can review the models and dates of their coins. Vacant postage stamps and coin albums stored on Mom's bedroom closet upper shelf serve as introductions. Filling in the blank spaces is a treasure hunt. Pursuing stamps with full fervor, I develop proficiency in naming and locating every country appearing on the world globe. There were a lot fewer than today.

Each year, attending the high holiday services with Pop, he prays while I roam the synagogue with the other children. These are my favorite days since it's just me and Pop sharing time. Mom attends the service a bit later, sitting segregated in the women's balcony. On the morning of the Jewish New Year, Pop awakens sickly, announcing that he isn't going to the prayer service. This is alarming, given the importance of holiday participation. Days later, he's hospitalized. I don't see him again for three months until mid-December when he returns home. He has lung cancer complicated by heart disease and has suffered another heart attack. Inhaled glue vapors used to assemble shoes, coupled with Pall Mall usage, contribute to the illness.

Pops' return home is of short duration. His health rapidly fails. Listening to the struggling breath and the unavoidable wheeze reverberating throughout the apartment, these moments are torturous for both of us. His frailty and lost invincibility break my heart. Understanding that he is dying, although no one bothers to prepare me, speaking with Mom out of his hearing range, I implore her to take him back to the hospital. "Mom, I can't take it seeing and hearing Pop breathe like this." Unable to cope at home, he returns to the hospital.

Godfather, who's a physician on staff, takes me to see Pop at the bedside. Children visitation at the hospital is forbidden, but he breaks the rules. I surmise he knows Pop's life is ending. Sadness and silence engulf the room. I stand alongside, dwarfed by the surroundings and intimidated by the tubes, needles, and the enormity of the moment. I want to cry but don't.

Mom wakes me during the wee hours of the morning with instructions not to attend school. I'm left alone. She and Bernard leave for the hospital. Reawakening hours later, huddled under the blanket, there's a knock at our hallway door. Aunt Freda is standing there, speechless, and enters hesitantly, her head bowed.

Looking at her sorrowful face, my crackling words emote, "Aunt Freda, don't feel bad. It's not your fault you need to tell me that my Pop is dead."

I'm barely able to stand. Crushing weight is pressing from within. Uncontrollably crying and sobbing, I rest my head on the kitchen counter, thinking of her discomfort and awkwardness during the worst moment of my life. That hospital visit was the last time I saw Pop. Pop died on January 2, 1964. He would have turned sixty in March.

Mom and Bernard return home. I open a paper bag found on the dining table and look at Pop's personal possessions, finding his wedding band, eyeglasses, and wristwatch. Anger and sadness consume me. I witness a shattered, demonstrative mom feeling sorry for herself while ignoring my presence. Angry with Pop for leaving me alone in this world, I have no one to turn to for a hug and feel that I'm in the way. The burial and initial mourning period lasts seven days. I'm offered no comfort. At the grave, I'm coached to read the mourner's prayer and drop small rocks on the coffin. Mom is propped up by her sisters, their reverberating hysteria drowning out the mourners' prayer. Love seems so complicated. Mom and Pop never demonstrated affection for one another. Now, she cries uncontrollably. Certainty is gone. We face the unknown.

After the funeral, I'm granted the opportunity to sleep over at a school friend's apartment two floors below ours. What a relief to escape the morbidity hovering in the air and not being an intrusion. President Kennedy and now Pop are gone. Longing and loss smother the present so that only memories and emotions remain. The crying and grief morph into deep-buried anger. Tears now gone don't resurface, no matter what the circumstance. I'm bitter.

Nathan and David, the twins, are a haven. They attend the yeshiva but are a year ahead. The family is receptive despite continuous intrusions, and they soon become a surrogate home. We forget the time playing board games. Pokeno is a favorite, with Risk coming in second. Miriam, their mom, wants to introduce Maxine, her daughter, to Bernard. It's their dream, and they want my help. Is this why I'm always welcomed?

Their neighbor, Aaron, owns a supermarket on Mermaid Avenue. He collects a myriad of consumer discount coupons in the daily cash register. He offers home employment where I sort the coupons by manufacturer for reimbursement. He wants to help. In front of the television, the work is tedious, but the Beatles on Ed Sullivan are a perk. The money helps Mom who appreciates the effort. "You are a natural businessman."

With Pop's death, I became an obsessed philatelist and numismatist. After school each day, I visit a local hobby shop that specializes in these items, stare at the displays for hours at a time, and converse with the owner who answers endless questions. This keeps me away from home, where I don't want to be. I often purchase stamps to justify the attention demanded.

Soliciting charity on the subway trains, the amounts delivered are impressive. If the Rabbi wants it to continue, we must renegotiate, and compensation increased to twenty percent.

Before handing over the charity box, I slightly bend open the slot and empty the coins, searching for rare models and dates. I can't help but think, "These are now mine." During recess, I hear coins rattling in the Rabbi's overcoat pockets that bulge from excessive weight. He left the coat hanging on a hook opposite his desk when exiting the classroom. I sneak back and, within seconds, extract a fistful. Fearing capture, I run unnoticed and rejoin the class line. We proceed to lunch. Driven by behavior, I don't want to stop, the results provide enrichment, which otherwise is so rare. Stealing breaks the rules, but I have no regrets. Self-talk justifies the behavior by rationalizing,

"It's no coincidence that I deliver coins, and his pockets are bulging with them. If he can steal money meant for charity, then I deserve to dip into his pocket and do the same. I'm entitled."

It's afternoon. The Rabbi confronts me and orders, "Empty your pockets now." Scattered on his desk are coins worth a couple of dollars. I can't adequately explain the source. Taken to the principal's office, I am expelled and sent home with a letter addressed to Mom. She forces a confession. Explaining how I stole funds for the stamp hobby has left her speechless.

The following morning, at the principal's office; frightened, spilling out my guts, I admit to stealing. I bow my head not to look at Mom when told to. I'm ashamed of what I might see. Her disgust, anger, and rejection are clear as day. The punishment:

"Report directly home each day after school, and you're never to participate in these hobbies again." Home before the Sabbath commences, the medical school student visiting for the weekend scornfully chastises me, "Don't ever try to speak with me after the disgusting behavior you engaged in."

Ashamed, in bed, not wanting dinner, I can't look at either

one of them. Throughout the weekend, lying there, I escape in books. I miss Pop.

As the designated family member, I'm given the responsibility of fulfilling Jewish law. I now include mourning prayers, remembering the deceased in the three-times-per-day, seven-day-a-week service. I never fail to attend. This obligation continues for eleven months. At school prayer services, I'm the sole person to stand up in the congregation and read aloud the mourners' prayer. I was eleven and a half years old when Kaddish began. I'm self-conscious of the fact that I'm drawing attention and wish I could hide away. Longing for and loving Pop so much, there's no hesitation. When leading the service, standing at the podium, I punch the surface vigorously, expounding on the prayer. Knuckles swell and bleed from scraped skin. The chest pain has no bounds. It's so intense.

Summer has arrived. I'm sent to a religious orthodox sleep-away camp that consists of male-only participants. My godparents at Chanukah time gave me a tin box with thirty dollars in coins so I could fund summer camp. It's for the deposit required. The orthodox community subsidizes the trip. I'm classified as an orphan. Longing for home, the need for comforting familiarity outweighs the excitement of the awaiting unknown. Introduced to nature, noisy insects and the heat make sleep difficult. During these endless hours, I recall memories of Pop. Dedicated to improving swimming skills, the pool is a favorite. Here, gravity has no effect. Bad feet, overweight, and all team sports aren't gratifying. I'm not having fun. Mom and Bernard extend the three-week session. No one asked if that's okay with me. Completing another cycle, I earn a certificate as an intermediate swimmer. The achievement doesn't offset the longing for my bedroom and the familiarity it provides.

Counselors discuss the escalating Vietnam War and their concerns with the draft. Questioning the morality and imperialism of American foreign pursuits, many plan to be conscientious objectors. Several individuals say that they would relocate to Canada if they were recruited. The veracity of our leaders is a concern; their policies are challenged. Issues outside the home affect young people for the first time, raising their consciousness. Exposed to events outside the home, the world expands.

Bernard visits on weekends to pick up clean laundry and a week's worth of prepared meals. Mom gave him no choice but to become a physician. We share a bedroom. Lights are on during endless hours of study. In the next bed, I indulge in reading books throughout the night. During summer vacation, the library permits borrowing up to ten books per visit. Indulging weekly, primary interests are biographies and World War II historical literature. Understanding the events behind the Holocaust and trying to fathom why a nation would annihilate six million Jews and a total of fifty million people makes no sense to this young mind.

This happened only a few years ago. It feels so real, like it occurred yesterday. If Mom and Pop had relatives residing in Europe during those years there, they are forever unknown. Unanswered thoughts about them are always within me. These thoughts never stop.

Opening one of Bernard's geology texts, I'm introduced to paleontology and discover that our planet formed several billion years ago. This contradicts the biblical teachings I'm subjected to. Challenging the hypothesis,

"How did science reach this conclusion? It dismisses everything taught about God and creation."

He explains, "Radioactive carbon 14 testing measures the level of isotope decay over time, revealing the age of fossils."

My beliefs now undermined, my foundation dissipating, "Do you believe in God?" "I'm an atheist," he responds. "What does that mean?"

For the first time, I hear the words atheist and agnostic. Their meaning is food for thought. I can't dismiss this perplexing news. All I've been taught about religion is suddenly false. The rituals we practice don't address the questions I have about God's existence. Bernard relishes my anguish. Immature cognition confuses me when I question respect for authority. He dismisses as absurd any belief in a God. I now question the sanctimonious teaching of the Rabbis. Certainty morphs into unbridled doubt.

During the summer season, Bernard heads up to the Catskills, working the ranks, first as a busboy and later as a head waiter. Having saved every penny, upon returning home, he counts and hands the cash to Mom for safekeeping. Money is designated to fulfill Mom's insistence that Bernard becomes a doctor. He doesn't enjoy the fruits of his summer efforts. Compliance is the only acceptable behavior. Mom makes sure I understand. How she raises us is all about how our achievements reflect upon her. Mom is proud of Bernard and lets everyone know.

ON THE OUTSIDE, LOOKING IN

CHAPTER 4.
ON THE OUTSIDE, LOOKING IN

Mom has to find employment. Family assistance will only last for so long. Sol, a butcher married to Aunt Paula's daughter Rosita, drops off meat and chicken products regularly, feeding us for two weeks at a time. Compensation is never expected. The extended family discreetly provides money. Mom finds work with a non-profit that hires people with disabilities and the elderly who are in financial distress or require occupational rehabilitation. Our apartment is within manageable walking distance. Earnings are based on production or piecework. A five-hour day is required, but if quotas aren't met to clear the floor of inventory, extended hours are available. Industrious Mom takes advantage of opportunities every chance she gets, and even though compensation is minimal, it adds up. Now that she's earning money, Mom proudly pays Cousin Sol upon delivery.

On a shortened Friday schedule, I'm home alone. Howling winds rattle the outer door to the hallway. The turbulence causes the steel door of our apartment to also vibrate. Hearing the sound, I'm convinced that a perpetrator is trying the door, and I'm in danger. Petrified, no one appears when looking through the peephole, and there's no response to repetitive shouts, "Who is it?" I overreact and phone the police. Accompanying the officers to the apartment entrance, the neighbors are not very sympathetic. The authorities conduct a casual search of the rooms to see if anyone else is present. Mom returns home and is hysterically angry because of the negative attention the neighbors witnessed. I've embarrassed her. I was scared.

At work, Mom operates a machine that applies heat to plastic sealing that is then pressed onto a cardboard backing. Razor blade blister packaging is a frequent item. She misjudges the movement of the insertion tray on an unfortunate day. Two of her right-hand fingertips burn off. Grafting is needed. As long as we reside together or when I visit, my chore is to scrub the dishes. I feel bad about her condition. I hate doing it. I've got it down to science. Efficiency expedites escape. The aluminum pot surfaces have to shine, no easy task given their natural dull finish. Steel wool and kosher bar soap do the trick.

I purchase food and household items under strict remote supervision. If an item is not to Mom's satisfaction, it's returned to the store. Correcting the error takes more than a mile to get there. The trek calls for pulling a cart to manage the bulk and weight. No longer viewed as in the way, I'm assigned duties.

"With Pop gone, the effort will ease Mom's difficulty coping with household burdens. She needs help."

Compliance gets me praise. I start to think that it is my obligation to be involved.

Mom's regimen represents the epitome of efficiency. Her fastidiousness and resulting cleanliness know no bounds. Each task follows a daily schedule that never veers. There's a designated time for laundry, ironing clothes, cleaning the toilet, or targeting the carpet and vinyl-tiled floors. Every week, she wipes the plastic covering on the upholstered living room furniture with a vinegar solution. Shabbat mornings, when sleeping in late, having read until the wee hours of the morning, Mom uses a dust feather, making certain to noisily strum the metal Venetian blinds. What nerve! The kitchen utensils are customarily kosher. Meat and dairy products never meet. Meals follow a rigid daily schedule. Mom's choice repeats on the designated day of the week at the same hour. Familiarity provides homeliness. Certainty after the loss of Pop is elusive, but the rituals are comforting as they wrap around me.

I've been preparing for my Bar Mitzvah Torah reading for months. I'm unexpectedly told that since we can't afford to celebrate like all the other kids, we must forgo the event and limit ourselves to the religious ceremony. I'm crushed. Seeing my godparents and sharing the news, they offer to fund a modest party and invite all the relatives. Having been through so much emotional hardship the past year, I want and need attention. The party takes place at the development's community center recreation room. The ambiance is institutional; the floors are linoleum-tiled, and the walls are beige-painted cinder blocks. The attendees are happy to participate, making the evening a success. Mom's family comes to celebrate Mom, whom they love, but I'll take whatever I can get. We share the limelight. Anticipating opening the presents: I'm looking forward to the evening's end. Liquor is available, along with cold cuts and complimentary side dishes. A keyboard and electric guitar provide music.

I don't like myself. The kids in my circle are mean. They taunt and make fun of my facial features, laughing and declaring that I resemble a chipmunk. Labeling and name-calling ensue. Full cheeks and a chubby torso add to the effect. Humiliation from imagined ugliness dismisses any chance of loving myself; it's hard to do when the people around you don't! Staring at the bathroom mirror, feeling ugly, I envision the description internalizing contempt. I wonder if any person can ever love such an ugly creature. Bernard reinforces the thought, constantly commenting on the blackheads and acne scattered all over. Mom forever points out how handsome her son

Bernard is while not being inclusive. Overall, I feel socially handicapped, inferior, and detached from others. With limited physical capabilities, I'm unable to hop, skip, or jump. Running fast is impossible. There is no spring or bounce when I try. Feet slap the ground with each step. Basketball, roller, and ice skating aren't possible with weak ankles. I can't rely on them to support me. Flat feet are declared the cause. Resigned to these limitations, the condition strengthens my break with the local kids.

Fear of academic failure and resulting anxiety trigger a flight response from study time. Avoidance makes me nervous, but I can't focus. Convinced rejection awaits if I don't measure up to Bernard's success, and guarantees failure. These thoughts cause my brain to freeze. I see words and equations that I can't process or retain. Existence is intimidating. I'm uptight all of the time. Mom didn't want me, yet my glass is half full. I'm here! Wanting love and appreciation from my family, I'm not feeling sorry, but anger lingers.

When Leon marries, I am the five-year-old top hat tuxedo-dressed ring boy at the ceremony. Afterwards, he moves with his bride to a new apartment in the same development where his in-laws reside. Since Pop's death, they often have me sleep over on the weekend. Their young, disabled son needs a playmate.

Leon, a contracted electrical engineer during the early years of his marriage, accumulated enough savings to join the newest suburban frontier in Manalapan, New Jersey.

They had a German Shepherd puppy that, even after death, is my loyal best friend. Love given in only the way a dog can love a person is timeless. Liebshun hasn't seen me for eight years. Knocking on the door, picking up the scent while I await, she's overwhelmed with excitement, realizing I've suddenly appeared. Memories of her still live inside me. It prevents me from ever having a housebound dog. A dog's needs require freedom only the outdoors can provide.

Occupancy takes place. The developer has not begun landscaping. Thorn-infested brush and foliage over the property line limit the backyard to a ten-foot depth. It extends an additional eighty feet but with no access. Liebshun by my side, excited to explore the woods, forcing through the dense foliage, I find a brook housing salamanders. Breathing, smelling, and touching nature; butterflies flutter around and inside me. The damp scent of the fallen leaves intensifies the sensation. With no tools available other than a hack saw and blunt hatchet, I cut down and clear the land up to the property line, at which point the treeline begins. This allows easy access to the woods. The cut rubbish scattered about will, over time, degrade into mulch. Wearing cut-up jean shorts, a tank top, and sneakers, I tan in the relentless heat and humidity with bugs everywhere. I'm tenaciously chopping away. The task takes multiple weekend visits. Complete, theirs is the only ranch house out of a row of a dozen properties to have the clearing. On the next visit, I see all the yards bulldozed to match the effort.

"Did I inspire this?" For once, I feel proud and important, but I wonder, "Was this just a dumb undertaking, or am I the hero?"

Eighth grade behind me, I intend to enroll in the local public high school. Mom challenges the plan, but I'm adamant. It's late afternoon. Exiting the shower wearing cutoff jeans that are side-slit, I'm also bare-chested. Responding to the chiming bell, I look through the peephole. Standing there are two orthodox Jewish men. Half-dressed and screaming, I refuse to open the door. Sequestered in the bathroom, I shout out,

"I will not go to the yeshiva high school. Tell them that when they have girls there, I'll go. It's time I went to school with girls and learn what they're all about."

Approaching Mom, I'm hysterical.

"After completing the ninth grade, I'm legally able to drop out of school. If you force me into a yeshiva again, I swear I'll be a high school dropout. The law requires that I only complete ninth grade to not be classified as a juvenile delinquent."

This declaration of independence releases the fury inside me. I've had enough of Mom's self-serving manipulation.

I'm seeking summer employment at the Coney Island amusement rides, but being young and with no connections, I'm turned away. Inquiring about options, the beach chair and umbrella people hire kids my age. Working papers are required. Their office is situated in a corrugated metal hut located under the boardwalk. It reeks of rust, must, and mildew. The elderly owner explains that earnings, in part, are based on a surcharge paid by the renter of ten cents for each chair and umbrella carried to their chosen spot. That's mine. Every second bay has a rental hut, and access to these areas is restricted. The hooded reclining wooden chairs are heavy. Often, I'm asked to carry up to four chairs and two umbrellas at a time. Reaching the chosen spot, I arrange the recliners according to the customer's specifications. I anchor the umbrella by placing its pointed metal post against the sand and rock back and forth as it penetrates downward. The depth reached determines its stability against the sea breeze. Over the summer, chubbiness melts away. The burning heat from rubbing sand against the balls of my feet aggravates my plantar warts. Determined to overcome the heat beating down on burning feet, I tell myself, "I'm earning money I'll use as I see fit." Resolve and attainment motivate my ambition and independence. Ringing in my head is Mom's mantra, "Your pocket is your best friend." Other than the family, Mom doesn't trust people.

Since commencing high school, I've had adjustment anxiety. Children attending parochial schools do not have a ninth-grade available. Continuing education means choosing enrollment in either a religious or a neighborhood public high school. Orthodox Jewish schools don't combine genders. I'm physically near girls for the first time! The occasional encounter with a female cousin didn't prepare me for this. I'm clumsy, shy, and a strange novelty. Most of the females are of Italian and Irish descent. They're a click. I attribute their distance to my unattractiveness. When the girls turn away, my clumsy social skills aren't considered the cause. I'm strange and foreign to them, not of interest to their behavior, and they give me a cold shoulder. I remain an observer during the school year. They remain busy with themselves.

Entering the teenage years, family interaction emphasized academic achievement and what they considered a noble career choice. This was life's objective. The dynamic defines self-worth and position in the family hierarchy. Little room is left for personal preference. The doctor is the ultimate goal. Achieving this brings about unbridled recognition and cult-like worship. The number of physician and medical student family members cannot be counted on just two hands. The opening greeting at all family functions is not, "How are you?" but rather, "What are you doing with yourself?" The undercurrent is quick judgment and a sentence of irrelevance if you aren't toeing the line. Competition and the inevitable rejection for not conforming would alienate any independent-thinking person. I don't want to be around these relatives. This dynamic defines Mom's way of relating to us.

Ninth grade complete, I show a cumulative A-minus report card, but the next year's outcome reflects all the frustration and unhappiness held within. Questioning the world's actions and internalizing social injustice corroborates harbored anger. Ramparts magazine, with its leftist radical orientation, is a ritual reading. Holden Caulfield, a troubled teenager described in "Catcher in the Rye" is a hero who identifies people's nature as phony. "Damian" by Hermann Hesse reinforces this understanding. Misplaced bourgeois middle-class values are the root cause of our discontent. Not knowing where to begin or how to bridge this conflict, I'm juxtaposing my values against the world around me, and the alienation intensifies. Where do I fit in? Rejecting the priorities I'm conditioned to pursue energizes nonconformity. It wears on me for all to see. Grades suffer as a result.

I reach out to my friends' parents, sharing with them the unhappiness my family causes me and how I feel I don't fit in. I feel guilty doing this. Mom often lectures me about not sharing home life with anyone, but I proceed anyway. I hope that empathy will provide relief from my sad state. The general response is, "Your mom loves you." What else could they say?

Summer approaches. Mom informs me that a lady residing on an upper floor wants to talk about a job. Knowing I'm fatherless, she offers me a messenger boy job for the summer months at the printing company where she's employed. Its name is Portland Printing. It's located on Canal Street, just off the Holland Tunnel.

"You're required to deliver printed proofs to different establishments in the Wall Street area and fly to Boston, where they serve a major client. Dress appropriately!"

Working from 8:30 to 5:00, receiving minimum wage, I can't

believe this good fortune. I'm just a kid. I'm flying unaccompanied to Boston, and I'm paid for it! Without a hitch, I wake up every weekday hoping I'll be on the shuttle. Often, the return flight to LaGuardia airport is delayed. We circle the airfield while I watch the night lights below and accrue hours of overtime pay. I'm so lucky!

Saving every penny, now that Bernard is gone on weekdays, I decorate the bedroom to my liking. Declaring independence, the decision is mine alone. I'm turning this space into my room. I trash the uncomfortable wire platform beds acquired before birth and purchase a metal frame, mattress, and box spring. No more hand-me-downs or lifting spirits by rearranging old furniture. Installing deep brown colored wood paneling on one wall, painting the opposite wall tangerine orange and the sides pale yellow, rust orange wall-to-wall carpet covers the vinyl tiled floor. I add a matching desk, chair, and dresser. At last, I possess my own room. The summer savings are now depleted. I'm not sorry. The changes bring a fleeting freshness, even as chest discomfort persists. It never leaves. Not for a moment.

Bernard visits on weekends. It's assumed I'll own these occasional sleepovers in Pop's bed. Mom rules. Bernard is king! I'm pissed. This loss of privacy and minimal separation from the person I disdain makes my blood boil. Blaming Mom for Pop's death, remembering how she'd berate him, negating any positive energy within, emaciating his spirit, and sealing the distance between them repels me. Presented a fait accompli, not taking my wants into account, feeds resentment.

Our ninth-grade English teacher doubles as an art instructor. Charged with grading the math midterms, she asks, "Would you like to be a volunteer aid assisting me?" It's Spring break, and we meet in the school's sculpture studio. The teachers are active there, and the most impressive-looking is Ron, the sculpture instructor, whose full-bearded, beatnik appearance stands out. He's friendly, engaging, and funny. While the others don't take notice, he bellows, "What grade are you in?" "Ninth grade," I meekly announce. "Freshy" follows. Walking the heavily trafficked hallways near the studio, whenever he sees me "Freshy," is yelled with a big smile to follow. I have an adult I can look up to and enjoy.

In the tenth grade, failing geometry, the midterm test grade barely reaches fifty percent. Ignoring all the homework assignments, it's impossible to apply even one formula. The New York State Regents finals are approaching. Passing Mr. Lerner, the elderly geometry teacher in the school hallway, he voices disappointment, riding me for poor class performance. Arrogantly replying, "I'm going to get a hundred on the State Geometry Regents exam in eighteen days."

He laughs. Pissed and motivated to take this as a challenge to prove him wrong, I want his approval and respect. Purchasing two geometry regent exam prep texts, I've memorized every formula studying day and night. No mathematical equation remains unsolved. I'm confident. Fear of failure doesn't come into play. Other than sleep and a quickly served meal, this is all I do. I'm determined to master the material with the test day lingering overhead. Nescafe instant coffee is a great help.

The exam concludes. Leaving the classroom, I'm certain the grade is one hundred. Running into Mr. Lerner, he announces ninety-four. I smirk, "Told you so," but I'm disappointed, believing that I made no mistakes. The ninth-grade English teacher charged with grading the exam allows a glimpse in the department chairman's presence. There aren't any conceptual mistakes, just missing simple signage on equations that cost points. The results confirm I'm a distracted underachiever. After a while, I forget all the memorized geometric formulas. It's like it never happened.

I enroll in the sculpture studio elective. The demand for this class is so great that acceptance requires Ron's approval and junior-year status in good academic standing. With no experience, I'm also in an advanced oil painting class. Familiarity evolves trust. Reaching out, revealing a sterile home life, the instructors become mentors. Under their tutelage, I spend after-school hours in the studio classrooms.

I'm comfortable around artistic peers, but connecting doesn't come easily. Ron is very outgoing and particularly receptive when classmates discuss social issues that are relevant and disturbing. His approach helps foster camaraderie among us. I slowly develop a bond with the group. The American literature teacher, Bill Cook, is a backwoodsman banjo and ukulele player who offers alternative views. He performs Woody Guthrie's songs often in the classroom. He's my grade advisor and confidante. Turning to him addressing anguished moments, sharing inner struggles, and looking for support, one visit, we discuss teenage sex and tongue kissing. He suggests, "Fornication and tongue kissing aren't any different. Think about it," leaving me to ponder the point. These nonjudgmental interactions are a breath of fresh air when the disconnect at home is unsettling. Obsessed with escaping the pain, suicide is a consideration. Opening their hearts and appealing brownstone homes make visits frequent. So is the chest discomfort.

I take frequent long walks enveloped in isolation at the ocean's edge. Even on the coldest days, the frigid blowing offshore winds I easily ignore. Anxiety and chest constriction constantly fuel thoughts seeking deliverance. There is no break. It's a strain interacting with classmates as the malaise doesn't ease. Bridging the disconnect seems unfathomable. Social skills are lacking. I see peers busy with exaggerated self-discourse. I judge them to be disregarded. Wanting to escape the pain, the teacher's refuge is a haven of understanding without commensurate lectures or critiques about sorrowful self-indulgence. Reaching out to these mentors achieves no relief. Talk doesn't dissipate emotions but engenders a connection with another human being. The assurances are helpful, and their mentorship is irreplaceable.

During class, I complete a still-life painting of inanimate objects placed on a wooden pedestal arranged at different angles. This oil is the first I've ever rendered. Months of devotion are behind the effort. Bathed in tones of red and ochre, the hues convey a melancholy emotional state. The painting instructor who guided me, Mr. Fletcher, decides to enter the rendition in the National Scholastic Art contest. One afternoon, I'm summoned to the principal's office, where I'm congratulated for winning a gold medal. It's announced at the weekly auditorium gatherings before the student body. The immediate family hearing the news does not bother to react with more than a simple acknowledgment. Art will lead to a wasted future. It's best not to encourage me with accolades. They hold on to the belief that this endeavor undermines any chance I'll pursue a medical career.

Learning the craft of wood carving, the first piece completed is an oak wood bust wearing a primitive African mask. The log is two feet in height. Not to share tools, I purchased a set of German-manufactured chisels, a mallet, a pouch, and various sharpening stones. It's the same brand used in Ron's home studio. When carving in class, the Italian forged tools splinter tiny fragments of the blade's tip. The steel is soft. This is the only German-manufactured product I've ever acquired. Ron carves tall totem-like shapes, reaching ten feet in height. Noguchi and Brancusi influence his approach. He's also an art instructor at both Pratt University and the Brooklyn Museum. His tough love and regimen help me hone my skills and believe in my untapped capabilities. The next completed piece is an abstract inspired by Henry Moore. It's carved out of a mahogany rectangle of two-by-twos glued together to form a block. The medium's softness allows me to replace the mallet with my palm for precise carving. After fine sanding, the silk-like finish, dust smell, and calloused hands provide refuge from the angst. Three completed forms emerge from the block mounted on a shiny black plexiglass platform. Both sculptures are selected for an exhibition presented by the Board of Education at the Lever House on Park Avenue. Receiving recognition and interacting with classmates slowly improves.

The art crowd click is my social refuge. We're anti-establishment. It's the era of American imperialism in Southeast Asia. Our passion in reaction to the wrongs in the world demands social change via organized mass protests. Peace and love are our mantras. We challenge social norms, claiming that traditional family life, centered on material possessions, brings us to this sorrowful state. A sizable portion of the nation is in an uproar. Radicalized against family and State values, we, the objectors and refuseniks, are nonviolently fighting back. We're seeking a shift in society's direction and actions. Belonging to this movement helps offset my disconnects, but it doesn't relieve the gnawing chest tightness. Attached to the ideology, but not the participants, being a nonconformist, I wear it proudly. The approach applies to individuals on both the left and the right. Our movement is righteous, but the participants are phony. Judging them comes naturally. Lonely, I rely on recreational drugs, specifically marijuana, to fill the emptiness. I'm on the outside looking in.

CHAPTER 5.
FIRST PUFF

After school dismissal, Paul, a classmate, invites me to join him at his parent's residence. Posters and a day-glow-covered bedroom, illuminated with fluorescent-inducing black lighting and incense, infuse the air, hinting at unforeseen possibilities. In comparison, my bedroom is sterile.

Jefferson Airplane heightens the senses as Paul asks, "Do you want to smoke some hash?" Pulling out a little brass pipe, he places a round mesh screen in the bowl and adds a small piece of brown-colored substance. Our peer group indulges in recreational drug use, but I never do. This is a first. I'm apprehensive that his parents will walk in and discover us. He assures me, "My parents allow me to smoke at home." Bedroom décor and personal appearance only confirm the declaration. Watching him and following suit, he smoothly holds the smoke in his lungs. Toking, choking, coughing, and fighting the smoke, forcing its way out of scorching membranes, after a few attempts, the drug's effect takes hold. Paul's voice is distant when he speaks, the glowing posters nearer and brighter, the penetrating music causing thoughts to drift with the senses. Generously, he offers to lend his pipe, which includes hash, to continue floating away upon arrival home. I think about how fortunate Paul is to have accepting, open-minded parents who love him as he is. Through his embrace and generosity, I feel we're friends.

Grooming less while letting hair grow, a seldom laundered sweatshirt, bleached jeans with an embroidered sewed-on cloth strip running down the outer side of one leg, and John Lennon-modeled gold metal-framed glasses are the signature look. The guise is hippy, but I consider the style to be politically based, not reflecting the communal norm of peace and love. Any similarity is a coincidence.

Reaching out to my godparents; they've always voiced concern for me. Riding the Long Island Railroad to North Woodmere, I'm hoping for a receptive audience with whom to explain my state of mind. The unhappiness is always there. Empathy might bring relief. To survive, escaping home is imperative. It's not a wholesome place for me. Chest knotted, I worry, "Will they understand and help?" I'm so preoccupied with my state of affairs that little else manages to enter my thoughts.

At the front door, Bernie derides my appearance, as it symbolizes a rejection of his aesthetics and values. He can't help but voice disdain. We sit at the dining room table; his response doesn't reflect any appreciation for the alienation and disconnect I bear. He only reinforces the anger I hold for the adult world. His solution is to:

"Complete high school at Clark Academy in upstate New York. Adhering to their imposing military discipline, the structure will straighten you out. You'll be far from home. You must agree to abandon any interest in painting." Rejecting the generosity and leaving in dismay, all my hopes are dashed.

Weather permitting, in the evenings, the art click gathers one block away from the ocean at Sea Breeze Park. Our schoolmates primarily reside in three major housing cooperatives located nearby.

We gravitate to the open grass field distant from the walkways, seeking a modicum of isolation. Sitting without blankets on the fresh, damp grass, forming a circle sometimes small and often large, we sing anti-war songs accompanied by an acoustic guitar. Frankie, a strikingly handsome man of small physical stature, sporting wavy, shoulder-length black hair and a beard, shares his great voice, entertaining us throughout the evenings. We sing along. A waif, he's addicted to barbiturates, and as the evening grows late, he nods off while our prodding attempts to keep him focused. Sometimes, we fail. He's referred to as Frankie "Roach" since there's always the end of a joint protruding from his lips. His romantic aura has the girls crooning for him, and on any evening while under his spell, he has the choice of the group. Joints are rolled and passed around as he serenades the crowd. Judging these shallow girls offering their bodies to a pill-popping drug addict is behavior I don't get. Life seems so unreal. Where do I belong?

Love at first sight strikes when Paula passes in the hallway. Enquiring around, discovering she's a merit scholar honor student eligible to graduate after completion of the eleventh grade, bubbly, vivacious, and outgoing, I attempt to befriend her enticing smile. I'm immediately taken. She's overly friendly but applies brakes when eliciting a response. I'm in her control. When she brushes me off, my resolve doesn't waver. Like an addict satisfied yet wanting more, I'm intoxicated when we interact even briefly. I won't accept her rebuffs. I find her hot.

Paula seeks attention from other male students, and in loneliness, I begin to stalk her. She is unaware. I wander about aimlessly, pain-driven, walking the distance until landing under her bedroom window, looking for any sign of a presence. Riveted and confused, not knowing what to expect with pressure gnawing inside and no relief in sight, I rationalize,

"At least I'm killing a little bit of torturous time. Don't know what else to do. There's no escape. I'm not sure how to respond if a neighbor appears." Searching for a sign of life or form of comfort, feeling foolish and frustrated with no solution forthcoming, I head back home.

The gnawing in my chest intensifies. It propels my behavior to persist despite no contact. Buried in thoughts,

"Having met her parents, who were holocaust survivors, my chosen fashion revolting, running into them again would be disastrous. They want their daughter to have nothing to do with this slovenly-looking hippy." Rebellious, she won't release me from her hold. She's a cheerleader, not my crowd. Knowing this adds to my doubt that she would like me. Nervous energy and lust propel me in my pursuit.

The war in Southeast Asia continues to rage relentlessly. The dead and wounded American count reported on the evening news is a daily reminder that our imperialistic government wantonly annihilates innocent citizen populations while rationalizing away the cost of our young men's lives. I don't identify as a hippy and reject the quid pro quo as a government hater. Not part of any group or dogma, attachments aren't in the lexicon. Although nonconformism is my prime concern, I join in anti-government demonstrations. The authority's rationale behind its foreign policy pursuit is another example of a phony world's disdain for people, both the enemies and ours. Negatively affected by events that are not part of daily life is the new norm. The draft hangs over this generation's heads. I'm angry and disenfranchised, not belonging anywhere.

The school administration scheduled annual elections for class officers during the spring semester. Disturbed, I decide to be a candidate for student body president. The intent is to raise the political awareness of my peers. I'm an unknown. The platform I present ignores extracurricular and after-school programming. I believe students will use their vote to make a political statement if their consciousness is raised. How could it be otherwise? The oration presented at the general assembly has to be faculty-reviewed and approved. The speech undergoes a heavy rewrite. It's deemed an inappropriate lecture lacking enthusiasm or pertinent to student life. One of three candidates, when it is my turn to stand at the podium, scared and intimidated, I freeze up but struggle and fumble through to the conclusion. The most important rhetoric was edited to erase the words meant to motivate the audience. Having flopped and ashamed of the performance, I now walk the corridors, avoiding eye contact.

Summer has arrived. The alternative hangout, populated by "the crowd," is the Trump shopping center. Selective attire serves as a symbol of our alternative values. This strip of twenty shops has a large supermarket situated at the far end. We gravitate to car hoods and the sidewalk curb. Fried rice takeout costs .95 cents and is shared as its most popular when stoned. It helps alleviate the munchies. Teenagers stealing pills from home medicine chests and night table drawers make their wares available. The purchasers are indiscriminate in their choice regardless of fashion style. Tuinal, Seconal, and Phenobarbital are available for five dollars a pill. For a month's time, these are the drugs of choice. For a quick kick, capsules are opened, and the powder is snorted. Nostrils on fire, taste bitter, and throat dry, I stumble about, slurring words and uttering nonsense. The effect numbs anxieties but doesn't eliminate them. I'm an embarrassment to myself. On mornings with no memory of arriving home, unable to wake, I eliminated these narcotics.

Exercising a degree of self-control instead of considering ending this miserable life, apparently, death isn't yet an option.

It's the summer of hippiedom. Experimentation with hallucinogens is our rite of passage. Kramer sells me a dose of Sunshine acid that's on a paper tab. He's a National Honor Society member and my Timothy Leary. I'm impressed and trusting. It's known that LSD is cut with speed. It causes the users to grit their teeth. Strychnine is also a danger. Folklore claims that in this form, the dose is pure. The effect I get is an intense heightening of senses but no hallucinations. With no exposure to rock music or lighting effects, the trip is limited, but others indulge in meandering about glassy-eyed and elated. A friend experienced psychotic episodes that remained after the drug wore off. She zealously found God. Weighing the drug's potential serves as a warning to be cautious, not flippant. Repeatedly, I witness these changes in kids and apply brakes to slow me down.

Our daylight playground is Bay One at the far end of Brighton Beach. There's a barrier that limits access allowing for privacy. Bohemians sunbathe there, so it's natural that young freaks gravitate to the spot. Most wear cut jeans, tie-dyed t-shirts, and flip-flops. Getting high on pot, basking in the sun, riding the waves, joyously throwing frisbees, we're in touch with nature and free-spirited. These images reflect our character.

At Bay One on July 20, 1969, while ingesting a gelatin capsule packed with magenta crystal, I'm told, "It's mescaline." Les, who is in his early twenties, married to Kari, is mature, reserved, and serious. I trust him. The supplier is a ringer for Sonny Bono, hairdo, mustache, long hair, and all. It's an overcast day. Sitting directly on the sand with no covering underneath and losing all sense of time, the drug takes effect. It starts to rain. Not noticing the approaching storm, I'm prompted to seek shelter. Walking off the beach, grains of sand appear as huge boulders towering above that I weave through to reach the boardwalk. With guidance, I arrive at Les and Kari's nearby residence to ride out the trip.

The hallucinations are mellow yet exhilarating, as are the physical sensations. Music assists. Everything is pristine, colorful, and sharp. There is no sense of time. The rain subsides. Sun breaking through the clouds, I head home knowing that Mom expects me at the scheduled dinner hour. Walking along the streets, looking upward at the vista, I see images of the heavens, angels dancing around the scales of justice, and a bearded 'god' like figure. The sun's rays bounce off a gold-gilded throne. Alongside scales of justice, God, upright, hovers over the entire scene. The vision accompanies me on the two-mile walk. The hallucination was so real to this day that it's vividly recalled.

Reaching home, sitting withdrawn opposite Mom, I attempt to appear normal, eating a favorite steak and rice dinner. It's an ordeal. Throat constricted, no saliva, unable to swallow the charred, well-done steak; it is the consistency of leather. Mom takes notice but says nothing. Scrubbing the dinner plates and broiler pan, when done, I escape to the park.

Frankie and I hook up and head to Les and Karis' place to watch a man's landing on the moon. Crowded around the television, we explode, exhilarated as Neil Armstrong says, "That's one small step for man, one giant step for mankind." We smoke pot, spaced out, mesmerized, sharing pride in our country in spite of its imperialist adventures. We don't stop carrying on about how wonderful the moon looks in black and white. The mescaline trip taken earlier that day was so pleasant I purchase five doses from Les. Available only in magenta powdered form, I visit the local pharmacist to purchase empty capsules. When popping one tab doesn't do the trick, I drop the remaining four at once, but to no avail. The images I search for are elusive. This is the end of tripping for me. What a wonderful day July 20, 1969, is for all the world.

It's the summer of Woodstock. I have no money to purchase an entry; I must be there. Frankie feels the same. We enter a pact to travel together and convince Les and Kari that we're accompanying them in their psychedelic-covered Volkswagen van. We depart the Brighton Beach neighborhood on Wednesday morning. The concert is scheduled to begin on Friday evening. Arriving, we park in an open field, a short hike from the campgrounds closest to the stage area. Les and Kari, being nature buffs, pitch an igloo-shaped tent that sleeps four. Providing us with a small two-man tent, after setting up base camp, I wander off to explore the larger site.

Fantasy fashion, naked children, and colorful, psychedelic-covered vehicles, including recycled school buses, are everywhere. The organizers haven't erected fences where the performance will be held. Communal groups construct the stage and tower housing the sound systems. There's constant movement as they progress towards the Friday deadline. A beautiful young woman wearing an open suede leather vest with no underlying cover grabs my gaze as she stands alongside a redecorated Merry Prankster communal bus. I'm thinking, "Frankie has got to see this!"

Returning to our campsite, Les brings out tarred black goo that he claims is opium. Sitting in their tent, Les passes the pipe around, and within minutes of the first puff, I'm floating off into the distance. Next consciousness: dawn has arrived. Within a damp sleeping bag squished alongside a covered bundle, awakened by bladder pain, I desperately need to pee. Groggy, struggling to get out of the tight space outside, facing this gray morning, I proceed to hop onto warm mud piles, squishing through my toes. It's chilly dawn in the Catskills, and I'm grateful for the effect. Coming back to myself gingerly after the night before has me in a fog. Needing an outhouse, there aren't any, so I relieve myself in a secluded spot. Wandering to the nearest pond and finding naked people bathing in this natural setting, stripping down, and joining them even though there are no means to dry off, engaging in this newfound abandonment of inhibitions supersedes all concern for absent comforts.

Returning to the tent, Frankie introduces me to the half-naked, suede-vested woman spotted the day before. She just spent the night sandwiched between us. Given Frank's Italian lover-boy successes, this isn't a surprise. Gloating to Les how I luckily discovered and enjoyed the warm mud piles, I'm told, "It's cow shit." Instead of laughing with them, I want to crawl into myself.

Life magazine publishes a commemorative issue dedicated to the Woodstock festival, and our free-spirited pixie appears in a solo photo dancing and sporting the open suede vest. Coming across this picture, I'm thrilled knowing that the world is introduced to the young lady with whom I shared a tent while comatose. This, I imagine, was a celebrity moment.

Paula attends a summer camp in Monticello, not too far away by hiking. Obsessed thoughts intrude. I'm ordained to search for her no matter what. Loneliness propels me even though so many people surround me. There's no respite for even a little while. Destination reached; upon arrival, I'm told, "Her group is camping in the backwoods, so she isn't available." Trekking back under the hot afternoon sun wearing leather sandals, my feet blister and turn raw. Physically uncomfortable for days, I'm forced to wonder if pursuing unrequited love is worth the effort. I'm resolved not to relent.

Behind schedule, fences to prevent gates from crashing still haven't been erected. Stepping over the trampled chained links lying flat on the ground, I find an unoccupied spot three hundred feet up the inclining hill facing the stage. The concert hasn't begun, and this is the closest I'm going to get.

Limitless numbers keep streaming in. Pot is everywhere. Strangers pass around a constant supply of joints. Previously attending concerts at Billy Graham's Fillmore East in the Village can't compare with the unfolding event. Richie Havens, the opening act, controls the crowd. Civility and neighborliness enable total strangers packed together to peacefully share this happening.

Enjoying act after act, the two-man tent is not very restful. Sunday morning, as rain threatens the sky, I manage to locate a ride back to the city, but Frankie remains behind. Surrounded by people, detachment hovers stronger than ever. I'm withdrawn and lonely. Burnt out, I'm grateful to leave before the masses later that day exit all at once.

Foregoing the Sunday afternoon acts, thunderstorms threaten with no shelter available. Mud is everywhere. Hunger is an issue, and the uncertainty of available food is a concern. Lying on my bed, I sleep until the next day.

CHAPTER 6.
LEAVING HOME

Bernard relocates to Los Angeles to complete an internship as part of his curriculum. The emotional distance between me and Mom intensifies. Anger is readily shown by both sides. My pursuits aren't making her proud; she steadily complains to Leon, my older brother, and her sisters. "He's heading down a shameful path." A year has passed. Bernard plans to drive cross-country, returning to New York City. He's been accepted into a radiology residency program at Albert Einstein Hospital. My godparents agree to fund a one-way ticket so I can accompany him on the long trip. The rational I present,

"It's not safe to drive alone three thousand miles." The unspoken agenda is to be alone with him, bond, and reveal Mom's true selfish nature.

"Bernard, she doesn't love us. Mom exercises control so that we satisfy expectations that impress her family. Our achievements are her accomplishments. That's all she cares about."

Driving along Route 66 heading East, I fantasize about living in the popular television show. Few stops are taken; the trip is completed in three days. I want to linger, but to no avail; he's impatient. We've now agreed that our mother is a selfish parent. From that point onward, when together interacting with or discussing Mom, we commiserate and complain. This common ground supports our newfound friendship.

It's November. Bernard flies back to LA for a ten-day vacation. The depression, unabated, is crushing. Feeling all alone in this world, the stalking continues only to increase in frequency. Daylight leads me to Bay One, where, head bowed, I traverse the windblown, ice-cold shore looking to burn time. I associate passing each second with anguish. Hating home life with pain gnawing in my chest there's no escape; suicide is the thought. Searching inward for answers, finding no solution, I'm tormented.

Sunday arrives, and Leon's family scheduled a visit for the early afternoon. My sister-in-law, disliking Mom, always manages to be tardy. Since Pop's death, Sunday afternoon visits with Mom are mandatory. Leon insists against his wife's wishes. The early afternoon promised arrival never happens. They float in at any time. Eager to see them, deciding not to go out, every few minutes, I jump to the window and search for their car, musing, "Where are they already?" Boredom and loneliness control the hours. I stare blankly out the window into the distance. Parallel to the Belt Parkway beside a mammoth Brooklyn Union gas tank, the barely flowing, polluted Coney Island Creek depresses me even more. The indentation where I'm prone on the carpet in front of the television marks the time.

Pissed off by this disrespectful behavior targeting Mom, I leave, heading for the shoreline. Hours later, returning for dinner, the visitors anticipate my arrival. Leon worked up complains about my lack of grooming and overall appearance. Derision spills over into the political arena. He's a caricature of Archie Bunker. Nixon and Agnew are his inspiring heroes. Angrily, I state, "This look is an anti-establishment protest for all that's wrong with our country."

Referencing corrupt vice-president Agnew, Leon's response heats up the air between us. Mom serves food, and the argument escalates into threats. Accusingly, I blurt out, "Obviously, Mom has talked about me while you waited and has you all riled up. If she continues, I'll end up leaving home even though I'm not done attending high school."

His aggressive response is, "Get out now." "This isn't your house," I scream back. Pointing disrespectfully at Mom, I say, "Let her throw me out."

The audacity of these words still rings in my head. We both rise. I'm punched in the face, pushed against the wall, and pummeled. Falling to the floor, shocked, instantly, a cheek swells, and an eye socket turns black.

Not saying a word, scared for my life, I telephone Paul. "My older brother beat me. Can I come over?" It's a forty-minute walk in the sobering, chilly night air. My face and head hurt. Hitting rock bottom, traumatized, physically stunned, and aware of the depression worn like a neon sign, I don't think it's right to bring this disposition into a friend's home. Not lingering, the next day skipping school and walking along the beach mulling over options, I conclude that the next step is to share the altercation with Bernard. Returning home, screaming at Mom, "Don't dare even look at me," I await him. It takes two days. Given our recent mutual conclusions about Mom's priorities, empathy is expected. Triggering Leon doesn't help her explanations. Bernard views him as a bully.

I correctly anticipated his stopping in to see Mom on the drive back to the Bronx apartment. Hearing the outer hallway door open, I jump to our entrance and greet him by pointing to the blackened eye and start to sob. He asks,

"What happened?" "Leon finally did what I told you he threatened to do, and Mom was the instigator." Pleading, "Bernard, I can't stay here another minute. Please take me with you!"

"Danny, give me a minute to come inside." Speaking Yiddish, they start arguing. Bernard turns, appearing perplexed, seeing the desperation, "Danny, give me tonight to settle in, and I'll pick you up tomorrow."

I leave Mom behind. During the drive, Bernard doesn't offer conversation. An hour passes. In either direction, the subway commute from the last station in the Bronx, where I am now located, to the Brighton Beach school stop takes two hours. The train pulls up, not heated, at 5:30 in the morning after parking overnight in an outdoor train yard. I shiver to the bone. The hard plastic seats are ice cold. Returning late afternoons, I often purchase takeout hamburgers at White Castle and then walk half a mile to the basement hovel. When arriving, I warm up the tiny basement studio by turning on the gas oven and lighting the pilot situated underneath with a match. The bedroom has just enough room for two narrow beds, a night table placed in between, and a small white dresser. There are no windows. It's the start of winter. My graduation is ten weeks away.

After the first night, I don't see Bernard for days and don't know his whereabouts. Searching in the bedroom dresser for pot, I notice an odd appearing envelope. Hesitating to invade Bernard's privacy, I curiously open and read the insert.

It's a letter from a psychiatrist addressed to the Selective Service stating, "Bernard Suster is a practicing homosexual and draft exempt." Shocked and crushed by the knowledge, I see him as a non-responsive, aloof, female-attracting stud. He's my male role model, even though we never in any manner reference the other sex. We leave the subject to our imaginations. A virgin, I now question my sexuality. When a young yeshiva boy, I mutually fooled around with members of my own sex when we curiously explored our anatomies.

These recollections cause me to doubt gender preferences. Arriving, a few words are exchanged. Lying on his bed, back turned to me, he forms a fetal position.

"Bernard, what's wrong?" I intuitively ask. "I can't tell you, and if I do, you won't understand." "Does it have to do with you not coming home the last few nights? Where have you been?" Struggling for words, he doesn't answer. "Bernard, I know what's wrong." Looking at me confused, I continue, "Don't be angry. Looking for pot, I found a letter from your psychiatrist addressed to the draft board."

He sighs in relief and starts to cry, the secret revealed, a weight off his chest. He now has a confidant other than the psychiatrist. He explains,

"The last few nights I spent at a bathhouse cruising naked men. We roam freely or pose in cubicles and, if there's mutual attraction, engage in impersonal sex. Inquisitive,

"When did you know you were gay?" "Danny, didn't you notice that since I was a young boy, I never missed a Tarzan movie starring Johnny Weissmuller?"

Our bond strengthens. He has an accepting family member who's also angry with Mom. Protesting this sexual orientation's illegality, the Stonewall riots happened six months prior. It's customary for police to raid gay establishments. Societal norms reject and shame homosexuality. Gays begin to fight back. They are coming out of the closet, asserting their natural right to be themselves. Adding to the depression and anti-establishment anger, this news causes me to feel completely lost. I'm trying to discover and adopt behaviors that seem the right fit. Virginity is troublesome, nourishing doubt and poor self-esteem. Marijuana is a companion helping to drift away from all the uncertainty and commensurate worry. I smoke whenever the opportunity comes my way, even though it's a crime. Breaking the law is unsettling, but I rationalize away this behavior since relief is paramount.

Pushing through it all, determined to persevere, I make it to graduation. The pre-dawn wake-ups, walks, and train rides in the frigid air are a benchmark to draw on when the going gets tough. Considering the ceremony superfluous, I don't attend or have a photo taken for the school yearbook. I matriculate at City College, a branch of the City University of New York. City residents attend tuition-free. This is my school of choice. The campus is in the Morning Heights neighborhood within walking distance of the Harlem community and Columbia University. The student body is more radicalized than at the other public campuses. This appeals to me.

We are relocating from Pelham Parkway to the Grand Concourse. A one-bedroom, Bernard has his room, and I sleep on the living room sofa. Most nights, he visits the bathhouses. Living in the Bronx, far from the neighborhood I know the isolation is absolute. Exploring Fordham Road, the window displays lack the ambiance of Brooklyn shopping. It's alienating. The fashion styles are not cool. The Brooklyn identity is missing. Familiarity is gone. The Bronx Botanical Garden offers a respite. It substitutes for the ocean surf. Bernard brings Larry home. Soon thereafter, he moves in and often naked struts about immodestly. This brings more discomfort. Graduating from smoking weed to my being wasted, blocking out uncertainties, and adding cheap sherry to the mix only deepens the darkness, vomiting the result. The bathroom sink overflows and I'm disgusted with myself. I'm miserable.

I receive a State-subsidized student loan. Desperate and without consultation, I rent an apartment further south on the Grand Concourse. The building and apartment are old and run-down, but were once stately. A couple of days after signing a lease and paying the agent, I explore the surrounding area. Discovering boarded and abandoned buildings nearby and failing to cancel the contract and receive a refund, the agent keeps the money while releasing any additional obligations. Escape is elusive. I feel like a fool for being so impulsive.

Devastated and longing to leave, I book a charter flight to join my peers when summer arrives. I'll enjoy the summer months hitchhiking across Europe. Starved for experiences, it would be good to get away from the situation.

Bernard and I never had an outing together, nor did he ever ask me to join him. Before Woodstock and the Fillmore East, I'd been a spectator at only three public events: Godfather taking me to see Barnum and Bailey's circus when I was seven years old, a Police Athletic League-sponsored outing at the Polo Grounds to see Willie Mays play center field for the NY Mets, when the pigeons bombed the PAL baseball cap just received, and at the age of fifteen Godfather took me along to watch the last game played at the old Madison Square Garden. The game versus the Red Wings ended in a 3-3 tie.

CHAPTER 7.
INDEPENDENCE

The school year ceases prematurely when the Ohio National Guard shoots and kills demonstrating anti-war students at Kent State. A mass protest at City College, inspired by the radical Students for a Democratic Society at Columbia University, takes to the streets. In solidarity, we shut down the campus and march down Amsterdam Avenue to join in. I'm part of a group that seizes our English Department facility. We access an unguarded indoor pool and naked, gender-ignored frolic in the water as a symbol of liberty. Not resting for three nights, ragged, I return home and, without disruption, sleep for fifteen hours. The academic semester remains unfinished. We're graded on a pass-fail basis.

With the rental monetary loss and cost of American Airlines charter tickets for a two hundred dollars round trip ticket, limited funds remain. I purchase equipment for the trip at the surplus Army-Navy store in Manhattan. Stocking up with a basic Boy Scout canvas backpack absent a metal frame, a simple sleeping bag, and an army gas mask shoulder bag in which I secure documents, American Express traveler checks worth three hundred and fifty dollars remain. These funds have to last eleven weeks. I can't alter the return flight date. Asking around, I learn that other budgets for the trip average about three times what I've available. There's no open ticket for train travel between countries for me. Euro pass is out of the question. Hitchhiking throughout Europe is very trendy, safe, and a fantastic way to learn about the inhabitants.

Landing in London, I walk around the city for days and sleep on park benches. Fish and chips and kidney pie are affordable cuisines. I loved the first but hated the latter. Wandering about with no destination in mind, riding the tubes searching for affordable youth hostels, directed by Fromm's guide, what's affordable is already booked solid. It's nighttime, and not finding lodging, I slumber on a bench alongside a double-decker bus stop. Morning arrives, and riding the upper deck, taking in the view, I find London too expensive as the day drags. Whipping out a road map of Europe, I decide to head south. Having read references about Dover and its historical importance during World War II, this is a must-see. Ambling through the countryside, reaching the shore to admire the famous white cliffs while traveling alone and restless, in short order, I reverse direction, deciding that Scotland is the destination. I stop in London to see Big Ben, visit Hyde Park, and find lodging. The tubes are my mode of transport. The park benches await me. Decisions are instinctual, with no plan in mind.

The lorry driver responds to the outstretched thumb and pulls to a stop on the busy road's shoulder. He'll take me as far north as Nottingham. My destination is Scotland. Keeping company while struggling to decipher his accented English, he urges visiting Edinburgh. Under the stars, I disembark. There's an open field across the road. In the thick, pitch-black surrounding air, opening the sleeping bag and crawling in, I keep my Chukka boots on just in case there's a sudden need to move fast. Wearing a hunting knife once belonging to Leon, I have no idea how to properly sheath it. Hearing roosters at dawn, I open my eyes and sit upright. There's a local in the near distance waving an arm, shotgun resting across his chest. Grabbing the backpack that serves as a pillow and flinging the dew-covered open sleeping bag around my neck, stumbling, I run towards the safety of the heavily trafficked open highway. The next stop is Edinburgh.

The lorry stops, and a hitchhiker accompanies the driver. Greg is two years older than I and resides in Sheepshead Bay, Brooklyn. This neighborhood is just a short distance from Coney Island. I find immediate comfort and security in the familiarity that comes with his presence. Coincidentally, we're heading for the same destination. Condescendingly referencing sexual exploits and hunger for female targets, having just met, the topic is discomforting, raising inferiorities; "I'm the only eighteen-year-old virgin on the planet." When male classmates speak of conquests, I doubt their words while remaining silent, believing no girl would share herself with someone like me.

Disembarking, we come across a young man with long hair. Striking up a conversation, he notes our backpacks and attached sleeping bags. "Do you need a place to stay?" he asks. We join him and are soon at a nearby third-floor walk-up. A large group of adults and children, all dressed in hippy style, warmly welcomes us. He introduces me to a woman referred to as his wife. They freely offer all types of recreational drugs. Beds are shared as well. Greg engages in sex that night. I remain enclosed within myself, happily settling on being stoned while music fills the air. Lacking experience and fearing rejection, the imagined intimidation prevents connecting with accessible sex.

We head off to the Edinburgh Royal Botanic Gardens. Our new-found friends join us. Children are brought along. The glass greenhouses engage us. The ambiance of the gardens reflects the peaceful, joyful, accepting character of the group. We visit the Castle; its historical significance and story keep us enthralled throughout the long day. Abandoning the guide, enjoying the freedom and opportunity to stay in character, and being loud while other visitors remain reserved, we playfully run about, satisfying our curiosities.

At the commune, we smoke to our heart's delight. Strobe lights flash throughout the communal room. A gaudy day-glow-colored rendition of stars in the night sky shows on the ceiling. Collapsed on a bed, our host's wife enters the room where I'm alone. Lying down beside me, she strokes the crotch of my tight jeans, and there's a quick climax. Inexperience is the enemy. Embarrassed, I want to disappear. Free love is the norm, yet I only think about how this young woman could engage me with her husband in the next room. He could enter at any moment!

I remain for days. Certainty provides comfort. Bored, compelled to move on, Greg remains. Recalling the dawn shotgun event in the open field, I decide to ignore the expense. Riding the train back to London is safest—enough of the British Isles. Reaching Heathrow airport, a short while later, I'm in Amsterdam. For someone like me, the city is the draw. Freedom at the moment means more than art, historical sites, or even culture. The storefront bordellos where women half-naked pose as window displays, smoke shops and cafes where you legally purchase and smoke pot or hashish, the electric trolleys, canals, pigeons, international travelers passing through, and throngs of young people wearing backpacks are like a movie set that's come to life.

This is not provincial Brooklyn, which is all I know. Bicycles and scooters are the primary modes of transportation. An inexpensive rental secures either one. Passports are the security deposit as I drive off on a scooter. The pedals are the brakes. The throttle is part of the handlebars. The top speed is thirty-five mph. Rotterdam is the destination. I'm following road signs, avoiding major thoroughfares containing heavy traffic. Sunlight reflects off double rows of thick foliage and tulips, radiating colors that illuminate the warm air. It's as if I'm in a Van Gogh painting and not the countryside. Singing "Born to Be Wild by Steppenwolf," I stand on the scooter seat, emulating an Easy Rider movie scene when the road's pavement suddenly turns to dirt. Butt quickly lowers to the seat. I enter a sharp bend in the road at 35mph. Losing traction, I'm in the wide turn and sail directly into a dry canal covered in shrubs. The embankment dips about five feet, the scooter flips, and I land head-first. The throttle jammed; the back wheel continues to spin. Upright, the machine pulls away. I struggle to get back on the seat. After several comical outcomes, the scooter falls on its side repeatedly, with me toppling over. I jump on it but can't disconnect the gas feed. To stop moving forward, I brake by standing on the pedals and pressing down. Speeding off, knowing I have to return the rental, the day is a failure.

Reaching the destination, jumping off, and dropping the bike on its side, thankfully, the back wheel stops spinning. The shop attendant, preoccupied with other customers, hands over the passport without inspecting the return. I hastily got out of there. Heading straight to a smoke shop, I purchase a large nugget of hash. Spending the next few nights grounded in Amsterdam, lodging at a youth hostel, the space between my skull and brain vibrates when I shake my head. I'm probably concussed.

Holland, I surmise, has a friendlier population. I'm comfortable thumbing once again. Reaching the border, I'm dropped off on the Dutch side. Carrying the nugget and walking around a bend in the road, a checkpoint appears. The Aachen, German border guard, stands one hundred yards away. Uniform immaculately pressed, shiny knee-high black boots reflecting sun rays, the perfectly worn outfit precipitates imaginary associations with the Nazi era. The caricature awaits approach. Apprehensive, I crouch towards a nearby bush and ingest the hash. Biting down on the lump, it pulverizes, drying up saliva, and I cough, choke, and wretch. Afraid the border guard will spot me, I try to be quick. Panicking, I attempt to spit out the pieces but with only partial success. Fighting dry mouth, spit disappearing, swallowing the remains, I proceed to the passport control, where I'm routinely stamped and waived on.

Behind me, carrying two young male passengers is a funny-sounding tiny car, its gears rattling chain-like sounds. Offering a ride, they ask if I'm here to attend the open-air concert happening down the road. The older one speaks heavily German-accented English. It's a free concert featuring Pink Floyd. The opening act is T-Rex with Marc Bolan. The ingested hash starts to hit me. Feeling with it, I continue rambling about owning their albums. The show is majestic. Flashing colored strobe lights reflecting off the rising mist to the cadence of the band make this day the highlight of the journey. The long concert ending, these stoned companions extend an invitation to their parents' home located in the countryside of Augsburg, Germany.

Their vehicle is a two-cylinder Citroen, its loud gears struggling up inclines. Nothing like this car exists in America, the nearest facsimile being a Volkswagen Beetle. The car drives like an oversized toy. There's now, early morning light. Looking out the window, traveling the winding, climbing road, the scenery is reminiscent of a trip to another era. Mountains touch the clouds, and homes at the cleared bases are few and far between. Green fields radiate contrasting colors against the bright, clear blue sky. The extent of nature's beauty is unfamiliar. For once, I'm speechless!

It's late at night. Their home is a villa. It's surrounded by forest landscaping, and the property has two large wooden barn-type structures. There's a running stream alongside a windmill. It appears like a throwback in time. The interior of the house was modernized and doesn't represent the exterior. When entering, a uniformed housekeeper instructs me, "Please take off your boots and leave your backpack. I take it. Danka." Stinky feet make me self-conscious. Leading me up narrow, steep steps to a small attic that serves as a guest room, shown a small adjacent washroom, I freshen up, wash my underwear in the sink, and go to bed.

Roosters wake me at sunrise. The uniformed maid serves breakfast in the kitchen area, where I'm introduced to their mother, who doesn't speak a word of English. The newly found friend translates. Sharing common Yiddish words pronounced in a different dialect, I search for minimal familiarity. The attempt is frustrating.

Informed that we're located near Munich, Austria, I ask to see this ancient city, and the brothers agree to guide me. The panorama is breathtaking. Mountain peaks press against azure skies. The dwellings on the steep slopes, quaint and tiny in the distance, have me reminiscing about children's book illustrations. Patches of forest are spread about. All is serene. It's so very different from urban settings. Here nature dwarfs man commanding recognition and respect. I feel tiny and inconsequential. This is breathtaking!

After touring St. Peter's church, we visit a beer hall. Never having indulged in alcoholic products other than sweet Passover wine and sherry, the taste of beer is a first-time experience. Served a stein in the Bavarian tradition, it's the largest drinking vessel I've ever seen. Lifted to my lips with two hands, the tepid, bitter taste is awful. "People like this?" I cry out in dismay.

The entire family sits together for lunch. With translation

assistance, I learn that the large barn is a stonework. Workers cut huge blocks of marble and other types of stone into manageable sizes. The material is chiseled, shaped, and polished, forming monuments earmarked to honor the deceased in cemeteries and other outdoor locations. Exaggerating, sharing that I'm a trained stone carver, they eagerly offer to show me the interior of the barn, pointing out a one-of-a-kind, crescent-shaped blade hanging down from the crossbeam. Without the presence of machinery, the blade precisely rocks back and forth. To prevent friction from overheating and damaging the blade, a constant flow of water is tapped from the adjoining spring. It's pumped onto the stone's incision. Claiming it's an original setup, no electricity involved, gravity and water are the power source. The pendulum and blade originated during the medieval ages.

Descending to the everyday living area, I walk around the room looking at art and other interesting objects. Family photos are scattered about. On the large marble mantelpiece are portraits of the father, including one proudly wearing a WW II Luftwaffe uniform. Upon arriving, I revealed my knowledge of Yiddish. No mention of the Jewish people's fate in Europe ever occurred like it didn't happen. Proudly displaying the photo demonstrates no regrets for how history played out. Abruptly, within one hour, I pack up and ask for a ride to the highway, explaining, "I'm meeting someone in Italy."

It takes time for a car to stop that's not local but is heading through the Alps. These outsized mountains are larger than anything I've seen so far. The snow-covered tips hide in the white clouds. Pulling out a road map of Europe, my destination is determined by the distance the driver travels. Nothing planned, movement is spontaneous. No forethought is freedom without accountability. The drive is long. Disembarking late at night in Venice alongside a stench-littered canal, searching for a place to bed down with Fromm's guide in hand, the place isn't hospitable. Observing two thugs assault another, tossing him into the murky water, signals, "Get the hell out of here."

Sleepless, acquiring a ride to Trieste, I chose to tap limited funds and catch a ferry to Bari. Slumbering on the damp deck alongside other young travelers, we share dark bread and cheese. It's been the main fare for weeks. Fatigue doesn't slow me down. At Bari, I catch another ferry large enough to accommodate automobiles and small trucks. It crosses the Adriatic Sea, and the destination is Split, Yugoslavia. Near the port are beautiful beaches covered in tar-stained, small, egg-shaped, white, smooth stones of varying sizes. Walking to the shoreline, I'm clumsy, slipping and falling. The distance is a struggle. The waters are clear turquoise, the most beautiful I've ever seen. The air is pristine, the seashore sparsely populated, and the few sunbathers present are nude. My feet are covered in petrol, smelling of tar, and the irony of the contrast is alarming.

After six weeks of traveling companionless, I'm lonely. Being on guard keeps me isolated from others. Aware Paula enrolled in a summer course at the American University in Jerusalem, fantasy morphs into obsession, knowing Mom and Dad are far away.

"Maybe these logistics will allow the opening to happen? She has no idea that I'll be looking for her."

Thrilled by the idea, I have no address or details, just the name of the school and the city. Reaching Greece, the Athens airport is the most expedient. Forty of the three hundred and fifty dollars remain. The flight from Athens to Lod Airport, Israel, costs thirty dollars. Destination outweighs money concerns. With romance in mind, I'm giddy, hopeful, and blinded by imagined possibilities.

Landing at Lod, I head straight for Jerusalem. Sleeping at a bed and breakfast in the Arab quarter of the recently liberated old city, the straw-filled mattress and accommodations cost two dollars U.S. for the night. It's morning. After a hot brew served from a Turkish Finjan coffee pot, I head straight for the school. Paula isn't in attendance, but visiting all the way from New York makes sharing her address acceptable. Tapping on the ground floor entrance of her abode, a strange face greets me. The housing arrangement is a share, and Paula is summoned to the door. More than I hoped for, the novelty of this adventurous undertaking sparks a vivacious welcome smothered with kisses. Leading me by hand to her room, the inquisitive receptivity prompts a babbling outburst. Suggesting we walk over to nearby Jerusalem Forest with a sleeping bag in hand; emotions run rampant. At a roadside stand, purchasing a huge melon and turning the jaunt into a picnic setting, the leg-hugging, long-bladed hunting knife carves the fruit. The trail takes us to an isolated spot. The ground cover is a bed of heavily scented pine needles fallen from the surrounding trees. Spreading out the sleeping bag, we talk and talk. The melon causes frantic peeing. We laugh about the urgency. Climbing into the sleeping bag, ignoring the prickly needles touching skin and coupling at last virginity ends. We pass the night under the stars.

Dawn arrives. Returning to the apartment, we see the rolling metal shutter designed to protect against enemy attack ripped out of its housing. Paula's room is in disarray. Nothing was stolen. We surmise that her jealous boyfriend caused the disturbance after learning from a roommate, "An American showed up, and they went off together." Later, he appears. They speak privately. Dark-complexioned, tall, thin, handsome, waves of anxiety and self-doubt ensue. Always there, the feeling just intensifies. Paula and I share a bed until the day London summons.

Her native family, who were early pioneers, live on a kibbutz near the Jerusalem-Tel Aviv Road. A must-visit; during the War of Independence, the road was under siege and essential to the reestablishment of the nation of Israel. Their greeting effuses strength, warmth, arrogance, and self-sacrifice. Individuality is a secondary priority considered only after the well-being of the community. The members nurture and raise the children. We eat meals in a shared dining hall. There are no kitchens in the apartments. It would be absurd to equate this setting with communes back home where the focus is recreational, be it drug use, music, or sex.

The elder son of this four-member family is wheelchair-bound. An officer injured during the 1967 war three years earlier is paralyzed from the waist down. His upper body demonstrates a physique reminiscent of a born warrior. If he could stand, he would tower over most people. He drives us to nearby ancient Latrun. Having no use of his legs, the vehicle's gas pedal and brakes are situated on the steering wheel and designed to be hand-operated. The ingenuity and resolve behind this innovation demonstrate Israeli love for its soldiers. Touring the surrounding ruins, busily scooting about in his wheelchair, the terrain is not a deterrent. Paula's cousin effusively describes the trials and achievements of the kibbutz. His limitations are never mentioned. He beams his ability to adapt for all to see. He says, "Not knowing what tomorrow brings, pursue your dreams and enjoy the moment."

Painting comes to mind.

The Federal government provides monthly Social Security survivor funds to fatherless orphans. It does not amount to much, but being it's from Pop justifies demanding Mom hand it over. The government earmarks the payment for full-time students until graduation or when they turn twenty-two. Wiring a modest amount accumulated while gone via American Express carries me until charter flight availability. While Paula attends classes, I regularly venture through the old city. By chance, at Jaffa Gate, I run into Mrs. Rapaport, a social studies teacher back at Lincoln High School.

Exchanging salutations,

"What a small world! Wow, seeing a Brooklyn face after so long brings on pangs. Every day is an adventure, but I miss home, Mrs. Rapaport."

Not refraining from holding back, I share the happy news that I've crossed through Europe only to find Paula after trying to be with her for so long.

Shopping in the alleyway markets requires negotiating skills. The Arab shopkeepers set the asking price high if interest in an item is shown. When turning away, they chase the prospect, shouting out a lower price. Negotiating begins. It's lots of fun. I purchase smelly, shaggy white sheepskin coats for myself and Paula, a four-foot-tall hubbly bubbly, and trinkets reflecting Arab culture. Days pass. A roommate responds to constant pestering. I'm directed to an Arab merchant where I acquire "five fingers," the accustomed measurement used in purchasing hashish. The price is ridiculously low compared to the States. The cost of a nugget in the USA equals five fingers here!

Contrasting this place with the urban concrete jungle I come from, modern Jerusalem is underdeveloped. There's no construction blocking views of the horizon. The area surrounding the Knesset buildings is barren. The highway is a single lane in either direction, with wide swaths of hard-packed red earth running alongside. Privately owned automobiles are sparse. Buses and taxis are the primary modes of transportation. The standard of living reflected by pedestrian attire compared to New Yorkers is basic, modest, and functional. The trip ends.

CHAPTER 8.
THE ONION

I return to New York City via London. Dismissing any possibility of going to Bernard's place with Larry, his lover living there, I have no other choice. Coney Island, here I come. Ordering Mom to keep her distance and determined to get out of there, I believe the stay will be brief. At the City College campus, I enroll in classes, selecting Anthropology, Sociology, Introductory Psychology, and two liberal arts required core classes. Claiming emancipated student status, I'm applying for financial aid assistance.

Playing frisbee on the open grounds in front of Finley Hall, the student union building, I ask an acquaintance if they know of anyone looking for a roommate. Introduced to Joel, a career student older than me, he appears detached from reality, starry-eyed. Unexpectedly, he's blurting that acid has burnt out his mind. Weary of him, "This is highly informative, but we just met! This is weird." He's passive, frightened, and struggles to concentrate when speaking.

Joel resides in a Brownstone, studio apartment situated in Park Slope, Brooklyn, which compromises the front half of the parlor floor. Raul, Joel's former roommate and his wife just reunited. Now situated in the above floor unit means there's a vacancy. We'll split the rent and share one large room, but I need to provide a bed. Furnishings are minimal. Without a moment's hesitation, I accept the offer to relocate on this day to Park Slope. The rent is half the one hundred and twenty-five dollar monthly survivors' benefit. There's no telephone hookup, and the electric bill is minimal. The municipality doesn't meter water and waste in these residential properties.

The large four-story brownstone built during the early 1900s had once been an opulent one-family home. After World War II, housing shortages everywhere intensified. Returning soldiers sought refuge. The owners converted it to a split-floor, eight-unit tenement. The hallway is neglected and smells like congested living quarters. The apartment is bare of furniture with a tiny linoleum-stained cockroach-infested kitchenette. The tight bathroom has a small sink, tub, and no cabinets but a mirrored two-inch-deep medicine chest. There's mildew and discoloration on all porcelain surfaces. The walls in the living quarters are scrawled with black graffiti. The ceiling is twelve feet above me. Deep scratches and scuff marks are evident all over the discolored parquet floor. Plasterboard seals the opening that once housed a marble fireplace. The thickly painted nailed wooden shutters are hidden in their housing. In better times, this was the parlor.

A bright, blinding light shining in the darkness kindles newfound freedom, Joel's insanity be damned. To be liberated from family, I jump at the opportunity, crazy and all. I remember that two high school mentors, Bill and Ron, are Park Slopers. Not affording a mattress or box spring, Joel directs me to the second-hand thrift shops on nearby Flatbush Avenue to search for a solution. Finding a folding cot with a two-inch foam mattress is the perfect solution; lacking storage space where I sleep, it costs only fifteen dollars. John's Bargain Store supplies towels and linens. Funds tapped, and without a pillow, the folded towel does the job.

Bringing along a change of clothing, hygienic accessories, and a transistor radio, the backpack serves as a closet. Overall, I can't believe my luck!

Eating a sandwich at the school campus cafeteria, a high school friend appears, walking hand in hand with a pony-tailed, tattoo-covered Latin-appearing guy. She shouts out, slurring the words for all present,

"There's Suster, who turned me onto the wonders of acid. He gave me the first tab of Sunshine."

In a hushed tone, she hands me a small glassine envelope with beige-colored powder, declaring,

"I owe you. Try this. It's unbelievable."

Returning to Park Slope, I'm opening the cot and turning on the transistor radio. Janis Joplin is dead. The news intensifies the gloom surrounding me. Seeking relief, I pour the powder on a covered book, snorting the substance as Sharon instructed. Heroin pleasures are unknown. I'm wondering why users rave about its effects. No nirvana for me. Dizzy and nauseated, overwhelmed, needing to lie down, the effects linger. Awakening the next morning with a splitting headache, my curiosity is satisfied. I swear off the stuff, disgusted that junkies surrender to it.

"They must hate themselves more than I do to stoop so low."

After completing two years at Lincoln High School, Paula matriculates at City College into a pre-med combined six-year program in conjunction with the Mt. Sinai School of Medicine. Her parents support her two-bedroom apartment on the Upper West Side. Enjoying each other's company in limitless Manhattan, the relationship flourishes.

Central Park is our favorite. Spending nights on her Castro convertible sofa bed, we're having a wonderful time. I'm in love.

Sharing the apartment with Joel quickly becomes problematic. Psychotic, often out of touch with reality, his severe bouts of depression don't ease my mental struggles. Raul, his Argentinian former roommate, now living in the unit above, privately speaks to me about the challenges and unpleasant environment around Joel. He's again separating from Lisa, his wife, and needs to cut expenses. Speaking broken, thick Spanish-accented English, sounding comical, he asks me to move in. The place is organized workshop-style, producing handcrafted custom jewelry and designer-inspired leather belts. The apartment was originally the brownstone master bedroom. A partitioned-off alcove creates a small bedroom. I'm restricted to placing the cot inconspicuously in an unoccupied corner of the larger room with the understanding I can set up an easel and paint whenever I chose. The room is the common studio, and his privacy is assured in the bedroom. The rent remains the same.

Riding the subway to Pearl Paints located on Canal Street, I purchase a sturdy oak wood easel, tubes of Grumbacher oil pigments, turpentine, brushes, a pallet of finely glossed paper sheets, a small metal spatula, yards of raw canvas, wooden stretchers, gesso, and a heavy-duty staple gun with a box of staples. To make do, a plier out of my toolbox serves to stretch the raw canvas over the wood. Not much money remains for groceries. The cuisine for the next few weeks will consist of macaroni and ketchup. Art supplies, more than food, are the priority.

Driven to pursue a dream vocation away from phony people I can't connect with, in front of the canvas, depression persists.

Replacing loneliness, entranced, concentrating on the moment, the pigments and the white canvas call out for life, the canvas my companion. When interacting with new acquaintances, they embellish, exaggerate, misrepresent, and are gratuitous. These traits repulse me. Canvas in front of me, what you see is what you get. Hidden agendas don't exist. For the artist, the relationship is very real. Interacting with the forming picture and the emotions tapped, I can't challenge or deny. It is my release. This is my refuge. I spend endless hours accompanied by a bottle of ice-cold Liebfraumilch wine, cheese, and bread, contemplating the next stroke and hue. I'm comically stereotypical. The silent, dark, late-night hours when the phonies sleep is the time to distance myself from negative thoughts and create something new and refreshing.

Pursuing academics is a secondary activity, but I'm completing the requirements to remain in good standing. The relationship with Paula continues, and this serves as an oasis. Raul, who is a business partner with his estranged wife, informs me that Lisa wants to reconcile since their custom-designed jewelry and belts are gaining traction. This development: Raul staying away most nights presents the opportunity to live alone and turn the room into a large painter's studio. Imagining painting mural-size canvases, I steadily pound Raul on the virtues of uniting with Lisa. It's December. The financial aid office notified me that for next semester, a financial aid package is waiting for acceptance. Receiving another NYS Higher Education loan coupled with a work-study grant, the timing couldn't be more fortuitous. Raul moves out, and without sharing space, the monthly rent is affordable. The college work-study grant amounts to one thousand dollars.

The stipulation: it's earned through on or off-campus employment. As a full-time student limited to a maximum fifteen-hour work week wanting stimulation, pursuing employment away from the campus library, tutoring, or cafeteria, I choose the NYC

Urban Corps program. The opportunity offers experience in municipal and non-profit agencies whereby recipients test career goals. It's the middle of the grant year, and placement selections are limited. I am assigned to and accept a research assistant position at the Harlem Research Center under the direction of Dr. Guttentag. She's measuring the achievements of student performance now that community control of local school boards gives parents curriculum input. I spend hours scoring completed surveys. It's tedious, mindless work, but nights in front of the easel more than offset feeling sorry. The academic semester is a success.

The brownstone consists of seven small one-bedroom apartments and a one-room parlor unit; each floor is divided in half. Residing there are contemporaries who share similar social values. Our responses to government policies foster solidarity. Individually, we pursue actions demonstrating rejection of American imperialism and the military draft.

Searching for people of similar views, a flier distributed in the neighborhood announces a gathering urging concerned individuals to attend. The meeting will be held on the second floor of an old vacant firehouse at 714 Union Street. The landlord donates the space with the understanding it might be rented. No furnishings available, we sit on old crates or the floor, a bare bulb throwing off a dim light, floors covered in broken, vinyl-stained tiles, and the glossy green wall paint cracked and peeling. The brass pole centered in the backroom opening allows for a quick exit. It's hot and musty, but we ignore the conditions and get to know one another and the reasons behind each one's presence. Being the youngest in attendance and insecure around a group of strangers, my radar is actively searching for phonies, I listen and don't speak.

On the outskirts, looking in, not wearing or espousing labels identifying inclinations either as a radical, socialist, communist, or hippy, I'm not doctrinaire. I find dogma and rigidity exclusionary. Fervor limits debate. The various social schools of thought discussed don't engage me. Despising the Nixon administration and wanting our country to get out of Southeast Asia, that's my passion. Fashion is rejectionist, so I appear to belong. We attend weekly meetings, collecting donations and rent for a nominal sum. The landlord is supportive of contributing space.

We need a name for our gathering place that projects an identity. Sitting in a circle, Salley, Deb, Joan, Giora, Ruth, Anne, Kip, and others have a turn throwing out their suggestion. A song I listen to is composed by the rock band Elephant's Memory. It's titled: "Mongoose." The little mongoose is a predator of large snakes. The cobra is its forte. The name serves metaphorically as a symbol of our mission. We vote on its acceptance, and it passes. We are now known as The Mongoose. This contribution doesn't gain me recognition in our social order. Not quoting leftist writings or preaching any ideology, I remain on the fringe. Visiting group members at their homes and communal living situations doesn't help bridge the gap. Their way of living is strange.

The group decides to purchase produce weekly at the Hunts Point market. It's a way for each attendee to acquire fresh organically grown produce at an affordable price. A consensus determines which items are in most demand. Selections are listed on a pre-order form collected the evening before the 5 a.m. trip. Minimum amounts of an item are mandatory to meet weight requirements and get the best price. Funds are collected on a prepaid basis. The food cooperative has a rotating core of volunteers who undertake the task of purchasing and delivering the crates. A set time when each purchaser has to pick up the produce at Mongoose is announced. Large orders are common and worthwhile. Most participants live in shared group settings. Living alone, with food requirements minimal, the program doesn't work for me. The Mongoose transformed itself from primarily a social meeting hall into a food cooperative. Today, it is the largest non-profit food cooperative in the USA.

Moving on, reuniting with the easel eliminates most social distractions. I refocus. When converted, the apartment's interior walls were constructed with plasterboard attached to a wooden 2x4 floor-to-ceiling inner frame. The frame holds the wall in place, separating the living room and bedroom. The ceiling is ten feet above the floor. Contemplating how this former master bedroom would make an ideal art studio if the walls were removed, I proceed. The alteration enables painting large abstract murals utilizing acrylic paints, a different medium to explore.

Without the landlord's approval or a building department permit, I remove the wall. Tools are a hammer, plier, and screwdriver. Punching holes with the hammer is easy, but the 2x4s are a challenge. The nail heads flush with the wood are two inches in length. Searching for heads, gouging the wood allows leverage to pull, nails squeaking. The effort snaps the hammer's wooden handle. A neighbor has a replacement. The empty garbage cans in front of the brownstone are made of metal and are heavy. Carrying them up to the apartment, I fill and top them off with plasterboard pieces. Too heavy to lift, I drag one across the hallway to the landing, a floor above ground level. Outside the entranceway, I descend another set of steps. Using both hands to firmly grasp the container's side handle while fighting gravity, I struggle to shimmy down each step one at a time. Filling four of the five cans, one remains untouched for resident rubbish. The disassembled frames are alongside. Garbage pickup takes many visits.

I head straight to Pearl Paints and purchase needed supplies, including the largest canvas stretchers in stock, reaching eight feet in length, jars of acrylic paints, a roll of canvas, and large nylon brushes two and three inches in width. I already have gesso used to prime canvas and a set of smaller brushes. Cheap clamped aluminum wide-shaded fixtures are found at a street vendor. I search for inexpensive spot-light bulbs that don't generate heat but with no luck. Trudging back to Park Slope on the subway, passengers stare at me, juggling to handle the dropped bundles. It is quite a spectacle.

May 1, is around the corner, I'm turning twenty-one. This milestone reignites the renovation effort. Renting a sander, the parquet floor is gouged but refinished. Satin varnish works wonders. Shudders are free from their housing. A red brick fireplace is revealed. To celebrate, I approached the other tenants, proposing that we have an open house party, inviting everyone we know.

We wedge open all the brownstone's doors, cook quantities of our favorite recipes, announce, "Bring your own drugs," and party all night.

Visitors roam from unit to unit. My simple stereo record player blasts music throughout the hallway. Every bit of space is packed with wall-to-wall freaky people. Bowls of sangria punch are easily located. Pete Peterson, our one-legged landlord, shows up and, seeing the altered apartment, just shrugs and smiles. Anne, a friend residing on the floor above, decorates an empty journal passed among the crowd for well-wishers to inscribe their thoughts and blessings.

The constricting tightness in my chest never subsides. Bernard's therapist is the Chief of Outpatient Psychiatry at Albert Einstein Hospital. With his referral, I see a resident psychiatrist for weekly counseling, diligently attending the sessions. The long train ride doesn't deter me. She is young, of firm demeanor, and energetic. I'm comfortable around her. She's engaging, but the time spent there provides no relief. She completes her training. I decline to continue with a new resident therapist.

Summer comes, and I'm offered another financial aid grant permitting a full-time work week. Again, selecting the Urban Corps, the chosen category of interest is field evaluator in the arts and health care. The choice opens the door for a career track in the health industry. Ironic, given I reject the profession. Physicians demeanor in their environment can be intimidating, but not for this young man, who's regularly been in and out of doctors' offices. It's a fitting selection. It requires visiting job sites, assessing the degree of training provided, and confirming that work duties aren't supplanting municipal employee functions. The labor unions, specifically District Council 37, allow the placement of these students alongside its members with the proviso their presence is strictly for training purposes. The seventeen public hospitals, the American Museum of Natural History, the Metropolitan Museum of Art, and the Brooklyn Museum are some of my assigned locations.

What an unusual opportunity to freely walk the corridors and sub-basements of these cultural institutions. I meet with department curators and learn about preserving, restoring, and exhibiting these valuable treasures. Accessing, with trainee assistance, dimly lit corridors, I view selected, stored items before placement in new exhibits. Witnessing the planning and construction is inspiring. Absent visitors, the lighting adds intimacy.

The general public will never be exposed to this. How lucky am I?

In contrast, the public hospital summer internships represent a diverse array of tragedy and hope. One day stands out among all others. Visiting the Belleview Hospital children's inpatient psychiatric ward and seeing the conditions the patients endure was awful. Rails enclose beds lined up in rows along opposite walls. Children stare into space, physically active within their enclosures. The milieu is stark, bare, sterile, and institutional.

I ponder, "In psychosis, are they aware of their surroundings or of human contact when it occurs? Is this therapy or confinement?"

Hospitals are understaffed, the workload is ever-increasing, and the training of potential future employees is a priority. That's why I'm here.

Each facility's human resource department coordinates placements. Locating the appropriate staff, explaining the purpose of the evaluation, announcing an imminent visit, and requesting trainee availability, reports are subsequently written and submitted to the Urban Corps program development director. Summer staffing requires ten field evaluators.

President Nixon implements a lottery for military draft selection. The Selective Service picks birth dates out of a drum. Numbers occur in sequence. Conscription is capped at 125. My number is 154. Full-time students receive a deferment if their number lands in the designated range, obligating conscription upon graduation. If you are in the annual eligibility pool and your number is not called, you have a lifetime exemption from military service. Fearful the war is escalating under U.S. imperialistic foreign policy, I intend to drop out of school that year, knowing that call-ups won't reach my announced number. If drafted like so many, I'll seek asylum, fleeing to another country. Military service isn't the only way to demonstrate love for the country. Public sector employment is an alternative.

Stanley Litow is the Executive Director of the Urban Corps. Being young, vibrant, intelligent, and dedicated to helping others, upon learning of my plight as an emancipated student with minimal family contact, he takes interest. I chase the attention that's wholeheartedly provided. He agrees, "The sabbatical is the way to go." The summer program is ending. I'm employed full-time as the assistant to Pamela Gwynn, the Director of Program Development. The salary is entry-level clerk grade. I'm grateful, excited, and ambitious. The agency reports to the deputy mayor, who endorses rapid expansion. The City of New York, the off-campus employer complying with federal guidelines, matches the funding with a twenty percent contribution. The deputy mayor's budget supports the expenditure. I'm tasked with developing clerkship openings throughout the five boroughs. The Housing Authority, under a borrowed line item, pays the salary. To gain receptivity, given my youth, I'm titled the Assistant Director of Program Development.

The Department of Health headquarters is within walking distance of our office that is situated across from City Hall. Visiting is fun when I work with and enjoy the company of Lenore Deutsch. She encourages and challenges me with a good cop, bad cop routine. I view Lenore as a mother figure with Bohemian values. She introduces me to Dr. Michael Baden, the Chief Medical Examiner who's eager to have qualified students observe and learn during autopsy and forensic procedures. Viewing slide specimens is a student activity. He's outgoing, talkative, positive, and very amusing; he's a bit of a kibitzer, which makes people comfortable, given his morbid task of signing off on death certificates. Frequently visiting her office, I'm teased and referred to as "the adopted" son.

Jack Moscou is the Director of Training at the Health and Hospital Corporation. He's the entry point to the directors of personnel at the seventeen municipal hospitals. He oversees the effort to place hundreds of student interns throughout the system. Conceptually, testing career goals could motivate candidates to pursue future municipal employment. This hope motivates us both to work as a team. Jack is personable, open-minded, and intolerant when personnel screw up. We are workplace friends.

With positive results in hand and no other work-related activity scheduled, canvas calls for freedom governs the clock. Returning to the office is a waste of valuable time. I find the minutes in the day to be rare and its utility to be used to the fullest. I look to get things done. Not reporting the absence to superiors is wrong, but the desire to paint offsets any hesitance. Guilty for violating their trust when, on City time, smoking softens conflicting thoughts. I drift away. The Allman Brothers energize. The canvas captivates.

When I appear, Mrs. Davidson, the Assistant Personnel Director at Coney Island Hospital, is effusive. Under her wing, I'm coached on the approach to pitching the advantages of training students in each service. Her popularity with hospital personnel as a lady who gets things done makes it easy to identify who to speak with or avoid. Within a short order, we reach over fifty placements throughout the facility. Located in the backyard of the neighborhood where I spent my teenage years, up the block from Lincoln High School, the building projects familiarity and comfort. With her and Jack Moscous' guidance, over three hundred students are scattered throughout the hospital system. Walking the corridors, salutations forthcoming, I'm now a hero.

Healthcare services aren't the only placements. Tutoring adults to earn their GED or learn English as a second language, working with children as a recreation aide, maintaining the greenhouses at the botanic gardens, conducting medical research at various labs, or marine research at the aquarium are only a sampling of what's available.

The year-long sabbatical, complete with no call-up, means I'll never be a military draftee. Stanley informs me, "There's the innovative University Without Walls program at New York University commencing this upcoming September."

He knows I intend to earn a college degree. As the Executive Director and my mentor, Stanley, composes a detailed letter describing my accomplishments and readiness to follow an independent study track. We became close, and until he left the agency, we spoke or met almost daily. His support was invaluable. He was more than a mentor. For a time, I had a big brother.

The program allows for designing the desired curriculum. It provides a Bachelor of Arts degree upon completion of the required credit hours. Participants are eligible to receive academic credit for work experiences when documented and presented. This is tailor-made for me. Both Herbert London and Vickie Pops administer the program enthusiastically, describing the students selected and their areas of interest. I choose to apply. With acceptance, self-esteem improves, but anticipated failure lurks above. I doubt myself. The NYU label is prestigious. Herb's commitment to student accomplishment reflecting his success is assuring. With both his and Stanley's faith and encouragement, I forge forward. Absent loving family guidance, these mentors direct me. Ambition is taking hold, countering melancholy.

NYU students can contact the administration to receive counseling services. I schedule an intake interview at the affiliated NYU hospital. An evaluation at intake occurs to match an appropriate treatment modality with the patient. Dr. Melanie Korn, a fourth-year resident assigned the case, arranges to see me at the Bellevue Hospital outpatient psychiatric department. The building and its interior are familiar. The downtrodden appearance reflects my mental state. Dr. Korn asks, "Why are you here?" Responding, "I no longer want to feel victimized by life."

This opening statement establishes a commitment to dig within, being honest, and not phony, no matter how difficult.

Seeing my determination, she accepts the mission. Dr. Korn explains that I suffer from global anxiety, which causes chest tightness; seeing the world through rose-colored lenses distorts understanding of experiences and messaging when interacting with people. The once-a-week session frustrates continuity. The doctor gains my trust, and progress leads us to twice-weekly encounters. This enables picking up right where we left off after the last meeting. Sparsely scheduled visits impede my progress. Layers of feelings and the mental processing behind them are peeled back like an onion. Tears flow with the wounds exposed. Relief comes with the knowledge and understanding that lies behind the veil. Mom and Pop are the focus. Losing him was painful for both of us.

As an NYU student, the co-pay is nominal, mandatory, and considered therapeutic. The expenditure gives added value to the meeting. The relationship is meant to be contractual, a give-and-receive mutual discourse where self-awareness brings relief. When a person buys something, it's cherished and valued. Its utility is put to use. The twice-weekly therapy sessions with Dr. Korn end after two years. The pain slowly dissipates until, during a session, one day, it's gone. No more global anxiety. When sensed, I'm now able to isolate the cause; introspection relieving the tension. I continue to smoke pot daily. Believing the indulgence represents a character flaw, I press the physician to address this illegal behavior only to have the topic brushed over, for this is the wrong time or place to address the subject. Not satisfied with the response leaves me frustrated and self-critical.

The citywide Urban Corps program for the upcoming summer projects an enrollment of three thousand students and a total of five thousand for the entire year. To manage the volume, the director has decentralized placement and evaluation functions to each borough. We still share the same physical quarters across the street from City Hall.

I'm appointed Coordinator of Brooklyn and Staten Island. To staff the unit, I glean through the early applicants who reside in these boroughs. The process I went through is repeated. However, experience has shown us how to be more than a processing center. We expand duties to include career goal assessment and placement counseling. For the recipient, placement is not only about earning a work-study grant. There is a two-week window to select and train staff in interviewing techniques and field evaluation. Grant recipients line up at our offices ten deep. We interview eight hundred students in the summertime and twelve hundred more during the academic year. A staff of six students is under my wing.

The Housing Authority eliminates the two job positions provided. The Health and Hospitals Corporation assumes the funding with a salary increase. Stroking the hand that feeds, I'm concerned these positions might, at any moment, also disappear. I prioritize hospital assignments, channeling students in that direction. Coney Island hospital numbers reach ninety, the entire municipal health care system five hundred. Harlem and Bellevue hospital programs rank second. I'm a Coney Island hospital hero.

At every opportunity, I slip away to paint. When not painting, I enjoy time with Paula, but I know that she doesn't love me. Unpredictable, I'm fun to play with. Being nonconventional intrigues her. I can't let go of this unrequited love. It fills the void. One afternoon, her mother unexpectedly knocks on the door while we're together. Her parents don't know about our relationship, and although I've conformed with employment-required grooming, hastily, I'm hidden behind a locked door in Peggy's space until I hear "all clear."

Excusing the slight, "I don't deserve better, but how low will I go?"

I'm empowered to implement administrative decisions affecting hospital resources and help people form their career direction and future. This sense of importance doesn't dampen the feeling of emptiness and the yearning for love. Proud but sad; that's me. Pot is my recluse where I find solace.

On the Day of Atonement, Yom Kippur, an invitation to end the twenty-five-hour fast at Paula's parents' home has us surmise the new appearance and work-school status bring acceptance. Everyone is cordial. We spend the evening glued to the news that's reporting the Egyptian invasion over the Sinai Canal. In religious observance, we were blacked out of knowing this. Shots of whiskey, part of the evening's custom, heighten emotions. Concern and dread take hold. Suddenly, Israel doesn't seem invincible.

Public school elementary teacher Bob, who resides below, shares my goal to upgrade our living quarters. A couple of blocks away, we find an affordable upper brownstone duplex. The apartment has working fireplaces, and I have a dining room and art studio in addition to a bedroom. We share the living room and kitchen. Residing together for a year, Bob is ill, has a psychotic breakdown, and can't work or pay his share. It's time I live alone.

Paula is consumed with pre-med studies. She distances herself by spending time with a male study partner. Unable to connect throughout the night, the smoking gun conclusion is obvious, "I'm now out of the picture." They share common goals. Initially denying the accusation, she, under pressure, succumbs. I end our romance. Infidelity is unforgivable. Containing the rage when at home, I smoke and catatonically stare out into space. The hours and days crawl on endlessly.

With properly prepared submissions, Vickie and Herb encourage me to take advantage of the up to one-year academic credit the University Without Walls curriculum awards for career experience.

Their assurances shake me out of the stupor. The assembled portfolio includes oil and acrylic paintings, photographs, and abstract collages of colored shapes. To qualify for thirty credits, a year's worth, the volume of work has to be extensive. There's an academic year to prepare the submission. In a written format, the effort must also encompass work experiences and the lessons gained.

Attending a modern art history course with William Rubin, the curator of the Museum of Modern Art, learning about the evolution of abstract art as a natural progression influences my painting style. Frank Stella's approach is now ideal, and for the year,

I render geometric presentations on canvas.

Conceptualization overrides esthetic consideration. Minimalism is the game. Production is the goal, so there'll be more volume to present for life experience credits. Ideas more than feelings stand between me and the canvas. It shows in the quality of work.

The primary color pallet is absent brushwork, plastic pigment applied with waning passion. It isn't long before career attainment replaces art. The portfolio and written presentations describing administrative and operational responsibilities earn a year's worth of credits.

Even with the year sabbatical, I graduate four years after completing high school. All's good. Ambition and recognition steer me.

The previous summer, financial aid referred four Downstate University medical students for work-study grant placement. Realizing that medical students in financial need could qualify for this aid package, I lobby their financial aid officers in the Metropolitan region, stressing the merits of increasing their federal work-study allotments.

"The Urban Corp will develop clerkship slots in the municipal hospital-accredited teaching departments. The third and fourth-year medical students in training ethos are: see one, do one, teach one. Here's an opportunity for them to earn income while gaining the attention of department chairpersons who, upon graduation, may offer a postgraduate position. Slots are very competitive to acquire. These externships will serve as recruitment tools for the municipal hospitals that traditionally aren't the first choice of graduates."

One hundred and four students participate. The Harlem Hospital externship program that has stayed active after losing funding, is saved. I remain the Brooklyn and Staten Island Borough Coordinator, overseeing the placement of one thousand students and the growth of municipal hospital placements throughout the city. I'm on a roll.

CHAPTER 9.
VENGEANCE

Leon and I reconcile. Mom is hospitalized. Her fall resulted in a broken ankle. Both he and Bernard are at work this afternoon. Not hesitating, I visit and assess the situation. Since leaving her residence, I've kept contact to a minimum. Seeing her lying in that Coney Island hospital bed, appearing aged and fragile, independence changed my perspective. Anger forgotten, and the desire to take care of Mom swells. Understanding the difficulty of wearing the Mom and Pop role alone, comes with the experiences maturity reaps. I now am able to accept her limitations. I still recognize her manipulative tendencies, which are no longer effective. I'm no longer angry. When she returns home, regular weekend lunch-hour visits begin, accompanied by bags of favorite groceries and produce. Leon offers to teach me how to drive. Is Mom behind this? Many weekends are spent at his home until I pass the New Jersey driver's road test. He provides the vehicle. It makes it easier to share Broadway musical matinees with Mom, of whom there is only one.

Leaving Bob behind, I find a vacant ground-floor brownstone apartment just off Prospect Park. The backyard is turned into a wood sculpture garden. A large hibachi is purchased to grill steaks and hamburgers that are now the daily fare. I own a mechanic-rebuilt stick shift Renault 12 station wagon with front wheel drive.

On Mother's Day, hosting Mom and her two sisters for a barbeque, several hours into the visit, there's an unexpected knock on the door. Paula effusively attempts to enter, guessing that Mom will be here. Blocking the path, grabbing her by the hair while leading her back out, I shove her body down the street while screaming,

"How dare you show up here when my family is visiting, believing I wouldn't confront you after you cheated on me. You take me for a schmuck! Get the fuck out of here!"

Drenched with adrenaline, I turn away and try to salvage the afternoon with my family. I must break her hold on me. Four months of chain smoking softens the blow. Paula was my first love. I'm heartbroken yet able to reject familiarity. Therapy showed me the way.

An Urban Corps exhibition is underway at City Hall Park. The entire staff attends. Recruitment booths representing many city agencies are placing their best foot forward. Coney Island Hospital has Annie and several nurse supervisors present. Mayor Beame is walking about and pausing for the news reporters. He approaches Annie and the uniformed ladies.

Catching his attention, I say, "Mr. Mayor, let's take a picture with the girls who make the program so successful."

The scene of Annie, the Mayor, and me hangs in her office, a gift of opportunity.

It's the summer of 1977. The brownstone garden apartment rent increases beyond affordability. A high school friend resides in a rent-stabilized one-bedroom on the other side of the park. A unit is available. Packing up and managing to minimize expenses, the little Renault is the transport. Fitting furniture in the wagon is a challenge. The schoolteacher-styled oak desk is taken apart and moved in sections. The queen-size mattress and box spring jutting out the sides are tied to the roof for separate runs. The new location is only two miles away. Undertaking the move without any assistance, stubborn independence prevents turning to anyone. The effort requires countless round trip. The heat outside is crushing. Spreading the move over two days, while caught up in the effort, suddenly everywhere, the lights go out. The elevator at the new address ceases to cooperate. The citywide Great Blackout of July 13, 1977, hits, and I'm up the creek without a paddle. I'm moving the furniture, the cinder block assembled floor-to-ceiling bookcases, packed cartons containing books, artwork, potted plants, and all the other items that comprise my home one step at a time. Climbing up to the small landing and then a full flight of stairs to the second floor, resting after each traversed step, allows a momentary wipe of sweat. The heat wave causes the non-air-conditioned building temperature to soar to well over one hundred degrees. Managing this day is one of the most difficult challenges I've ever faced.

Earning recognition, accolades, and developing a close personal relationship with Esther Smith, she invites me to a social gathering at her home. Saving the Harlem Hospital extern program is acknowledged there. David, her spouse, is the president of Penn South co-op housing in the Chelsea neighborhood. She is my protector at Health and Hospitals. She serves as Special Assistant to the President, "Mike," as his friends call him. Dr. John L.S. Holliman Jr. is a prominent civil rights leader, and Esther is a New York State Democratic Committee member and active civil rights advocate. They're both mentors and guides. I'm enamored by their demeanors and social values, which are anything but establishment-based.

It's a blustery Sunday winter day. Abbey, the Smiths' daughter, and I begin a friendship. Abbey and her newlywed husband, on their honeymoon, were driving cross-country when a fatal auto accident took the spouse's life while she was sitting alongside him. Withdrawn, sitting staring out into space, unfocused and scratching her scalp until bald spots form, her loss touches shared emptiness. We are two lonely people drawn together and needing a friend. Folk guitar and singing are her refuge. After several visits, accepting the invitation, she moves into the apartment. I spend summer weekends at the Smith vacation home on Fire Island. Congresswoman Bella Abzug, a leader of the anti-war protest movement, visits, and upon introduction, I'm overwhelmed, speechless, and tongue-tied in her presence.

"How did this lonely, isolated kid reach these circles? How is it that I'm digging with my bare feet searching for oysters in the Great South Bay?"

During the relationship with the Smith family, I felt out of place and intimidated, but not by their treatment of me. They were accepting. Challenging common values, leftist socialist doctrine in the extreme is a prime feature of their personalities. Orthodoxy of any kind makes me uncomfortable. Capitalism is not the root cause of all evil. Our romance, absent passion, evolves into routine cohabitation. Two summers pass; we separate.

Matriculating in the New York University Graduate School of Public Administration with a major in Health, Policy, and Analysis is advantageous, thanks to the experience gained interfacing with municipal health care. Attending the evening program while continuing full-time employment has me feeling proud of the professional standing earned since the hippy days. I'm busy making the world better! Visiting Mom regularly, sharing successes in detail, expecting recognition and approval that was previously absent, she responds by helping to defray the tuition cost. She provides her savings accumulated over the years. I couldn't afford the expense without her help. My newfound self-esteem feels like I'm walking on clouds. I'm energized.

Entering the lobby of 346 Broadway, I'm intimidated and anxious. The building seems ancient, a throwback to an earlier time. Taking in the soaring ceilings, yellowed chandeliers casting dim lighting, and cold stone flooring, I search for the elevator bank. The elevator demonstrates that it once had a human operator. It hesitantly crawls upward, causing me to fidget restlessly. Disembarking, I search the expansive hallway for the destination. The mammoth space in the past had been partitioned into offices, the flimsy walls clashing against the original building design. Taking a deep breath, I enter to see a large space divided by three-quarter partitions. Sounds of activity reverberate throughout. A receptionist greets me at her countertop desk.

Dismissively, I reply, "I'm Danny Suster, and I have an appointment with Mr. Brownstein. I'm Joan. Please wait a moment."

He's alerted, and after a short wait, we enter the only private office in the area. Standing tall, bespectacled, and lacking smooth-flowing movement, he's clumsy.

"Refer to me as Allan. You've been sent to me highly recommended by Esther Smith, who's my patron. Please elaborate on any experience or education qualifying you for employment under my direction during these trying times." He's stuffy!

As previously briefed, the urgent mission of the department is to identify, locate, claim, and collect grant funds owed to the municipality. I'm instructed to assist the director in this effort and maintain a direct pipeline to Mrs. Smith when deemed necessary. Divided loyalties within headquarters jeopardize everyone's security. Infighting among senior staff is rampant. Fiscally, the organization is a failure deep in deficit. Her edict "do what's right" is not a concern that I share with others. Lacking experience, I qualify for the pay grade entry-level position of assistant analyst. Involvement with Health and Hospitals, the Urban Corps, and earning the master's degree in public administration at New York University covers it all. I'm to report after providing the Urban Corps with a two-week notice. Graduate studies are complete. I defer taking the required final comprehensive all-day exam. Passing will take a round-the-clock effort. The City's plight I resolve is more urgent. After any future academic semester, I'll conveniently piggyback the exam.

The New York City government is facing imminent financial bankruptcy. Gerald Ford, the Republican-appointed President who replaced our corrupt leader, Richard Nixon, refuses to guarantee loans, a bank bailout requirement, given the municipality's low credit rating. The frightening outcome is endangering the citizenry. Essential services protecting life and property will not be provided. At a minute to midnight, New York State establishes the Municipal Assistance Corporation. Loans are subject to stringent monitoring and implementation of a Program to Eliminate the Gap (P.E.G.). The City must bring revenues into line with expenditures or face bankruptcy, and default will no longer be delayed.

There are three analysts on staff. Jack focuses on the National Institute of Health and Mental Health research grants awarded to the hospital's affiliated independent medical schools and teaching departments. These, to a degree, are administered on municipal property. An accounting or payment of funds never occurs. Health & Hospitals neglectfully subsidizes these Federal research activities by providing floor space, equipment, and manpower. Arlene works on state and city-mandated community drug treatment programs. Community groups manage and spend these funds without any accountability. I freelance, assisting the analysts.

I'm assigned to reconstruct a paper trail for the Woodhull Hospital federally funded CETA program grant valued at three million dollars. The hospital is under construction in the Greenpoint/Williamsburg community and was designed as a state-of-the-art facility. The training department personnel obtained a three-year training grant designed for nurse aides to meet the standards of State-licensed practical nurses. These folk reside in the community, and this upgrade in education provides upward mobility and greater income. The only reference found in our files is an empty W folder. The training is underway. HHC salaries the students anticipating federal reimbursement.

When meeting the department director, it becomes clear that to learn anything concrete about the status of the program, the HRA Department of Employment controlling the funds must get involved. Richard is a middle-aged, immaculately dressed gentleman who's diminutive as if I'm intruding on his domain.

"I have this in hand and don't need your help administering my responsibilities. Why don't you go back to Brownstein and tell him that I've got this under control."

I can't help but think, "Yep, to the detriment of HHC, you, up until now, have been in control. I know how to deal with this. I'll contact the DOE CETA administrator."

Richard replaced Jack Moscou around the time Woodhull's training was funded. Not in the least intimidated, I'm offended and on a mission to save the City from financial collapse. Esther's words come to mind, "Aren't we on the same page pursuing the common good?" Richard's associates address him as Dick. I can see why.

Gary Post greets me with warmth and civility.

"Where have you been? I've been waiting for HHC to send over a troubleshooter so that it can claim the money owed while accounting for the progress of the program. The total funding in jeopardy is three million dollars. This has been a royal fuck up on your agency's part. There are reporting requirements to meet before I release funds. My department controls the money!"

Revealing there are no records, including the grant application and its parameters unbeknownst to me, I appeal for help. Flavia, his assistant, is assigned the job. We commence at the starting line and reconstruct the paper trail. Grant division nonfeasance has caused a turf war with the HHC Department of Finance. Grants are set up as a standalone unit. Under the corporate organization chart, it reports to the vice president of medical affairs, who happens to be a physician with little, if any, management skills. Finance personnel's hostility and lack of cooperation enable the situation to fester. Most of Grant's paperwork is nonexistent, leading to tens of millions of unclaimed federal and state dollars. Woodhull Training neglect is "the tip of the iceberg." Acquiring incomplete miscellaneous forms from various sources, I spend countless hours piecing the program together and compiling a decipherable document. Without Flavia, the effort is fruitless.

The work's tedious and boring. I'm trusted with keys to our office entrance, which I require given the after-hour effort. Reporting to the cavernous building on weekends, the lobby is always accessible. The guard on duty maintains a sign-in log. Footsteps echo through the expanse, and the emptiness is eerie. Engaging in illegal activity on government property by lighting up at the desk, puffing away, and watching the smoke rise while anxious I'll be discovered; rebellion makes drudgery acceptable. Pot slows progress. Struggling to stay focused, stamina increases, and the surrounding dead silence weighs heavily. The effort is so intense that after hours, there is no time to socialize. However, slowly, over the weeks, a picture forms that will allow HHC to claim its first reimbursement.

Gary and I meet to gauge progress.

He says,

"A six hundred thousand dollar check will be cut to cover the invoicing you've submitted. I insist that you pick up the reimbursement. I'll not give it to Richard or anyone else. You've earned my unwavering trust."

Two days later, Flavia informs me, "The check is ready."

The Grants director offers congratulations. It's a nasty, cloudy, gray day as only wet New York can produce. Excited, I trudge over to their office on Hudson Street, with each step resonating; "I've conquered the world." Handed a cashier's check in an envelope and quickly heading to 125 Worth Street, the HHC headquarters, I'm carrying six hundred thousand dollars.

"Is this real? I can hardly believe it. Sums this large are only read about!"

Cutting through the red tape, I approach the Vice President of Finance, who challenges the interruption. He's patronizing as if the Grants director's clumsy bodily movements are indicative of our abilities. Handing over the envelope, he dismisses me with no acknowledgment. Unfazed and proud, his arrogance doesn't negate my elation for completing a job that belongs in his domain.

I continue to assist Jack and Arlene in their endeavors. Arlene is trying to help the Corporation gain control of the Lincoln Hospital detox program. Their response has been intimidating. I'm glad I don't speak Spanish. I help Jack construct a paper trail of research grants. He slowly obtains pertinent material from the HHC Executive Office of Medical Affairs. The finance people reluctantly lend a hand. We estimate that over twenty-eight million dollars in uncollected funds are owed to HHC by the grantors. It requires months of monotonous research and meetings to compile sufficient documentation supporting this. The magnitude of uncollected funds is staggering. It equals half of the HHC projected deficit for the fiscal year. All municipal agencies were ordered to comply with the PEG initiative. Grants is doing its part.

Mayor Beame forces Dr. Holliman to resign. Upon hearing the news I am distraught as both he and Esther Smith are the guardians who encourage me to go up against the grain. They believe in challenging the self-serving behavior of those around them. Our values coincide. "Phonies and selfishness have no place in the public sector." They are my mentors, keeping me focused on our mutual concerns.

The newly appointed president is affiliated with the New York Archdiocese. The move is politically motivated and not in the public's best interest. Brownstein decides to leave the organization, and Ms. Gladys Handy is the replacement, a middle-aged paper pusher who has relocated from the District of Columbia to assume the position. She spends her office time fiddling about instead of debriefing the staff. She doesn't effectively provide leadership as we pursue our agendas. Weeks pass. Ignored, I'm frustrated to no end.

Bringing the matter to a head, I step into her office, seeking attention. Impatiently received, her body language dismissive, she barely looks up from her desk.

"Ms. Handy, I've spent months pursuing the recovery of funds owed to the Corporation that, due to neglect, is not claimed. Don't you want to debrief me so that we continue these efforts under your leadership?"

She curtly responds, "I've been warned about you. You're to cease all activities, and failing to follow this directive will result in your immediate dismissal."

Quickly taking leave, suppressing the impulse to be confrontational, I exit the office and head to a public payphone.

Days prior, I spoke with a close friend about my unhappiness.

Angry and frustrated, I reach out once again.

"Hi, Iris, it's Danny. The other day, I hinted to you that I've information regarding HHC that your boss will find especially useful, and it will further his career. We need to talk. Gain his interest, and please set up a meeting, all the while protecting my identity."

Trusting me, Iris complies.

Iris is a volunteer student aid in State Assemblyman Schumer's neighborhood community office. Our friendship dates back to high school, and now we both attend the New York University graduate program in Public Administration. Sharing common interests and ambitiously mapping our futures, it's easy to confide in her. We both are very motivated and speak often. Sharing conflicts and searching for her advice is always sound. Unequivocally, I trust her propriety for choosing to associate with Schumer. He's known as a formidable opponent unhesitatingly exposing government malfeasance. My rebellious nature and tendency to challenge authority bring action. I'm not relenting after months of effort. I won't surrender to the edicts of a bureaucrat who wants to endear herself to Dick, a fellow minority member. Branded an outsider, a troublemaker, I need to find others of like mind. I'm pissed.

Disenfranchised when engaged with other people, on the outside looking in; a maverick, am I about to do this again? Is this an opportunity to interact with a respectable group and get things corrected? Altruism is in play, but there's a behavioral undertone driving me. Revenge aimed at those who rejected my good intentions is necessary. Whistleblowing, betraying loyalty is no easy decision. "I have a wrong to right." The predicament worries me. Nervous over the thought of getting caught, I proceed anyway. Revealing this scandal, exposing HHC mismanagement eases any doubts that arise. I am angry.

Initiating outreach, a meeting is set up with the director of Schumer's NYS Assembly subcommittee at 270 Broadway, located a hop, skip, and a jump away. The uniformed elevator operator ascends. Stepping onto the landing, I ask for directions. Unlike the municipal building décor, the surroundings are stately with buffed gleaming stone floors, no fluorescent lighting, high chandeliered ceilings, dark polished wood, and gleaming brass at every turn. The effect projects a wealthy history demanding respect. The hushed tones heard upon entering the office reflect the deference the setting deserves.

The NYS Subcommittee on City Management and Governance is headquartered here. Daniel Feldman, a bearded, bespectacled gentleman with an aura about him fitting the location, receives me. Introduced to his associate, a given name is offered to protect anonymity. Asking for a one-on-one private meeting, taken into a small conference room, I sit alone opposite Feldman and explain the purpose of the visit.

Emotional, I ramble on about the injustices HHC personnel subject me to, explaining how the nature and value of the information could boost Schumer's notoriety. This point gets undivided attention. Feldman is an astute listener, calmly asking me to slow down and address the dynamics that brought me to him. Appalled after hearing me out, his concern focuses on the ability to vet the veracity of the charges. We review the operational fragmentation that exists in HHC and their ineffective results.

Explaining the facts and dynamics behind Woodhull's nonfeasance, I assure Feldman, "I can obtain corroborating documentation confirming the charges."

We agree to pursue Health and Hospitals. Repeatedly, we reconstruct the accusations and their strength holding up against Corporate rebuttals, denials, and news media cross-examination.

Schumer will be challenged. His words must be defensible against all scrutiny. His concern outweighs the scandalous behavior of HHC. Press coverage is of paramount importance. Caught up in the unfolding events but noticing the unspoken dynamics behind the reception, I'm treated with deference thanks to the positive media exposure brought to the table.

Remaining at the office after hours, I stop weekend

attendance. Security is best avoided to not bring attention to any extracurricular activity. I was ordered to cease and desist. The words play back repeatedly.

The copying machine requires a meter that keeps a count when printing. I'm worried this could lead to my downfall. Copying documents while hands shake, I furtively glance around to see if anyone else is present, with ears perked up, listening for intruding sounds. If caught, the resulting consequences have me thinking of nothing else.

CHAPTER 10.
SCHUMER'S AGENDA

It's the initial meeting with Schumer. Youth, academic credentials, and dialect reflecting intelligence impress. Two years older than me, he's a political reformer, allowing for an imaginary bond of overlapping values. He's quite distant, not personable at all. He's energized and driven by an agenda. District politics and his maneuvers in navigating the local machine to gain a higher position appear paramount. His face happily gleams that my anonymity is assured. The utility of the moment is the focus, and I, the person, is of little consequence. We sit together and review the accusations and supporting material, constructing a picture of management neglect costing the municipality millions of dollars. A question-and-answer session is rehearsed. Feldman and I often commiserate reviewing the material. He interrogates whatever I bring to the table. Holding up well against intense scrutiny, we jointly draft a press release. The press conference is set with invited reporters who offer favorable coverage. Schumer dramatically sensationalizes the presentation, demonstrating an unrelenting desire to uncover corruption while sublimely drawing attention to himself in the name of government reform. Woodhull Hospital exposure is just a personal tool, nothing more.

Evening arrives. Driving to the neighborhood all-night newsstand awaiting the early edition of the New York Daily News, their reporter was present.

Anxious to see where the editor chose to place the story, "What page and position on the page did it justify?"

120

Pacing the sidewalk, awaiting the delivery truck to toss its bundle, I'm jumping out of my skin, knowing I precipitated this moment. I'm just an unknown, simple guy from Brooklyn affecting reform while achieving revenge on those who dismissed me as inconsequential. The empowerment experienced is indescribable. I'm physically soaring, or so it seems.

Asking Feldman, when describing the moment, "Do all whistleblowers feel this way?"

Now, when I enter their office, I'm the star of the moment. The Daily News 12/12/77 prints, "Schumer Says Hospital Corporation Operates Funds Poorly."

The NY Post editorial on 12/19/77 "City Hospitals' Waste Scored." Continuing media coverage emboldens, revealing an even bigger headline grabber. What a rush!

Employment at Health and Hospitals doesn't offer doing anything useful. I'm caught up in leading a double life. With Brownstein's interface, I know where the records are. Gathering a compilation documenting unclaimed federal research grant overhead and expenses under the HHC umbrella arms Schumer. He can charge the Corporation with gross incompetence for not collecting over twenty-eight million dollars. The report and press release are timed for the slowest news period of the year, December. The strategy is not to compete with other breaking news. Ed Koch is replacing Mayor Beame. Schumer's report draws the newly elected mayor's attention. The NY Times places the coverage on the front page of its second section. We're elated.

I share the action with Dennis, a close friend and confidant. He's an analyst in the Office of Loss Analysis and Prevention (OLAP) under the reign of Nicholas Scoppetta, the Director of the Department of Investigations. We're comparing our investigative talents, dueling back and forth for upmanship when he shows me a classified single-spaced two-page report just completed. It reveals the municipality is purchasing asphalt at an inflated cost to repave excavated streets and repair potholes. Colluding asphalt producers are rigging bids by inflating their prices so that the predetermined designee underbids and gets a windfall.

Revisiting Dennis, I bait him by dangling the opportunity to endear himself to this up-and-coming, brilliant Harvard graduate politician.

"Dennis, I memorized the asphalt study yesterday. One of us should present it to Schumer. I've exhausted documentable Corporation newsworthy material. If you're not game, I'll proceed alone, remaining a valuable resource." Excitement and peer notoriety are addictive. I'm not ready to let go. Schumer, with each new exposé, emphasizes the sustainability of the disclosure. This reinforces my wonder if the scandals are of secondary importance. Career upward mobility dominates his motivation. He may get good things done, but he is a phony. Dennis is now on board.

The seriousness of these revelations gives Schumer significant airtime. Nick Pileggi, an investigative crime reporter for New York magazine, turns this news into the weekly's cover story. Dennis volunteers at the Committee, revealing social security number integrity shortfalls that allow ineligible recipients to receive welfare payments. Media coverage continues. Debating which direction to take, public service messages from associates about the common good just masks people's selfish agendas. To date, the behavior of colleagues confirms these tendencies. As a kid, concluding that everyone is phony, I called it correctly when seeing behavior in either black or white. Turning to Feldman to vent and seek answers and never questioning his sincerity, he urges me onward. He suggests I accept an analyst position on the NYS Assembly subcommittee. I think "Schumer can be a means to an end. Why not?"

Driving north to the state capital, I realize that drug testing is mandatory. I regret the undertaking. Living a double life, professional by day, and being an abusive pothead during leisure time, trepidation, guilt, and shame prevent accepting the opportunity. Imagining wearing those investigative shoes makes me uptight. It isn't only the illegality of drug use but also the inability to control cravings when alone at home that causes doubt. Completing the about-face, arriving back in the city, I explain to Feldman, "I'm having second thoughts about the offer. I'll defer." I move on, and Iris, two years later, marries Chuck. I'm not at all surprised. They make an ambitious couple.

Most evenings, I'm bored, and restlessness builds up. Struggling against the urge, I tell myself, "Today, no nightly run to buy grass. The quality is horrible." The effort entails driving a short distance from home to a metal door that faces pedestrians on busy Church Avenue. A buzzer controls entry. Any presence standing there waiting is conspicuous. At this hour, I'm the rare white person on the street. The dread of getting caught gnaws at me. Climbing up the five-step landing, I perch at the top, facing a one-way viewing glass pane with a small slot, and pass five dollars through the opening. A paper nickel bag appears. There are more seeds than green. The taste is awful, but the burning smell is familiar. Skunk weed doesn't do the job, but craving controls any logic that I can't muster.

Under certain conditions, marijuana is psychologically addictive and habit-forming. It's been that way for me. Every evening, I say, "Not today," eventually caving in. The lack of control is disappointing. Smoking up the envelope's content, searching for an elusive buzz, the effect saps what little energy loneliness permits. Still in streetwear, my head buried on bedroom pillows, I sleep for lengthy periods and awake more depressed than ever. Believing I'm not worthy or able to meet the expectations or requirements of a New York State investigative analyst, professionally associating with a lawbreaker could endanger careers.

"If discovered, wouldn't I be one of the bad guys? It's time to move on."

Resigning from HHC and spending months dabbling with different options, I land employment with the Manhattan Borough President's office. Leveraging Schumer's media coverage to entice Andrew Stein, I remain ambitious.

The time spent as an analyst on Andrew Stein's staff is sedentary on the surface but tumultuous underneath. The stately ambiance of the office is settling. Upon introduction, Stein is combative, addressing me as "kid" while pressing for a response on how I will obtain the media attention enjoyed by Chuck. He views Schumer as a competitor in the Democratic party-political arena. Both politicians are rising stars. Stein's persona is glamorous, portraying a noble Upper East Side lifestyle compared to Chuck's, who comes across as a Brooklyn streetfighter.

I report directly to Barbara, the Deputy Borough President. The core group consists of Barbara, Ron, the Chief of Staff, Jesse, the counsel, and Ken, the publicist. Potheads are on board! Naively thinking that their level of professional attainment precludes drug use; awareness eliminates my flight response.

The borough president's primary duty is to, during Board of Estimate sessions, approve or deny by vote all contracts executed between vendors and the municipality. I've several proposals. One of them is to fund the conversion of police department mobile communication equipment from patrol car mounted to portable units worn by police officers. The federal government provides a sizable portion of the multimillion-dollar funding matched by the city. RCA and Motorola corporations competitively bid to win the deal.

Consideration and debate occur at the Board of Estimate. Staff seating is assigned by section. The dated architecture resonates with the years of arguments witnessed. Climbing steps to join waiting team members, the battle is on. We commiserate in hushed tones, reviewing positions taken. Voting members include the council president, city comptroller, mayor's office, and five borough presidents. It doesn't get more stimulating.

During daytime hours, I'm an analyst. During my free time, I'm with State Assembly candidate Murray Weinstein. The after-hour activity comprises brainstorming and addressing community issues, formulating responses, and drafting press releases. Insecure, doubting my ability, the experience at Schumer's limited me to assisting Feldman while under his wing. Stein attributes Schumer's recent media exposure to my efforts; no contradiction is offered. Helene Weinstein, Murray's daughter, was the original candidate, but a residency challenge bumps her off the ticket. Murray, a successful litigation attorney, replaces her. They intend to end the Steingut family's forty-year imperial stranglehold on the state assembly legislative agenda. Steingut is the Brooklyn Democratic boss and the Speaker of the State Assembly. He controls the voting calendar. He and Stein have an active dislike for one another. Stein's mission statement is to help the Weinsteins defeat this nemesis.

Stein is viewed as a maverick reformer. He, without hesitation, challenges political power brokers. In 1976, he was famously known for exposing Rabbi Bernard Bergman, a Medicaid, nursing home fraudster. This led to an indictment and conviction. This is the motivating factor behind seeking employment under his leadership. Spending considerable time with the Weinstein family both at their Canarsie district headquarters and home, witnessing a wholesome family environment, and dreaming of belonging, I'm just an assigned guest. Helene and my political thinking concur. For a brief time, we have been active friends. Murray wins the election. It's time for me to move on.

At the Board of Estimate sessions, I continue to study and recommend a position vis a vis citywide communication equipment conversion. Two manufacturers are competing for the contract. Lobbied by RCA representatives, they make a compelling case. Their equipment costs less than the Motorola model, but their technology is not as advanced. If a unit needs servicing, replacement parts have to be soldered, a process that requires a repair shop to take considerable downtime until the equipment returns to the field. RCA offers extra replacement units at no cost to minimize inconvenience. The Motorola equipment is factory-assembled with modular plug-in parts, so their efficacy is obvious. Contract voting is held in abeyance by any Board member if still in review. I suggest to our executive staff that Stein can justify tabling the vote even though Police Commissioner McGuire is lobbying for quick passage favoring Motorola. Motorola is the better purchase, but given the edict to generate press exposure for Stein, the immediate goal is to gain attention, friction attracting the media. This would further his persona as independent-minded, not influenced by powerful public figures.

The holiday weekend is coming up. Assuming the Board of Estimate will not schedule a session, I take a Friday vacation day. Reporting back to work, Barbara and Ron summon me. With smirking faces quickly turning to frowns, I hear,

"Andrew was on a Caribbean weekend retreat when McGuire got him on the phone. He bought Stein's favorable vote for the Motorola contract by authorizing the installation of a red flasher and police siren in his municipal car. This enables Andrew to cut through morning traffic on the FDR when he leaves his Sutton Place residence for the office."

I'm dumbfounded! "I thought there was no scheduled session."

"The Council President unexpectedly called for one."

The irony of this outcome is that my values, disdain for duplicity, and selfish goals lead to the obvious conclusion.

"Toys! He sold his vote for toys!" I resign.

Employment under the direction of Harriet Dronska, the assistant administrator at the Human Resources Administration, doesn't pan out. She buries me in administrative drudgery. She won't allow me to pursue social security integrity issues Dennis had shared with the committee. Esther Smith refers me to Madeline Bowman, the Executive Director of Bellevue Hospital. I'm to complete administrative residency training under her wing. I'm placed with an underling who doesn't know what to do with me. I can't help but miss the recent action. I need a challenge. Impatient with the slow daily pace, it doesn't work out well.

Unemployed, idleness is the routine. To escape, Mom and Bernard gift me a brand new color television console. Avoidance is the preferred way to address this world. I haven't watched the tube since leaving home. Regular programs don't interest me. Yesterday, today, and tomorrow, humanity never changes for the better, so why stay informed? The news only makes for sadness. The television sits idle on the dresser top.

Now respectable in Godfather's eyes, we confer on a regular basis. I brag about undertakings to gain praise. Painting canvases stopped when graduate school commenced. Career advancement is prioritized; there just aren't enough hours in the day to do it all. I'm soaring. Channeling creativity, I'm pursuing non-conventional activities. Positive results legitimize the loss of painting. Praises set off a dopamine rush.

In self-talk, I rationalize and reconcile the internal debate that ensues. "Am I being true to myself?"

Outside reinforcement surmounts any conflict or doubt. Swept away from artistic pursuits, the dynamics of unfolding events determine my direction.

Surprisingly, Godfather informs me, "The ideal job is waiting if you're willing to take a chance on something new."

PART 2

CHAPTER 11.
ROSS MEDICAL SCHOOL

Acceptance into a U.S. medical school is so academically competitive, most applicants are rejected. A World Health Organization-recognized school located in a foreign country is an option. Requirements for acceptance are not stringent. Mexico's proximity to the USA and the multitude of medical schools there make this locale a favored alternative. Earning a degree in the USA requires two years of science, anatomy, and lab curriculum, plus two years of patient contact. Once free of the classroom, the initial step is learning to take and record a patient history while projecting a confidence-inducing bedside manner. Training at Mexican and Dominican Republic schools requires completion of a six-year curriculum. Candidates enroll in European universities as well. American participation in these programs is profuse. Due to pressure from stateside regulators and institutional concerns, the Fifth Pathway program was introduced. Participants complete the fifth year of training in an accredited U.S. hospital teaching department, and the required sixth year is waived.

Bernie, the Director of Medical Education and Chief of Surgery at Rockaway Peninsula Hospital, is an active player. Jerry B.'s son enrolled in a Santo Domingo school that trains in Far Rockaway and lives at home. The father conceptualizes establishing a medical school on the island of Dominica. It will cater to foreign students and require only four years of study. It would mirror the stateside curriculum. He shares this idea with Bob Ross, but before he can act, he suffers a stroke. After years of friendship, Ross brushes him to the side. The seed is planted! Ross commences the first-year class with thirteen students in attendance at an island hotel in Portsmouth, Dominica. Godfather is a contracted consultant and is later appointed Trustee. The school has no clinical training, and the Island hospital cannot offer any. The facility provides only basic health care services.

The interview with Bob Ross is unusual, to say the least. His office comprises a large shared space and a smaller room. Paper and files are stacked everywhere in total disorganization. His oversized desk crowds the small office. There is a secretary and two employees. The main space lacks the capacity for more. The interview is anything but professionally conducted.

Ross spends time talking exuberantly about himself while puffing a Cohiba that's a foot long. White-haired, overweight, sporting pronounced suspenders, the dialogue centers around claiming he's a successful commodities barterer who trades contracts like pantyhose for coal. He's an eccentric throwback to an earlier time. Referring to me as "young man," the cigar demands deference to all that's pontificated. He's long-winded and boring. Smoke blankets the mess.

Employed as the Assistant Dean for Clinical Affairs, I'm to acquire clerkships throughout the country. This will enable students returning to the states to undergo hospital-based patient contact. Using the nationwide residency program directory, I will selectively cold-call teaching departments, purposely referencing the new job title to project prestige and open the way. Programs of lesser reputation or with no medical school affiliation are receptive to gaining the recruitment tool, but question the capabilities of foreign-trained individuals when undergraduate grades don't reach the stateside threshold. The NYC metropolitan area is the prime target.

Pressured to prove myself, Mrs. Davidson at Coney Island Hospital is the obvious first contact. The process is slow. Cutting through stoic physician prejudices is a challenge; she greases the way.

A Miami-based Cuban exile who is both a physician and student recruiter for a Dominican Republic medical school cuts a deal with Ross for a lateral transfer of eighty students into clerkship training. Official school transcripts follow after studies commence. This is not an ethical way to start a school. Ross, a fighting businessman, is scrambling for money. Academicians are hired. A gateway for student acceptance hasn't yet been set in place. These students have community hospital clerkships in non-teaching specialties already underway. The reward for switching schools is graduating after four academic years of training instead of six, while also reducing tuition. A for-profit business, the school is starting to generate cash flow. Overhead expense during the clerkship years is minimal, and the tuition collected is considerable. Three sixteen-week semesters generate three revenue cycles per calendar year. Ross University administration relocates to the Empire State Building.

Ross the showman believes the image this location creates builds credibility with prospective applicants. He has a recruitment video produced with E.G. Marshall, a popular Hollywood actor, narrating. James Cassidy, the Dean at Tufts Dental School, is appointed Chancellor, accompanied by Maureen McCarthy, his assistant and future wife. Architectural plans to install prefabricated classrooms and housing are presented to Ross. To assuage State licensing agency accusations that the school is a paper mill, credentialed, high-profile medical educators comprise the Board of Trustees, lobby State officials, and are hired as basic science instructors and department chairpersons.

Bob announces he's won a lawsuit against the Federal Republic of Nigeria. During the 1970s, he signed a contract to have concrete delivered to the port city of Lagos. The military incompetently runs the country. Four hundred ships were idle at the port waiting to unload. The docks don't have the capacity to accept the delivery. Lengthy delays cause the concrete sitting in moist salt air to turn into unusable, hardened solid blocks. Unloading the commodity never occurred. Ross sued the Nigerian government in the NYS court. He claims that not going through the international legal system and winning is a precedent. Ross holds up a check for all the staff to see, in the sum of two million four hundred thousand dollars. His investment was in the thousands. Funding to seed construction is now in hand. Emboldened to hire a full-time chauffeur and stretch limousine, Bob believes that flashing wealth brings respectability, credibility, and the recognition he hungers for. Visiting the Breakers in Palm Beach, Florida, he loves advertising the fact.

Appointment setting is a grind. With a cluster of responses, I jet to locations, rent an automobile, and visit with the decision-makers. I target economically distressed communities. The competition to secure resident specialty training is minimal compared to other places. Quality of life after years of round-the-clock study for the average domestic graduate is paramount. In contrast, foreign medical graduates are grateful to secure any accredited program, no matter the location. Youngstown, Flint, Detroit, Harlan County, Cook County, Cleveland, Miami, Bartow, Camarillo, Los Angeles, Jersey City, Elizabeth; the inner city is of no consequence to the committed.

I propose to Bob that we start paying the departments of medical education that accept students. It's immediately approved.

To nurture goodwill, I visit the various participating facilities. Playing one off against the other, instilling envy, results in acquiring additional sites. Friendly discourse with physicians is a load of fun. I'm confident but humble and secure knowing that I have what they want: trainees and money. These educators are chronically underfunded. Off-campus resources drive the profitability of the school. Farming out training at a minimum expense is a slam dunk for Ross University. This eliminates overhead cost.

The news that Ross has clerkships drives the enrollment of transfer students who want to repatriate. Core clerkship requirements include Internal Medicine, Surgery, Obs/Gyn, Pediatrics, Family Medicine, and Psychiatry. Clerkship requirements are from six to twelve weeks, totaling forty-two weeks. Accredited teaching department clerkships are difficult to obtain. Alternate sites are in small 150-200-bed community hospital facilities. Traveling to Dominica repeatedly over a six-year period, I interview students about to complete their basic science studies. I assign the better performers to accredited teaching departments, and the remainder to community hospitals.

The hero: helping the deserving, I'm predisposed to view students as winners and losers. Negative categorization becomes part of the lexicon. In the Manhattan office, I witness parental solicitation; their presence as an intrusion. Parents, often physicians, insist that their unqualified children become doctors. Grades barely passing; MCAT scores are an ineffective evaluation tool. Character flaws are obvious, no motivation is shown, and these parents insist that their offspring become physicians! Staring at a parent physician, I asked,

"How selfish can people be if a person who swore the

Hippocratic Oath to further health care and medical science is prepared to place a person's life in their incompetent child's hands?" The father stood up and left the interview. Ignoring this Dad's response, the applicant's sincerity and passion won me over.

These parents are not out of the norm. Many candidates have no business joining the profession. A moron with enough effort and memory can pass the Education Commission for Foreign Medical Graduates (ECFMG) exam. I'm aiding, abetting, and endangering proper patient care. Unsettled over continuing employment, wherever I turn, people compromise correctness. The duplicity of incompetent would-be healers wantonly seeking social status reinforces my estrangement. It's so personally familiar. I don't like people very much. Is everyone full of shit? Marijuana remains a close friend.

Nothing growing up in America or when hitchhiking through Europe prepared me for the realities of Dominica. The underdevelopment and lack of infrastructure are startling. Automobiles are rare. Sidewalks and drainage barely exist. Some roads are paved. Gravel is common. Structures are assembled with tin and corrugated metal sheets. Palm trees and dense tropical rainforests cover dormant volcanic mountain sides. Hurricane David stripped trees of their foliage, and scars in the terrain are everywhere. Coconuts, bananas, papayas, mangos, avocados, pineapples, and more grow unfettered. The 200-foot-high Trafalgar Falls and Titou Gorges are nature's wonders. Birds talk, and colors hover in the air. The parrots are very happy, swarming about in groups. The airport landing strip only accommodates propeller-driven airplanes.

My initial impression: "Albert Schweitzer would find

practicing medicine here challenging." Dominica is referred to as the breadbasket of the Caribbean.

Transfer students maintain contact with friends left behind. Happily, resettled, it's common to recruit friends on the benefits of returning stateside and reducing curriculum requirements by one or two years. To earn favor and better clerkships, industrious students set up presentations for me near campus. Guadalajara, Juarez, and Santa Domingo are scheduled. Never exposed to commission-based compensation, the concept is foreign to me. Helping the school expand casts me as the hero. Acceptance and recognition are compensation enough.

The job is anything but boring, yet a corrosive routine sets in. When at home, intense feelings of emptiness take over. Marijuana is my companion. The quality is nominal. No spacey drift. Without it, the buzz is still craved, and I remain agitated. Removing the seeds with a strainer, then folding and packing the cigarette paper, fingers twisting and rolling in an upward direction, licking the glue, and lighting up finally brings about a modicum of relaxation. The ritual served its purpose. Smoking inferior quality stuff wears me down to where I sleep away endless time. Ten to twelve hours out cold is common, but so is waking mornings with a foul taste. I hate this lack of self-control.

CHAPTER 12.
LOVE AGAIN

It's a Friday afternoon visit to the Internal Medicine department at Jamaica Hospital. Sol, when seeing me, exuberantly latches on. He's cunning, believing that if we're friends, I'll place him in the best locations. He invites me to join him the following evening at a disco. He'll introduce me to a beautiful young Israeli woman. She's completed her army stint and is touring the country. He's so persistent, I acquiesce.

At first sight, it doesn't seem that either of us wants to communicate with the other. Our fashion choices clash. She wears skin-tight velour pants tucked into knee-high boots, accompanied by a one-button blazer exposing flesh between small breasts. Her overall appearance includes eyeliner and lashes, red lipstick, perfectly applied nail polish, and a scent of perfume that emotes sensuality. I, a nerd, don't own casual clothing appropriate for a disco setting. Sol hands us cocktails. Barely communicating and bored, a short while later, I extricate from the scene.

Delivering a payment at Jamaica Hospital, I run into Sol. He insists I accompany him to where the Israeli woman is temporarily staying.

"It's just a five-minute drive. She needs to find other accommodations until a scheduled return home is made; she has nowhere to go. The Israeli male roommate bullies her."

Weakly resisting Sols' overtures, his persistence wins out. Entering the apartment and seeing her down on her knees in a bathrobe, barefoot and without makeup, she's occupied behind the pulled-out refrigerator and stove, scrubbing grime off the old linoleum floor. Custom requires a clean home and kitchen in honor of the Sabbath. This picture is so familiar and touching. It reminds me of my mom's cleanliness.

I whisper in Sol's ear, "She can sleep on the large pillows in the living room and tell her I won't touch her. I'll return later this evening."

There is something cute, innocent, and playful about her. Alone for so long, starving for companionship, this woman is exotic! Rudimentary and heavily accented English brings us laughs. Our cultural differences cause friction, awe, and appeal in sharing perspectives, experiences, and possibilities. Over cups of coffee until the wee hours of the morning, we sit side by side at the two-seater, squeezed into the kitchen area. Our aid: an English-Hebrew dictionary. We refer to it as "The Bible." Searching for appropriate words to converse with is fun. Fatigue eventually takes over. Introducing Orly to Dylan, The Beatles, Zeppelin, and similar genres, I intend to captivate her. Orly smokes grass for the first time.

Miami-based facilities need attention. More clerkships translate into expanded enrollment and greater profits. With a blank check to travel the States, results are the ticket. I offer Orly an all-expense-paid trip to accompany me to Miami. Eagerly, she accepts. Hotel room, car rental, and shared meals are the school's expense, the remainder mine. I try to be cavalier with the invite, but feel otherwise. Anticipation runs high. I had reserved a room at the famous Diplomat Hotel, where Sinatra, Martin, and other famous acts once performed. We eagerly head to the pool deck, cocktails forthcoming. Her Mediterranean-styled bikini resembles band-aids covering the important parts. Her skin tans so deeply, the following day it peels off in sheets. Her words flaunt that she's not a novice around men, but that night, I show her otherwise. The trip is a success in every way.

Returning to New York, I leave her behind to enjoy the hot rays of South Florida. Absent mentor guidance, trusting Orly is the manly thing to do. Orly doesn't return on the ticketed flight. Days later, I ignore a knock on the door until a voice calls out. Opening it a crack with the chain in place and peeking outside, I turn Orly away only to surrender when she voices, "I have nowhere else to go." She returned to the other apartment only to find a macho person awaiting her. Pissed but enjoying her company, enamored I can't refuse.

Without fail, we visit Manhattan. Orly, upon entering Duane Reade or similar stores, stares wide-eyed at the variety of personal care products on the shelves. Import tariffs are so high in Israel that the populace doesn't demand product availability. I'm the enabler. Items mentioned unceremoniously appear in quantity: three bottles of this, four tubes of that, and so on. I purchase an additional suitcase to store the booty for eventual transport. Out of control with little experience, reference points or mentors, I'm in the dark. I don't know the right way to grow or secure a love relationship.

Nightlife is pursued at every opportunity that arises. Walking the streets of Manhattan, if there are avant-garde garments in a window display, we enter. Soho and the West Village are favorite targets. Orly's appearance is sexy but not cheap. Arriving home, I crop the dresses. High-heeled boots complete the trick.

Parking the Renault 12 station wagon at a metered space on

the Avenue of the Americas in Greenwich Village, the engine catches fire. I'm not upset. Not exposed to cars as a kid, there's no interest in them. It's just a means of transport, nothing more. Removing the license plates, I abandon the vehicle. Orly reacts, "You're crazy!" Her bewildered eyes glance up and down the street, perplexed by my spontaneity and indifference.

Orly is returning to Israel. I want her to see me as the next best thing since sliced bread. Wanting her yearning for me while not cognizant of the possibility she might not look back, I'm tapped out. The day after she left, Con Edison turned off the electricity. In the dark for two days with only candlelight available, I feel victimized. Considering how I reached this state, I blame the gold-digger, assuming no responsibility for poor choices. It's comforting to blame someone else.

Absorbed at work, the repetition is a grind. The long flights to the island, accompanied by a Sony Walkman and Jason Bourne, are no longer engaging. Butterflies are a memory. Smoking pot is more prevalent than ever. Binge eating after smoking is the routine. Entenmann's sour cream cake and Häagen-Dazs ice cream are my favorites. The chocolate ice cream takes me back to Amsterdam. Personal appearance is a concern. The munchies are hard to contain. To control calorie intake, I'm now bulimic. When satiated, I lean over the toilet, press the handle of a toothbrush against my throat, spasm and release. Weight loss is quick. Evenings after work, I body build at Lou Ferrigno's gym located under the El on McDonald Avenue. With a thirty-inch waist, spandex swimsuits are the style. London Fog, Cerruti, and Boss dominate the work wardrobe. The time spent with the Israeli woman causes me to be fastidious about appearance.

Purchasing a white Toyota Celica GT five-speed stick with

mag wheels completes the look. Not riding the subway is a privilege. Taking the required comprehensive exam produces the NYU master's degree. Having been away from classes for years, I relearned all the material. I'm feeling good. The upgraded physique, toys, and belief that I'm now desirable drive me.

Looking in on Bernard at his Upper West Side apartment, yearning for his love and attention never ceases. During our upbringing, Mom conditioned us to think that career choice and attainment earn respect and love. Personal achievements fool me into believing that our interaction will be wholesome and on equal footing.

There are two topics that our conversations revolve around: complaints about Mom's selfish games and his gay nighttime social life infused with inhaled poppers and parsley-soaked angel dust.

Handing me a rolled herb, "Take a puff of this angel dust. The taste is repulsive, and the effect is totally disorienting, but you'll get high!"

All that I remember afterward is his acclaim for the unfettered sex enjoyed during nighttime excursions. Bernard's demeanor evolves into flaunting debauchery. This behavior is his freedom declaration. He, too, was Mom's captive. She is the topic that draws us together. We have little in common. He has no interest in my activities but is always ready to pass judgment on my choices. He's noble, I'm not. I try to bridge the gap and am frustrated at not recognizing the futility of the effort.

Dr. Bernstein, his former therapist during the intake session years earlier, said, "Forget your brother. There's nothing there for you."

Those words fell on deaf ears.

Smoking a fatty, Bernard confesses that one day, when I was little, resentful of cleaning and diapering me, he pressed the back of my hand against a steaming hot radiator. He held it there to blister, ignoring my screams and cries. Upon inspection, freckled pigmentation is obvious, and so is the guilt he's wearing.

Two envelopes arrive months apart, sent from Israel. Clearly, they're from Orly. Written in Hebrew, I can't decipher them. Housed in my suit's inner breast pocket, I await Sol, the student who introduced us, to show up at the office and translate. As predicted, his unscheduled appearance to pick up transcripts prompts us to seek privacy. We descend to his illegally parked car. Israeli culture doesn't foster civility. He translates. Orly gushingly addresses the visit, stating she hasn't come across anyone so special. Abba Bentzi, having heard stories of our time together, emboldens her to attempt renewed contact. I telephone. It's fun conversing. Concluding, I can handle her more effectively this time, I'm assertive and confident, and there's nothing to lose. Good times await. The flight is booked.

Carmen's son attends Ross, and his father makes it a point that I'm aware of. At his office, he excitedly shares maps of oil well drilling in Texas, offering me the opportunity to participate. A prominent citizen of Fairfield, Connecticut, he seeks assurance that his son receives training in accredited teaching departments. One good favor deserves another is his maxim. Seizing the opportunity, I make certain Peter is placed in the best locations. In turn, Carmen offers the use of his beachfront condominium on St. Croix. Assessing work ethic and results, requesting time off is never questioned by Ross.

Orly and I have been back together for about a week. I enter the apartment. Orly is conversing on the phone in Hebrew. Even though I don't understand the language, I'm confrontational. Her tone sounds solicitous. She admits her hashish connection called to inquire about her. He's her father's age, and they made an acquaintance through her dad. Angry that she would give my phone number out implies that he's important. An older guy checking in is a red flag. Confronting her, it's made clear that if they ever have contact again, she'll be on the next flight to Israel. Raging, I punch a hole in the sheetrock wall. Brushing a beam dislocates a pinky. Exiting, muttering curses, the injured hand feels no pain.

Our bags packed, we head for the airport. In St. Croix, collecting our luggage and exiting the terminal, the surrounding ambience reflects the island's serenity. The taxi driver, ever so polite, is a caricature of this. The apartment entrance is near the shoreline. Without visitors, we have our own private beach. Feeling special, we treat every moment accordingly. Romance in a dream-like state intensifies. Neither of us uses birth control. We're not responsible enough to weigh the implications and just live to fully enjoy the moment. Ignoring the consequences of our choices become the foundation of the relationship.

Adding a little adventure, Orly, who's not a great swimmer, is convinced no harm will come if we snorkel at the Buck Island reef. Arms wrapped around each other's waist, we climb down the chartered boat's ladder, adjust our masks, and push off the side, entering a world of unfettered beauty. Tropical fish swim within inches of us with no concerns. We avoid getting close to the coral, the boat's crew warning that it's sharp and easily cuts skin. Orly needs to constantly feel assured. She's impressionable. Earning her trust, the outing brings us closer. I am the enabler, she the receiver. The interaction makes me heady. It's our precursor for mutual dependency and the need for certainty.

The isolation has us jaded. Aiming for action, we abandon laid-back St. Croix, catch a commuter flight, and hop over to San Juan. Orly is fastidious, absorbed with self-appearance. Scheduled commitments always take a second seat. There's little concern for others, vanity taking over. She believes her entrance will be so captivating that any tardiness is readily forgiven. This assumption might apply to friends but not to booked flights. Ignored, I pace and curse until there's clearance to order a taxi. A yellow flag thrown on the playing field is warranted but denied.

With only minutes to spare, I'm forced to carry the luggage directly to the runway. There's no porter available. Resting Orly's huge suitcase upright on my shoulder, I carry the smaller pieces with the other hand. Knees buckling under the weight while racing to the plane before the doors close takes an absurd effort. About to collapse, somehow making it, the last one on, we catch the flight and laugh, releasing the tension. She doesn't give the scenario a second thought. Instead of justifiably missing the flight, I'm the angry enabler. Denying any ill will, I'm content with the fun we're having.

Lodging at the Caribe Hilton hotel and casino is like a honeymoon without commitment. Poolside, we befriend a middle-aged couple who also live in Brooklyn. They love to party and treat us by sharing their cocaine. The drug is a first for both of us. We limit gambling to slot machines. I'm an adverse risk-taker with money on the line; the fear of loss overrides the joy of gain. Ironically, though, I throw caution to the wind when my well-being is compromised by unfettered behavior. Without mentor guidance, I'm feeling, but not seeing, the paths I chose.

Back in Brooklyn, shopping for clothes on the streets of

Bensonhurst, smiling and walking towards me is Sharon and a bearish appearing fellow who towers over her. The last time we met, she was stoned on heroin in the City College cafeteria, and Janis Joplin died. She introduces me to Ralph, her husband. Making small talk, she volunteers, "We deal grass." Agreeing to reacquaint ourselves, I jot down her Manhattan Beach address and phone number.

"We reside on the upper floor of a two-family house. The homeowner is an unassuming, elderly lady living on the lower floor. There are separate entrances in the hallway. This is essential given the type and extent of trade we pursue. Danny, we hope to see you soon."

The entranceway is dim, musty, and smells of sea salt and mildew. Reaching the second landing, their home serves as a living space and warehouse. Everywhere, there are bales of marijuana stored in labeled, large black plastic trash can liners. Boxes of Glad bags and scales, both large and small, are scattered about. Bundles of cash are everywhere, labeled, rubber-banded, and stacked. Incense fills the air, combating the pungent marijuana odor. Seating is limited to a large mattress and throw pillows set on oriental-style rugs. Furnishings are a secondary concern; commerce is primary.

Sharon explains that weed types come in varying strains of quality, and the most popular is California Sen similia. Questioning, I learn that one client alone moves one hundred pounds weekly! High up in the wholesale marijuana supply chain, Ralph's side business is moving cocaine in lesser amounts. It's not long before my purchases for personal use turn into a dealership. The quality is great, and the price is right. Bales are offloaded at the Long Island shoreline and then sold to them. Limited actors in the chain allow for great pricing. Sharon offers to front the product thanks to a friendship that traces back to high school and shared times. Like so many others, I fund personal use by selling to friends and acquaintances.

There are a dozen regular clients who indulge. The effort turns into a modest profit. Open for more action, my secluded lifestyle doesn't produce potential clients. The consequences aren't considered at all. The rush of easy cash blinds me. Moral compass in disarray, ambition reigns. In my pursuits, the medical school is ranked second. There are no mentors.

Impulsively, I concoct a plan to seek employment managing a Crazy Eddie electronics store, the largest retailer in the tri-state area. The owner and core personnel are Jewish Syrian transplants. Many of them attended our neighborhood high school. They're clannish and exclusionary. I'm intimidated but ready to break in! The application process requires submitting to a lie detector test to ascertain if the applicant is a theft risk. I'm required to take a drug test. It's not going to happen. I'll be discovered as a two-time loser, both for toking and stealing. This is 'Crazy' given the group's reputation as a party crowd. The name is fitting. Hearing me out, the interviewer suggests I contact David.

Providing his contact information, he alludes, "You might be of help in another capacity."

David is part of Eddie's inner group. Eddie wants to diversify. He's convinced the profit-producing foreign medical school business is the way to go. The St. Lucia government is prepared to charter a school with WHO recognition under its sponsorship. Upfront funding, a euphemism for payoff, will go to the decision-makers on the island. Interaction with David blossoms into a friendship.

Wanting my services, he says, "Initially, you'll be retained as a consultant and later full-time employment once student applications are solicited."

The offer is lucrative and appealing, but in the back of my mind, being an outsider, doubt festers. I'll be temporarily utilized and when they're done with me, tossed away. There's no certainty in his words, "consultant" or "later."

The NYS Medical Board is aggressively labeling and reviewing these schools, referring to them as paper mills. Seeing only in black, white, and cared for by the best of the best, my standards are uncompromising; foreign schools are in a precarious position. Meeting with Eddie and his entourage, I urge abandoning the idea. The existence of for-profit Caribbean medical schools is ending. The authorities will conclude the same. Inferior candidates with adequate test preparation qualify for licensure. This dilutes the quality of care. Regulators won't let this go on indefinitely. Ross University is familiar to me and appears more secure. I defer the offer. For reasons not shared with me, their initiative is abandoned, but I'm viewed endearingly. Years later, Eddie Antar is imprisoned for fraud.

David and I like to smoke together. Revealing that I can acquire pot in substantial amounts, he becomes a client. Pick up in Manhattan Beach and drop off at his Neponsit address, the markup is small per pound, but in five and ten-pound amounts, the profit adds up. Living a dual persona, I'm Assistant Dean during the day and a drug distributor at night. I purchase a triple-beam balance scale to properly manage the expanding business. David is the largest customer.

Involved in a whirlwind of activity, my infatuation with Orly is constant. Making her happy often leads to compromising better judgment. Exposed to high-end shopping, this indulgence becomes a basic staple not to be denied. This standard of living doesn't exist in Israel, where all imports are subjected to a high value-added tax in addition to tariffs. Bloomingdale's, Tiffany, and Saks Fifth Avenue are anticipated weekend excursions. Standing by the cosmetic counters, too eager to please, this will come back to haunt me. What I intended to be episodic is now an expectation.

She's open to whatever I introduce. Sex is an activity we mutually enjoy. Music and concerts are an integral part of our leisure. We smoke with regularity but don't consider harder drugs an option. Bouncing down streets with our arms wrapped around each other's waists, heads turn to take notice of this couple exuding happiness. Orly whose taller than me without high-heeled shoes is a looker. In the evenings, we sit over coffee with a joint and an English-Hebrew dictionary, talking and laughing until exhaustion takes over. The closeness is intense.

Leon's unemployed spouse sits on my mind as a sore point. The situation is viewed resentfully by me on Leon's behalf. I insist that if Orly intends to marry, she must return to Israel and enroll in technical training that will lead to a career. "You'll never be content as only a homemaker." Beautiful nails are her forte. We locate a cosmetology school in Tel Aviv that accepts her, even though the program had started the previous week. Handing over tuition fees and a little extra, we pack the now overloaded suitcase and send her off.

The cost of a long-distance telephone minute from Brooklyn to Ramat Gan is exorbitant. Days pass before checking on Orly. She hasn't started the program. The reasons are lame. Funds meant for tuition squandered, I'm disappointed and angry, but I soon forget. I miss her. We agree she will return after a two-month stay. Attending school is forgotten. She complains that the Northeast frigid winter temperature turns her feet blue, which she hates but will put up with. Flight booked, her arrival time approaching, I attack the disaster that reflects bachelorhood neglect. I had piled every garment onto the bedroom lounge chairs, some clean, others needing laundering.

It's midnight on the early morning of her arrival. Visiting the 24-hour Pathmark supermarket, I fill the kitchen cabinets with all sorts of products. The apartment is domesticated after months of neglect that began when she left. Entering the apartment, the Phone Mate answering machine's red indicator light is blinking in the darkness. I have a bad premonition. Orly states, "There's a problem. Call me." Israel airport security caught her not renewing the multiple-entry visa to the USA and turned her away. Not believing the explanation, I'm terse and keep the costly conversation short in response to the "get back to me message." I can't help but question, "Am I being taken for a ride? Is this girl sincere? Is there an Israeli boyfriend in the picture?"

Hatching a plot to discover her true intentions, I inform Ross, "Given it's the Christmas holiday season, I'm taking time off to visit my girlfriend in Israel."

The only immediate booking available is a Christmas Eve flight on Alitalia with a stopover in Rome. Telephoning Orly, "My boss is giving me a holiday reward, the use of the office phone on Christmas day. We'll have an unlimited conversation, and you must answer the call at the designated time."

Factoring in the ETA and taxi drive to her home, the mailing address serves me well. During the Rome layover, a number of priests and nuns in full dress board the plane for the annual pilgrimage. I stare, pondering their presence. It dawns on me that we're sharing a journey of love. I can't help but laugh.

Catching Orly unaware, I believe signs of dishonesty will leak through any façade spontaneously erected. At the four-story apartment building, buzzing the lobby intercom, there's no response when I'm asked to identify myself. Investigating, her youngest sister descending the staircase allows me entry, staring with sudden recognition, and takes off racing upwards.

On her heels, shouting the Hebrew word, 'sheket' for silence, I enter right behind.

Orly is standing in the kitchen, bent leg on a chair. She's tying her laces. Looking up confused and trying to focus, she's speechless, jumping up and down, her body shaking, managing, "I can't believe it! What are you doing here? I can't believe it. Somebody get Abba."

No explanation offered; we embrace. She struggles to take it all in and phones Bentzi. Within minutes, he leaves his kiosk situated around the corner to make an acquaintance. A parade of girlfriends ensues and continues until dawn. They all heard about me. This is all the assurance needed. The visit lasts ten days, exposing me to a community of friendships nonexistent in Brooklyn. Visits aren't prearranged. Friends just show up at the door, assuming a welcome. Refreshments are readily served. It's a custom to have "goodies" stored in the cubby for the unexpected.

It's winter and the weather is wet, cold, and nasty. There is limited outdoor recreation available in the Tel Aviv area.

Restaurants and discotheques are plentifully resonating until the early morning hours. Although I don't speak Hebrew, her friends and relatives have a basic knowledge of English. They stimulate and charm me until it's time to return home.

Orly complains about the frigid winter awaiting her in Brooklyn. Her feet turning blue in the cold is a constant tease. We're in love. I'll grant her anything she wants if it's doable. We agree she'll delay returning for an additional six weeks. Leaving alone, disappointed, feelings denied, the instinctual parameters of love are foreign. "Shouldn't love tame the cold weather?" Elated, I have her masks the truth. Winter's ferocity over, when she returns, I'll find her a diamond engagement ring. I know just where to shop. Vinnie, a Ross student, referred me to a connection, his cousin, who's counter borders Little Italy at the Bowery Jewelry Exchange. This is so in character. First Carmen, now Vinnie. Good teaching clerkships are hard to find.

Entering the dimly lit, silent apartment, emptiness saturates the air. Flashing on yesterday, I'm hit with the contrast in realities. Threatening loneliness lingers in the shadows. Quiet triggers memories of emptiness that unexpectedly arise. There's a history of shallow, disconnected relationships that I hope I left behind. Yearning to be untouched by the foibles of the past, I'm driven to move forward and propose.

"I'll surprise Orly with half-carat diamond stud earrings."

Thoughts of companionship dampen the intensity of the enduring silence. Global anxiety is just a memory. Certainty is in play.

I can hew, shape, and polish this rough diamond. I'm so

happy to have found her. I'm liberated from a life so empty. Empowered, invulnerable, governing choices, and anticipating only positive outcomes, there isn't room for any other result. I'm on a roll. I won't fail and never have. I throw caution to the wind. Poor self-esteem is a thing of the past, or so I think, and yet I smoke pot daily. Am I driven by the pains of the past? This act only adds to my awareness that I'm still struggling inwardly. Am I being phony with myself? Pot clouds cognitive abilities. Impulsive action renders my judgment questionable. There is no one to consult with, no alternate perspective. Mentors I relied on are now not around. The mania joy feeds is working like a drug, grasping, forming, and holding onto my decisions. The brakes are gone. I sway onto a dangerous path. Self-talk isn't part of the equation. Feelings govern me.

Dropping the luggage, playing Enrique Masias and Julio Iglesias songs, Orly introduced, I'm rolling a joint and drifting to visions of the trip provides relief. Adjusting to the seven-hour time zone difference, my body clock is out of sync, so I take the next day off before resuming work.

CHAPTER 13.
I DO!

Back to the routine. The contrast with last week's events spent in Israel is glaring. Medical school responsibilities during the day, weed after hours. Smoking and commerce, curtailing the mundane, keep me occupied. Days morph into a holding pattern. I'm waiting for Orly. Disliking employment, pot commerce, and easy profit is an alternative outlet that numbs the discontent. Spending evenings toking away, social visits with Sharon and Ralph are more frequent. Business is minimal but steady.

Counting the days till her return, Orly and Bentzi are planning an August wedding on the Tel Aviv shore at the Hotel Diplomat. Meeting Orly at the airport, presenting her with the diamond studs, she's in shock.

I ask, "Would you please put these on?"

Her face glowing, our kissing is not meant for public consumption.

Within days of reuniting, we visit Vinnies' cousin at the jewelry exchange. It's a midweek sunny afternoon, but dark and gloomy inside. The place is vast with counters everywhere and void of traffic. No matter, the proprietors are earnest in their greeting. I mention Vinnie, and they promise satisfaction. Suggesting a price range, trays are pulled out of the unlocked display cases and set before us. We discuss the different cuts available. I'm specific in wanting a teardrop that sacrifices depth for surface. We find a 1.1-carat pink diamond without visible inclusions for half its assessed value. Orly distracted makes it easy to admire the emerald jewelry in the adjoining glass case. Intoxicated by the moment, in a hushed voice, I negotiate the package price for two rings that speak the perfect gesture. I want to be sure that Orly is also intoxicated.

It's time to leave the bachelor pad and establish a shared setting we mold together. Purchasing our Middle Eastern groceries at a row of ethnic stores on Kings Highway, above one of these shops, a freshly renovated, small two-bedroom apartment is available. We're acquainted with the owners, having visited the location often. Two units are situated on the second floor, with the entrances facing one another. Our neighbors are a young Israeli couple of Moroccan and Libyan ancestry. Orly is both Iraqi and Bukhari, and I'm Lithuanian and Polish. We befriend them given the shared Israeli desire to socialize. Venues before me are as enticing as the strongest narcotic. With a beautiful, exotic fiancé, foreign cuisine and music, illicit drugs, fashionable clothes, nightlife, friends, and shared religion from diverse cultures, I can do no wrong. The draw: Israelis are genuine, not phony.

The renovated apartment is raw. The plywood floors need covering. This is the tenant's responsibility. Walnut wooden tiling is installed at the entrance. Plush black wall-to-wall carpeting is selected for the living room and off-white for the bedroom. A thick Berber rug and an installed mirrored wall, free weights, and a bench, all placed in the other room, serve as a gym. A two-drawer dresser, the only furniture in this room, serves as a pot storage cabinet, also housing a three-beam scale.

Commerce isn't robust but steady. So is smoking.

Across the road, facing our second-story windows, is a row of public telephone booths. Placing stereo speakers at the windows blasting Middle Eastern Israeli music resonating onto the thoroughfare, I often notice cars parked alongside while occupants spend hours taking turns on the phone. Elie, the store owner's son, informs me that a code sequence obtained on the street for a price allows unlimited international calling free of charge. This criminal behavior circulates below our new residence. The thought of gaining expensive service at no cost gives me a rush. Something for nothing is great. Not requiring it now, the availability is reassuring.

His mom overhearing us interjects, "There's an old Lebanese proverb: show me who your friends are, and I'll know who you are."

I wonder why she said that?

Neglecting California trainees and needing to expand the program out there, a flight to San Francisco is booked. Orly accompanies, room and board, a business charge, only her flight is an out-of-pocket expense. Her Israeli girlfriend, our neighbor, joins us to keep Orly company during the times work calls. We visit tourist sites, ride the cable car, and make the Hard Rock café a mandatory stop. Employment requires her Brooklyn-based girlfriends' return.

Renting a car, we traverse the Pacific Coast Highway, gawking at nature's beauty, our smoking augments. We lodge within easy striking distance of the scheduled hospital meetings at the Sheraton Universal City. Touring Universal Studios, a short walk from the hotel and overlooking the hills, we eat the best Chinese cuisine at Fung Lum. We both run into and chat with actor Telly Savalas when he exists his mother's suite. His face is missing in the photo I take of Orly and Telly together, arm in arm. Taller than her, the last frame doesn't catch his head. There was another celebrity moment.

Visiting Rodeo Drive, lunching at a restaurant with sidewalk seating, the surrounding wealth feeds our imagination that one day we'll join the ranks. We visit Saks Fifth Avenue, and Orly is taken by the high-end fashions. Admiring the designer bags, she exits the store before I can react, not drawing attention with one tucked under her arm. The bag has no anti-theft device. I unlock our rented auto, and we are confronted by two plainclothes security personnel. The Beverly Hills police arrive, search the vehicle and find a gram of hashish. Arrested for shoplifting and drug possession, we're jailed overnight. Never before in contact with law enforcement, the incarceration is fortunately a one-night stand, and we're released with a probationary sentence. Furious with Orly, love erases anger. A part of me admires her rebellious behavior. No event can come between us, or so I believe. She knows that infidelity is the exception. Wanting to one day live with the rich and glamorous, we spend a night in the Beverly Hills jailhouse!

Settled in our new abode, it's time for Orly to return and set the wedding arrangements in motion. Before this occurs, we need wedding bands fitted. The Cartier intertwined tri-colored gold rings are the choice. Foregoing the Cartier inner signature makes this affordable. The jeweler I locate assures me that he knows exactly what I want. The end result is flawless.

Friendly with our next-door neighbors and introduced to Mirela's brother Bruno, we become acquainted while smoking grass. Local Israelis need a connection, and Bruno now has a source. He doesn't purchase much but views me as an American asset. The association is a novelty for both of us. Israelis gravitate toward one another, mistrusting outsiders. They're cliquish. I'm in. A rebellious Jewish drug dealer thief engaged to an Israeli woman of Iraqi ancestry is acceptable. In fact, I'm valuable. Bruno provides the telephone black box codes. It's a gratuity meant to solidify the burgeoning relationship. Now in Israel, Orly is reachable free of charge whenever the public phones across the way are unoccupied. The lack of Hebrew language is a hindrance, but I belong.

Wedding arrangements are in full swing. Forwarding cash via Air Post to augment Abba's budget allows Orly to purchase clothing, both hers and mine. Flowers, a live band, filming, still photos, and liquor are on me. A team of three, including two video cameramen, is hired, and no expense is spared. In my absence, Orly manages to size an outfit and shoes perfectly, the accuracy amazing. Purchases occur at the ritziest shops on Presidents Circle and Dizengoff Street in Tel-Aviv. Her father manages to retain the chief rabbi of Netanya, Rabbi Ysrael Meir Lau, to conduct the marriage ceremony. Bentzi selected him to honor my Eastern European ancestry. He's a Polish concentration camp holocaust survivor. We plan our ten-day honeymoon to take place at the Sonesta hotel in Taba, which happens to be Israeli-occupied Egyptian territory bordering the southern city of Eilat.

Marrying six thousand miles away from family and friends who won't be in attendance even if invited is not an issue. Without seeking confirmation, I know this given family history. There are no inquiries regarding logistics, and I don't raise the possibility as a fundamental concern. Starting a new relationship with Orly that's all-consuming and distant from the past is the way to go. I'm also receiving unbridled attention from my new family. They love me.

Purchasing an eight ball from Ralph and wrapping it hermetically, I insert the small package into an opaque bottle of J&J fragranced talc. Smuggling is not limited to this. Shopping in Manhattan, a huge suitcase is meticulously filled with presents that only a wealthy Israeli can afford. All items must be compatible with a 210 electrical current, unlike what's used in America. I find these in Hasidic-owned shops on the Lower East Side near the Bowery: a multisystem VCR by Akai, Pac-Man arcade console, toaster oven, blender, walkie-talkie for her young sisters, and more.

Not declaring these items at border control is a serious offense. Aside from a fine, the items are subject to triple taxation or, for nonpayment, confiscation. The suitcase is so heavy that the handle tears off when attempting to lift it off the luggage conveyor belt. Forced to shimmy the weight so it falls to the ground, placing it on a luggage cart is backbreaking. I'm fumbling about while trying to move rapidly, hoping airport customs won't notice the unmanageable load. There are two lines leading to the exit, one red and one green. Observing movement towards both, when custom agents stop a large religious family that is between lines, during the confusion, I dash through the green and make it to the street. Moving away from the exit quickly, hailing a taxi, and sighing in relief, the throat constrictions dissipate. Deep breathing calms trembling hands. I can't believe I made it!

During the 1930s, my uncle, his wife, and children immigrated to Palestine from Cuba. He was a bread baker who refused to follow local customs, bribing police to sell his goods. Fleeing an arrest warrant, his fate was to be killed during an Arab riot targeting Jews in the city of Jaffa. His wife died soon thereafter from a broken heart. Leaving four orphaned children, three boys and the oldest, a girl, in an insecure reality replete with violence, Channah set a positive example by anchoring her brothers while they raised themselves. Visiting Cousin Channah to reacquaint and invite the Israeli family members to the wedding, we met fourteen years ago when chasing Paula. Back then, she was critically vocal in discussing our family hierarchy's priorities. I consider her an ally.

Bentzi, Rabbi Lau and an uninvited Rabbi who represents the municipality await me in the Diplomat Hotel lower lobby. It's time to sign the Ketubah. Defining the marital commitment, I believe the wedding contract is sacred. A monetary pledge is required of the groom. Rabbi Lau laughs as I hesitate, caught by surprise at the request and quote a five-figure amount. I fret over future earnings and Abba Bentzi suggests a sum. I, apprehensively, agree.

Prior to the reception, after viewing the unoccupied decorated hall, I am escorted to our suite. Tension hovers in the air. Orly, surrounded by young women in front of a full-length mirror, is assisted in getting her appearance right. With a bouquet of orchids in hand, topping off the sight of her radiant face, I'm frozen. Snapping to, I roll up a hundred-dollar bill, place cocaine on the glass table, and hit each nostril. The photographers below can wait! Orly wisely just rubs the crystals on her gums and teeth.

After the photo session, entering the ballroom to an effusive throng of family and friends, everyone is standing noisily in anticipation. David and Barbara flew over from Neponsit to surprise us. The entourage lines up. I march down the center aisle to the awaiting Rabbi Lau, who is standing under the chuppah. Avraham is the best man. He's Channah's brother. All four siblings, their wives, and adult children are present. An unknown, I'm a blood relative, acknowledged and honored on this special occasion. What an amazing reception, absent familiar family members. I'm their baby first cousin, and they're eager to join me. I belong.

Legs are wobbly at the knees; the drug is affecting gait. Walking is difficult. Avraham provides balance for our forearms are intertwined. His wife, Pnina, is marching alongside the other arm.

Reaching the platform, steadying to step up and wait for Orly, the lights bring on profuse sweating. Bug eyed from the drug and dripping sweat, it's a struggle to focus. Eyes furtively search the crowd seeking familiarity. Persevering under the influence during these venerated moments, Orly joins alongside, and upon the conclusion of the Rabbi's singing, I place the wedding ring on her finger. I'm required to smash a glass that's wrapped in a cloth napkin. Wearing soft Italian loafers with feet unsteady, the glass is thick, and it takes three attempts before breaking. My face flushed red; this is a bad omen.

It takes effort to tour the tables with few available Hebrew words, but a smile goes a long way. Fulfilling the host's obligation to individually welcome and thank everyone for joining us, over one hundred guests attended, an extended family that didn't seem possible. Visiting each table, there's little opportunity for Orly or me to taste the food. Aside from the smorgasbord, the guests have three main dishes to select from. Nonstop dancing to live, high-powered Middle Eastern Israeli music fuels the attendees. Eventually exhausted, I lift Orly off the wooden dance floor and cuddle up off we go to the elevator. The party continues both below and above. Sisters and friends join us. They open gifts. The invitees and I have a few lines.

We fly to Eilat. The Sonesta is a sought-after location for honeymoons in Israel.

I tell Orly, "This time we're making a baby. Birth control options don't come into play. It'll be okay."

Orly responds, "I can't get pregnant. I never miss a cycle. I don't use birth control and believe it won't happen. There's nothing I want more."

Children are my impetus for giving up bachelorhood. Cohabitating separately with two women had been optimal. A free spirit struggling to raise myself, when imagining parenthood responsibilities, a blank impression forms. I have no idea how to begin. The thought is frightening. Without a reference point to call upon, I'm at a loss. Together, I'm ready and eager to take on the responsibility. Loving Orly, certainty will prevail. Believing she'll be a wonderful mother and partner overcomes any hesitation or doubts that linger.

We spend ten days in Eilat smoking hashish and indulging in the remaining cocaine. The drug is uncut and quite strong. It symbolizes our celebratory spirit. Not feeling a care in the world, we're having fun together. We tour the city, the underwater observatory, and visit a different restaurant whenever room service feels like a lazy indulgence. My absence from Ross University lasts twenty-three days.

Back in Manhattan, an intensive international and domestic travel schedule awaits. Completion of the basic science curriculum and transfers from other schools create a shortage of clerkships. Local grass clients are also waiting. Evenings run into early morning hours, energy bursting at the seams. Orly and I feed off one another. We are inseparable. The mornings start off otherwise. A few hours of sleep can't erase the effects of smoke and love. Driving to work instead of riding the subway and listening to loud rock music offers no relief. The grogs are in the way. Pushing on: El Paso/Juárez, Guadalajara, Santo Domingo, Montserrat, St. Kitts, and Dominica comprise the foreign itinerary.

Stops scheduled, student contacts announce hotel-based conferences with handwritten posters and fliers. The mission: to

161

convince students they can condense the medical school curriculum by one to two years if switching to Ross while completing their training at stateside hospitals. At the El Camino in Guadalajara, drinking a Coke while proud of the wise caution exercised, stupid me, the ice cubes bring on Montezuma's revenge. Sickness shortens the stay, and the return home can't occur quickly enough.

Arriving in Santo Domingo, I land during a nationwide lockdown and strike prompted by the government's announced reduction of bread subsidies. With armed soldiers everywhere, the population's freedom of movement is limited. Driving around photographing the turmoil, I find the school campus vacant. Witnessing and documenting live military gunfire aimed at the rioters, I cut the trip short. Prospects can't be found.

Sol hooks me up with students in El Paso/Juarez. The trip is a recruitment success thanks to Sol's hustle. What I remember most from the trip is my purchase of Tony Llama lizard skin boots. They become a favorite wardrobe selection.

At home, our friendships center around marijuana. Cocaine is the glamor drug of the moment, energizing pleasures into the early morning hours. Studio 54, the Palladium, Limelight, and others are our nightlife rage. Orly's appearance makes for an easy entry. With access to hard drugs but no interest in indulging, expanded commerce is another matter.

Bruno is linked to a young Israeli group on visitor visas. They seek arranged marriages with U.S. citizens. Wanting legal status, criminal behavior is their modus operandi. Orly and I often spend evenings with Bruno and Eva. We share nightlife in and out of our apartments. "Once Upon A Time In America" and "Scarface" are our favorite films. We glorify criminal behavior. We sit around smoking and watching films. Enjoying one another's camaraderie, one weekend we drive down to Washington D.C., tour and photograph monuments, the Lincoln Memorial a favorite. Always feeling disconnected and unable to maintain meaningful attachments, this friendship has made me heady. I've lost sight of where I'm going. Deprived of love for so long, now inebriated with concerns thrown to the wind, there are no anchors to ground me. Is this what Elie's Lebanese mom meant about the choice of friends?

Visiting Ralph and Sharon at their home in Manhattan Beach, we sit and smoke surrounded by bales of weed. Ralph prefers lines of coke, making it clear that this department is his to run. Sharon's behavior can be dominating. The division of labor allows Ralph to be assertive, establishing status within their relationship. His shoulder-length curly black hair, beard, bulk, and gentle demeanor resemble a cuddly bear. There are Greenbacks piled up in the living room, rubber-banded with tops marked in black indicating the value of each bundle. The sight of all this money has me both agitated and excited.

"I'll find ways to score significant sums as well. Nothing can go wrong. It's so inviting and easy!"

When retailing marijuana, profits are incremental and small. To score larger sums, cocaine is the obvious option.

Days prior to the wedding, Orly introduced me to Niko, whom she dated during our two-year hiatus. He speaks heavily accented English.

She wants him to meet her cool new husband. He's our hashish source until we return to Brooklyn. Marijuana is nonexistent in Israel, but hashish is prevalent if you know where to go. There's synergy between us. We share interests and recent personal histories. Niko's criminal activities take place in Europe, specifically Denmark, where he's resided for years. He has a Danish wife and two children living there, but when in Israel, he lives alone in a small Givatayim apartment. Entrepreneurial, he lives off undeclared activities. Impressed with my comfort level facing airport security, we explore possibilities and my willingness to carry contraband across borders. An enticing proposal, I defer the offer, conveying that it will receive consideration. Cocky, I'm certain of success, the possible outcomes are also frightening. I'm not ready to commit. The awaiting cash is compelling.

Money is addictive, and there's never enough. With it, I can be the hero. Marriage is more expensive than being single. Asking for a bump in salary while sponsoring my nephew who attends Ross tuition-free, I'm turned down and reminded that I need to be grateful that he attends. Over the course of thirty-two months, the scholarship covering tuition, room, and board is worth over fifty thousand dollars. Losing interest and not valuing Ross and my coworkers, I want to quit. Employment history, references, and contacts make this appealing. However, my nephew's free education would terminate, leaving my brother and his son hanging by a thread. The alternative is clear. I'll fulfill my family commitment.

Our marriage alone is not driving the need for money. We need to fund infertility treatment. Not using contraceptives, Orly's menstrual cycle never wavers. Physically, the physicians find nothing preventing pregnancy. Health insurance doesn't cover treatments. The doctor visits where she undergoes lab work and hormone injections are costly. Wanting only the best for Orly, we pursue this at Women's Hospital, a Columbia University affiliate in Manhattan.

The ill effects brought on by Pergonal don't dissuade continued treatment. Increased ovulation is the goal. The hormone helps. Weight gain is apparent, muscle pain recurring, irritability, and complaints are constant, and tears readily flow, but Orly's determination doesn't falter. Soothing encouragement is all I've got to offer.

The battle underway within is hers alone to endure. In protest, shouting against the injustice that menstruating women bear, "It's so unfair that men don't suffer the monthly hormonal cycles that women do!"

Chuckling in response, "I feel lucky."

Turning to Niko, I declare, "It's a go." For safety reasons, there isn't much to detail on an international phone call to Israel without jeopardizing secrecy. We agree that he'll stay at our Brooklyn apartment. Although on a first-time visit to New York, he has local resources. On a need-to-know basis to protect me and any links in the chain, Niko offers little information. I want none. Not only do the authorities concern me, but the suppliers are also potentially a greater threat. I won't forget this for a moment. Orly understands that I'm involved in drug smuggling, but is not privy to our conversations. She believes Niko and I make a formidable team.

CHAPTER 14.
LIVING DANGEROUSLY

Niko leaves for the day. Returning to the apartment, he has a supplier fronted eight ball ready for testing. Startled at the size of the sample, "That's an expensive maybe! What happens if it's lousy?" A novice, tension within has me scared. Not in powder form, the chunk of glittery rock is eye-opening. He casually responds, "Got this stuff gratis." He doesn't offer any explanation. Asking for benzene is an unusual request; fortunately, it's available given past pursuits. An old soup spoon follows. Removing a scale from his backpack, weighing out a small amount, and dropping it onto the solution resting on the spoon, lighter in hand, the solution heats and bubbles until the liquid evaporates. Niko weighs the remaining rocks, and the drug is ninety-three percent pure. We enjoy a couple of lines. The powder enters smoothly with no burning effect. The business has begun.

Niko is concerned that I'm new at smuggling. He's pleased to know I'm not a cokehead. Users make mistakes, leading to retribution or incarceration. Imagining the consequences after snorting up your supplier's contraband and drawing attention near airport security doesn't enter the discussion. I'm drilled with questions regarding how security is handled. Rejecting the use of any sort of baggage as a prop, I decide to stuff the drug behind the front of pleated pants, loose fit the criteria. Niko makes it clear that, since this is a trial run, the quantity is small. One hundred and fifty grams are hermetically packed in plastic wrap. The mule's compensation is three thousand dollars. Destination Tel Aviv!

The costume worn is key to passing through the airport and

166

blending peacefully on the long flight. Inflections are as important as clothes. Security, plain clothes, and uniforms are everywhere. Choosing to fly with El Al, where security is most intense, obscurity is the name of the game. Keeping talks simple and friendly when answering questions, the most difficult leg is passing through Israeli security at both airports and upon returning, clearing U.S. customs. At JFK, El Al check-in, all passengers are subject to a security interview.

Disembarking from an Israel-secured airliner draws less attention from uniforms on the ground. So I hope. Eyeglasses are black plastic-framed with thick lenses, and contact lenses remain at home. Hair is full and a little disheveled. Woolen charcoal gray pleated cuffed slacks with penny loafer brown shoes, a dress shirt, and a dark, baggy two-toned sweater make the grade. It is late Autumn. I drape a London Fog raincoat over my forearm and wedge the package below my belly button. Niko and I will meet at his apartment.

Sitting on the plane for eleven hours, it's imperative not to get fidgety, restless, or in any way draw attention. It's the time of the air marshal. A Sony Walkman with cassettes and an espionage novel as the preferred diversions isn't good company. The intensity doesn't allow focus on anything other than the task. Trying to maintain discipline these long hours, I pee a lot. Keeping the parcel stable in the tight lavatory is a struggle. Nothing to declare, the customs agent waves me on. Under the gray, cloudy sky, breathing fresh air after hours of more than physical seclusion, I exit the terminal. Having successfully masked the emotional intensity boiling within, I'm now naturally smooth without working at it. What a relief.

Taxiing to Niko, knocking on the door, our voices rise

overjoyed and relieved to have safely ended the journey. The anticipated compensation is foremost on my mind. Money! Money! Money! We hug, pounding backs, accompanied by salutary blessings. Sitting in the living room, smoking hashish, he inspects the package, making sure the seal is secure. Insisting on a detailed description of the trip, he laughs ceaselessly at the reenactment of the rigid posture held for so many hours in an airline seat.

Passing a Pagaz, 'bomb in English', I form a similarly closed fist, placing the cone in between the index and middle fingers, the tip reaching my palm. Cupping a hand over the other and placing them against my lips, inhaling, the embers turn red hot, and a deep breath holds smoke until my lungs scream for air. Lightheaded, reclining on the sofa while gathering my senses, drifting thoughts are challenging.

Using sheets of cigarette rolling paper and joining them after licking to form a large surface is the perfect housing for a mixture of tobacco and hashish. Warm the hash with a flame momentarily and then rub the softened substance into the tobacco. Pack the mixture tightly and roll the paper forming a cone wide at the top. Leave a small opening at the bottom. The ritual is alien to me.

Boarding on Niko's sofa for two nights after concluding the short business trip, the return stamps on the passport are innocuous. Leaving the country hours after completing the drop would be conspicuous. Better safe than sorry. Carrying thirty hundred-dollar bills in the same compartment that held the coke, there are more trips to follow.

No one at Ross nor family members other than Orly knows about the trip. I resume work duties after a long weekend break. The entire operation took four days. Stepping back on the ground at JFK is like walking on air. Euphoric and eager to share these exploits with Bruno, I keep my words brief with Orly. News travels fast among Bruno's small circle. An English-only speaking educated American with no criminal history, an anomaly, I've passed a rite of passage. Acceptance is complete.

Funds are available, and Orly undergoes hormonal treatments to enhance ovulation. This leads to an increased egg count. Her menstrual cycle functions like clockwork, irrespective of the treatments. We make love regularly. Weeks pass. Negative results. Reacting by breaking down and sobbing, her face anguished, Orly shouts, "This is Hashem punishing me for transgressions committed by an unknown ancestor. This is not fair."

Holding onto her tightly while encouraging us to continue the treatments, she wails that the side effects aren't worth enduring if each month the results are a failure. We don't give up.

There's an Israeli restaurant at the end of the block where we reside. Bruno and his associates routinely meet there, sitting for hours alongside a row of Formica-topped tables. That's where we make contact. The fluorescent lighting glares, reflecting off the cream white wall paneling, giving the place a naked, bare character. The worn, yellowish tourism posters featuring Israel don't add any offsetting feature. Upon entering, the aroma of deep frying and grilling immediately attaches to clothes. There, I meet Shimon, Bruno's partner in nefarious undertakings. He's introduced as Shimon the Satan. His demeanor reflects the name with a gangster gait, projecting a mean streak. Being the tough guy provides status in their social order. In his mid-twenties, his older brother is serving a long prison sentence in Israel for international heroin smuggling. Well-known in the criminal underworld, Shimon wears the family badge proudly. I'm filled in to not think he's a petty criminal.

Surprised to hear that I'm the Assistant Dean of a medical school engaged in regular international travel, "Ya gotta be kiddin' me," he blurts out in surprise.

In poor broken English, he explains,

"Michelle, the love of my life, she is stranded in Montreal with no means of entry into America. She doesn't have a visa. I'll pay well if she's brought to me. Could you do this?"

Playing tough, he warns, "You'll face consequences if she falls into immigration's hands."

Offered two thousand dollars upon delivery, relative to drugs, the punitive repercussions seem minimal. After the Israel run with confidence inflated, comparing the airport scenario against the ease of crossing the border in my car makes it a deal.

The drive north on the thruway is a straight line into monotony. The roadsides hold scenic moments, but part of the trip is a daytime lullaby droning on and on. I smoked before leaving Brooklyn. The initial stretch passes pleasantly, but soon thereafter, my eyelids are heavy. Letting in the battering ice-cold wind is the only way I'll reach the destination. Approaching the border after traversing back roads, I reach an unmanned wooden booth representing Canadian border control. The posted instructions require the use of the Out-of-Order telephone to check in and declare identity. Jittery, I ponder the consequences of moving forward without reporting, and then I get stopped. "Not my responsibility," I rationalize and continue happily knowing there's no record of the crossing.

Seeing Michelle, I realize Shimon's passion. This young woman, wearing no cosmetics, has sculptured Middle Eastern features that demand a second look. Her naturally dark olive-colored skin is smooth like silk. At first hesitant since my appearance doesn't fit the part, she accepts me after I share facts about Shimon and his professed love for her. Her broken accented English acknowledges that we'll disembark as soon as I freshen up. Her luggage consists of a large suitcase and a carry-on vanity.

It's a couple of hours before dawn. This is the time I set for running the back road border crossing.

Hoping to catch the border patrol napping, if stopped and questioned, "Michelle is my fiancée and we're on a romantic tryst."

Pitch black outside and surrounded by nighttime forest, the winding road is difficult to navigate. A lump of fear wedges in my throat. Eyes dart between the windshield and the rearview mirror, anticipating flashing lights and loudspeaker barking instructions. Reaching the interstate without any intervention, we stop at the first rest area, attending to our needs and picking up snacks. During the long trip we don't converse much. Her English and my Hebrew proficiency are limited.

Shimon greets us at David's restaurant. Kisses and hugs, winding down, he turns and thanks me for ending his lonely nights.

Responding in his ear. "Shimon, you are full of shit. There are no lonely nights."

His macho swagger tells me otherwise. Excusing himself, accompanying me down the block to the apartment entrance, he counts out twenty one-hundred-dollar bills. Slapping me on the back, he claims, "You're now part of us." Exhausted, I drag up the staircase, enter the apartment, and briefly hug Orly. I say little and go to bed without showering. Uncleanliness is a cardinal sin in our home, but tonight it's forgiven. The power of money goes far, and I just delivered a good sum for a twenty-four-hour effort.

Word spreads among the Brooklyn criminal Israeli element. On the street in front of our usual meeting place, I run into Shimon and a short, swarthy, facially pockmarked character named Rafi. It's summertime, and his scantily dressed tattoos are glaring. They extend an invitation to sit down at the eatery, explaining they have a proposal to discuss.

"If you'll agree to meet with Rafi in Amsterdam and transport a package back to Brooklyn, he'll pay ten thousand dollars."

Rafi intimidates me with his presence.

Shimon assures me,

"My friend can be trusted. Compared to Israeli security methods, you'll have no trouble with U.S. customs. Handling the Americans will be easy for you." The tone is upbeat.

Orly has her heart set on seeing Bruce Springsteen perform live at the New Jersey Meadowlands. Large outdoor venues are the craze. We've attended concerts including Turner, Collins, Clapton, UB40, and others, but Bruce is our favorite. We featured the Born in the USA album on our wedding night. The performance date conflicts with the scheduling and planning of the European trip. She hates these criminal characters that I associate with, and can't assuage her feelings of rejection. "Bruno and Eva are okay; the others are garbage." Undertaking the trip without her blessing, in fact, she won't talk to me.

Rafi provides cash to purchase tickets. The route is JFK to Brussels, where I travel by rail to Amsterdam. Taking a circuitous route avoids direct Amsterdam-New York custom stamps from appearing on the passport. These are red flags when viewed at U.S. border crossings. We agree to meet at the Sofitel hotel in Amsterdam. The flight is uneventful. Anticipation is anything but. I'm on high alert since Rafi's explanations back in Brooklyn were vague. His English is poor. It's presumed I'm smuggling cocaine strapped to my body. Rafi assures me, "Everything will be okay." The room has two queen-size beds. He removes rolls of beige colored surgical adhesive tape, each three inches wide, from a duffel bag.

He explains, "With the surgical tape, I'm constructing a vest that holds the packages you wear."

Gaping at his hands, he assembles the vest. He tries to comfort me. It doesn't work.

The tape emits a strong, concentrated odor associated with hospital emergency rooms. The room reeks. Voicing objections, he insists perfume disguises the smell. I respond, "The odor draws attention. Don't take me for a fool."

While I anguish over whether to proceed, he tailors the vest to size it properly. Dreading this guy whose inclinations disregard my well-being is justified when he fills the openings in the vest with packets of beige powder. No one ever mentioned heroin. In a panic, wanting to extricate myself from the situation, I associate heroin with the inevitable final sentence. Fearing the consequences if either remaining or leaving, I decide to get away fast. The profit realized from the two kilos packed in this vest is worth more than both my life and the heroin. His chutzpah dooms the plan. Lacking a return flight ticket with only pocket money available, I'm trapped and lost without a plan of escape. "Would he harm me if I choose to leave?" I fret.

Niko resides in Amsterdam. He's been there for a time, and I have the local telephone number. Leaving the room with the excuse that I need air, I search for a phone. It's provided at the lobby front desk. Blurting out the situation semi-coherently, we agree to meet at the location where he's staying.

Returning to the room, I see Rafi hunched over his creation assembled on the carpet.

Before he speaks, I state, "You're setting me up for failure. Shalom."

Exiting, carry-on bag in hand, before he can respond, I'm gone.

Greeted with an embrace and lighting up when describing the situation, Niko says, "Business is slow, but a drop off needs to be done in Copenhagen. The money isn't much. You want it?"

Compensation upfront enables a return flight to the States. Instructed to reach Denmark by train, the least suspicious travel method, the ride lasts forever. The package is small and hidden in my favorite spot. The European exit stamp on the passport will read Copenhagen, the perfect ruse for hiding the Amsterdam stay. The latter city is known for its proliferation of drug use at coffee houses licensed by the government. Caution governs every move. Dozing off in the sparsely traveled carriage, the ride requires fourteen hours of patience. Wedging the ticket on the top of the seat before me, the conductor doesn't disturb me each time there is a hole punched in the designated spot.

Pick up is at a bed and breakfast where I pay for a two-night stay. Niko instructed me to wait patiently in the room until I am visited at a random time. He didn't provide a name or any other details. The less one knows, the safer it is for everyone. Uptight as I've ever been, the stuffiness and absence of natural light are claustrophobic. Insidious loneliness slowly takes over. No distractions available as time drags, I swig bottles of Torburg that are in the mini fridge. The alcoholic content is greater than that of stateside beer. I'm quickly overcome with fatigue. Head pounding, I awaken in total darkness. Perhaps I missed a knock on the door? Cramped after endless hours riding trains and sequestered in second-rate hotel rooms triggers an attack of melancholy. I flash back on Rafi assembling the stinky vest with no regard for me or my family. Dawn arrives, and the package is picked up. No dialogue ensues.

It's a new day. Heading for Tivoli Gardens, custom fitted leather sandals aren't proper when hiking long distances. Feet blister quickly. The day is sunny and warm. Viewing the topped-off barrels lined up along the wharf; fish odor, brine, and saltwater permeate the air. This reminds me of the barrelled pickles and herring displayed at the Belmont Avenue pushcarts during early childhood. Drudging forward with loneliness draining any mustered energy, I give up on reaching Tivoli and turn back.

Coordination is complicated. I have to wait a day to book a flight and return home. With only cash in hand, the airline agents insist on payment with either plastic or traveler's checks. Having neither and desperate, I telephone Sharon and Ralph, guaranteeing reimbursement if they help. "We want to remain under the radar," they turn me down. Bernard is an option. "If you purchase a ticket, I have cash in hand to reimburse you." Impatient and disagreeable, not concerned that I'm stranded, demanding to know, "What are you doing in Denmark?" Punting, emphasizing the phone expense per minute, and that I'll explain everything in person, a booked flight soon awaits at the airline counter. When I reimburse the funds, Bernard makes no reference to the trip. Typical of him to not take more than a superficial interest in me.

Haggard, after this wasted venture, I blast Shimon Satan for bringing me Rafi. I keep my distance. Orly offers no solace over this failure. We remain tight with Bruno and Eva. David and Barbara become more than customers. Sharon and Ralph regularly have me over to share weed and pick up merchandise.

Not neglecting work responsibilities and personal commitments, self-interest leads me to have the Chief of Surgery at Jersey Medical Center appointed the chairman of the Ross department. This is an honorarium that includes a monthly stipend. My nephew is completing the curriculum at the hospital, and I feel obligated to help him obtain the post-graduate training licensing boards require before opening an independent medical practice. His education is a wasted effort if it doesn't lead to a gainful career. The supervising physician for the required twelve-week clerkship is satisfied with his progress. Words not spoken, it's mutually understood that the physician associates with Ross academics, and my familial obligation is satisfied. Leon's son becomes a doctor. Job done.

Alternate medications bring no results, only tears every cycle. The doctor assures us that Orly has no physical indicators that would explain her infertility. She ovulates like clockwork. The in vitro fertility process reaps disappointments, frustrations, and adverse physical effects. Sperm analysis gives no indication that we should have difficulty conceiving. Orly is convinced she will remain barren, and if so, I should divorce her.

Reassuring her, "I could never be so hurtful; no kids and no husband because you can't get pregnant isn't happening."

Too painful to even consider, I'm not going down that path. "We're going to make a baby!"

She cries in spite of the words. I comfort her. She sleeps each night with her head resting on my shoulder and her leg draped over my thigh. The intimacy of her natural fragrance is my magnet for certainty.

We walk the streets of Manhattan selecting all the scenic locations I'm familiar with. Photography wasn't stored away like the other arts. The Minolta and lens selection give me purpose. Orly and I are inseparable. The simplest housekeeping chores shared are as much fun as any other activity. The lingering loneliness is gone. I have a buddy. Infatuation with one another evolves into the pull and tug of a lasting relationship. Frequently, the insistence on high-end purchases turns into a yelling match. Orly's inclinations challenge my instincts. Her expectations result in angry outbursts by me and a rage response in turn. Feeling guilty, I quickly dismiss the discomfort, seeking amends, I surrender. My self-esteem and being her hero are interconnected.

Our cultural differences keep us entertained. I compare our sexual engagements to playing a musical instrument, and the tunes are harmonious and complete. Enjoying the Honeymooners television show, I'm crowned Norton, who's a municipal employee working underground in sewers. The humor is that I'm anything but that character. We laugh, kiss, and tightly hold one another, relishing the moment. Her touch, skin, and smell intoxicate me.

There's constant pressure to generate revenue. Eager to hook up with Niko once again, the local drug trade generates steady but limited income. A solution is readily at hand.

It's a cold, nasty winter in New York. To keep Orly from turning blue, it's time to visit Israel. Responding to my telephone inquiry, Niko shows up at the front door the following week. Orly leaves days later. Caution dictates that we do not fly together while I'm carrying contraband. Having proven trustworthy and competent, the next amount will be greater, but once again compact enough to conceal on my torso. Niko doesn't know that the rules of the game have changed. Payout to the courier after the previous run was not commensurate with the risk undertaken. Realization drives me to find and enlist a solution. I line up Bruno to fund a three-way partnership if I'm to continue with Niko. He'll fund two-thirds of the next purchase. Out of the profits, I'll pay him back and still walk away with a considerable sum. Only a kilo justifies a generous three-way split. Bruno is game, wanting to get in on the action.

Before Orly leaves for Israel, Niko shops for merchandise, bringing eight balls to the apartment at no expense. His suppliers want the business. On the sofa until the early morning hours, while testing the white crystals, Niko offers me the glass pipe. Having never free-based cocaine, curiosity takes hold. Stoned on pot and not recognizing the effect of the vapor, again and again, I crave the pipe. "Where's the high?" repeats in my head while I relentlessly puff away.

The party continues for hours until Orly bursts out of the bedroom, screaming, "How dare you do this in my home?"

She lifts the thick oven-proof plate resting on the coffee table. Covered in powder, it's flung frisbee style towards the wall. Impacting just above my eyebrow, it shatters. Stunned, I'm shaking off the dizzying effect of the hit. I'm laughing! Running to a mirror, I see the wound. Its swollen skin opens, oozing blood.

Standing there thinking, "Her action is admirable. She hit me in the head with a plate."

Her fury, a sign of more to come, doesn't deter the direction I've chosen.

Angry, I insist, "It's an hour before dawn. It's best that I drive alone to the Coney Island hospital emergency room. It'll be easier to handle triage when questioned about the wound."

Physically wired, not feeling any pain, I struggle to hold a compress, clutch, steer, and shift the five gears. "I walked into a glass door" isn't received well, the nurse's head shaking in disbelief. Thirteen stitches later, I'm on the way home.

The next day at the office, I'm sporting gauze and surgical tape covering my brow; it contrasts well with the suit and tie. The look draws attention. I explain, the lame excuse about the unseen glass door. It's in line with the judgmental view management has of me, as if they need a reason. Nonconformity and independence don't sit well with them. They tolerate me because I deliver. It's been a while since I've had a vacation. I inform Ross that with the winter lull, this is an opportune time for me to visit Israel. No objections are voiced. The plan proceeds.

Niko obtains a kilo of cocaine that meets his standards. It's not cut with additives and is solid as a rock. Never having seen a brick like this, the first thing I do is place it against my lower stomach to gauge if it appears discrete. Doubts arise. Niko asserts, "Elastic ace bandages wrapped around your torso while holding your gut flat will look natural."

On the long flight, difficulty ensues when body heat causes the bandages to cut into my back. A line of water-filled blisters forms. Reaching to soothe the burning pain could draw the air marshal's attention. Adjustments in the restroom offer no respite. Suffering quietly while maintaining my composure, the trip goes smoothly. Greeting Orly at the family residence, we take privacy in her bedroom. Hastily removing the sweater and bandages exposes a blister, horizontally running across my entire back. Already broken, the oozing liquid dramatizes the damage.

The wound is swabbed; I comfort Orly, who is overly concerned. "I'm safe and that's all that matters."

Sitting down and rehashing events that happened the last few days, Orly informs me, "I have a great contact who wants to help distribute the Coke."

I go ballistic.

"You're an idiot mixing into a business that you're incapable of handling. You broke the chain of secrecy."

She responds, "I'm scared and just want to finish with this."

Orly thinks this friend's participation will help unload the contraband quickly. Avi heard from Orly's manicurist that she's in town.

Distraught, when opening the apartment door, she reveals to Avi, "Danny is on a plane this very moment with a kilo of coke." Comforting words declaring that he has coke user clients and can help are now in play.

Moshe, our close friend, and Niko's clients await delivery. Patronage is comprised of professional sports figures and industrial entrepreneurs. Remaining anonymous, their names are publicly known. I'm faced with a decision regarding Avi. Do I include or ignore him, hoping he isn't a loose cannon? This is the same guy who, from Israel, telephoned Orly during her return to Brooklyn. I forbade further contact then, and now here he is.

An awful mistake has been made. I need to maintain control. The choice is obvious. Avi needs to be included. He owns a beverage truck selling cased bottles to residential customers on a door-to-door route. His spoken English is poor. Trying to understand him, I turn to Orly. Requiring a precision scale, Avi directs me to the Diamond Exchange, which is conveniently within walking distance of the apartment. The three-beam scale purchased is perfect. The minimum acceptable order is one hundred grams priced at ten thousand dollars. The uncut quality of the product makes this a great buy, both for enjoyment and resale. The greater each transaction, the sooner I'm free. Less traffic minimizes danger. This assumption gives me a modicum of comfort.

Niko arrives two days later. Informing him about Avi doesn't go over well. He declares, "Avi only knows you and it must remain this way."

Fronting Avi products, it doesn't take long for him to return with a problem. In Israel, the word coke is associated with Coke Parsi, a form of heroin smoked, not injected. The user places a small amount of the flesh-colored powder on aluminum foil, then takes a straw or rolled up currency, and while heating underneath the foil, running the melted powder back and forth, it glides about. The smoker pulls on the tube, inhaling the vapor with tight lips until it evaporates. This ritual's addictive power is absolute. Avi has no clientele for Coke Crystal. He tries repeatedly but has no bites within his circles. Following failed attempts, I diplomatically extricated him from the business, but I remain concerned that he's a loose end out of my control.

The airwaves flood with the news; the spaceship Challenger has blown up, leaving no survivors. The event affects me deeply. Sadness overtakes everything. In mourning, I love America and what it stands for, but the people are another matter. That's why I'm not conflicted by holding these values and pursuing the drug trade. No one is honest; most are phony. Everyone is selfish, yet I love my country.

Moshe is one of our closest friends, and Orly has many that date back to childhood. Friendship is the way Israeli society copes with ongoing threats to its existence. We are all an extended family. Random terrorist stabbings are rampant. When on the street, everyone is on heightened alert to their fullest capability. The mantra is to live fully today. Tomorrow may not come. Uniformed soldiers in full gear are stationed everywhere. Sitting on a wooden public bench, the foot traffic and bustling cars buzzing by are engaging. I await the completion of Moshe's shift in the famous soccer player Sinai's sporting goods store. Rechov Sokolov in Cholon is a working-class neighborhood. Within a couple of meters is a rifle slung across a chest, ready to respond in an instant. In the gas mask canvas bag clinging to my side are three packages of cocaine weighing one hundred grams each. When the soldiers turn their backs and walk away, I sigh in relief. Angst surged through my veins when they stood near me. Alert like them, adrenaline bathing my innards, they represent the law. I'm an outlaw.

Moshe joins me and we head off to his apartment in Bat Yam to conclude our transaction. After a short wait, his client joins us. Moshe samples the product both by snorting and rubbing it on his gums. He's not a connoisseur but still can appreciate the quality. No introductions required; this is a cash-and-carry exchange. The customer doesn't speak English. Moshe translates. After testing and weighing the results, ten thousand dollars is handed over in exchange for one parcel. The crisp, newly issued currency is counted out as I fumble to separate the banknotes. This delays my desire to escape quickly.

Heading to Niko's to share the outcome of the effort and drop off the other two packages, his compatriot Roni, who supplies a famous professional basketball player, a name I recognize, is waiting for me as well. The two hundred grams taken, Niko holds onto all the cash.

Keeping cash and the supply in the same location simultaneously endangers both. The remaining load stays with me. Over the next ten days, Niko's and Moshe's customers take the remainder. Niko and I divide up the spoils. Bruno's share is set aside.

Flying El Al into JFK is the way to go. Orly and I clear customs separately. She goes first. A five-minute delay between us limits danger to only me. I placed two bundles totaling six hundred bills into the two front pockets of the leather jacket I am now wearing. Brazen, the obvious seems the best hiding place. Customs will search luggage before emptying pockets. This money is not declared!

Climbing up the stairwell to our front door, the key won't grant entry, and the doorpost isn't aligned. The noise on this chilly early morning brings Bruno with sleepy eyes to the entrance. Eva is under the blanket in our unmade bed. I understand something is wrong. They declare,

"We're in hiding. Uri is dead, shot and murdered outside a Mill Basin disco. We Israelis partied to Shimi Tivori, and we are not involved. The police want to question everyone from that night."

So they say.

The apartment is too small to accommodate four adults. We divide the cash and move their personal belongings next door to Mirela and Asher's apartment. Bruno also removes a large silver revolver hidden in the dropped ceiling above the vestibule in the hallway. Mulling their explanation over for crashing our home, "Is it really the police that concerns them?"

Sporadic contact with Shimon the Satan, who lives in the neighborhood, is unavoidable. Approaching friendly, he asks if I'd bring Rafi's Brazilian girlfriend to Brooklyn from Montreal? Pointing out that Rafi respects and never reproached me about the misadventure in Amsterdam, I'll be compensated with cash in an amount matching the last trip. This is all happening so rapidly, my reasoning is congested. I'm running with events as they're presented, consequences be damned.

Picking up the Brazilian beauty who doesn't speak a word of English goes smoothly at first. An unanticipated hitch occurs heading south on the back roads of New York State. Spotting flashing red lights in the rear view mirror, a loudspeaker announces, "Pull over. Remain in the vehicle."

It's the border patrol. "Are you aware you've entered the United States illegally?"

Taken to headquarters, we both present our IDs. Naive sounding, weaving a story,

"She's a buddy's fiancée. He asked me to bring her down to Brooklyn since getting away from his job is impossible. She only speaks Portuguese, so that's all I know."

The interrogation goes on and on. I don't budge. They legally assign me recognizance and require a signature and verbal commitment that she's leaving the States within 30 days. After a harrowing few hours, the long trip is over, the delivery made, and compensation paid. Everyone's happy.

The belief I can't fail is driving my decisions. Not considering mine or anyone else's well-being avoids applying the brakes. I'm thinking, "The possibilities seem limitless. Ross University is a turnoff. Now that Orly is a part of me, loneliness and depression are memories. Money is pouring in. Doing well, there's no stopping me."

Ongoing hormone treatments and resulting failures mean we're escalating intervention. Urging Orly to persevere, knowing it'll require a large sum of money to continue treatment, cocaine buyers are ready. The time is right to make another jump. Passover holidays are around the corner, and Spring is the perfect time to visit. Medical file in hand, we'll consult with the foremost fertility specialists in the country. Israel's a world leader in achieving positive results.

Niko's ready to return to Brooklyn. The kilo glitters like a monster-sized jewel. The flaked pieces he tests are pinkish and ninety-five percent pure.

Niko says,

"It's from Peru. We're paying twenty-nine thousand dollars a kilo, wholesaling untouched at one hundred dollars per gram. Accumulating cash, you'll have funds to emigrate and obtain the medical treatment that ends your nightmare."

This reasoning makes the undertaking acceptable. Life was so empty and joyless before Orly's presence and all that came with her. Country, family, camaraderie, and more are now mine.

Ten weeks have passed since the last trip, and my back is still scabbed. We logistically place the block so that the elastic Ace bandage avoids the wound. Friction will cause bleeding. Bruno assists.

The costume worn is similar to before, but the weather on the flight day isn't conducive.

"Will I blend in or draw attention?"

Cocky after completing cross-border trips I think it'll be advantageous this time to travel as a couple. Facing border control, it'll distract attention away from solo globe-trotting. We're pursuing a holiday vacation with our family. The navy-blue cashmere overcoat draped over my arm is out of place. Aware, I'm concerned.

Exiting the taxi curbside in front of the terminal at JFK, it's startling to see uniformed Israeli personnel armed with Uzis guarding the entranceway. The heightened security directs us to a small counter off the side of the main thoroughfare. Comforting Orly requires total concentration to hide my agitation when the agent takes our passports through a secured door. We stand stiffly in place. We're not questioned. Overdressed on this unexpectedly warm spring day, I sweat salt that stings my eyes.

Questioning the delay, "A terrorist named Hindawi had earlier today tried to carry a bomb-laden suitcase onto a plane in the British Isles."

The wait at the counter drags. I instruct Orly, "Refrain from aggressively bitching but appear impatient with the delay."

Fighting to stay calm, the kilo secured weighs a ton. Passports are handed back; without explanation, we're instructed to approach the inspection tables near the ticket counter to undergo the security check. Relieved, I whisper to Orly, "We're back on track. This, from now on, is standard operating procedure." The words address the helplessness I just endured.

At the family apartment in Ramat Gan, we shout a greeting and immediately sequester in the bathroom, releasing the hard white brick. Hiding it in the crawl space used for storage within the ceiling above the bathtub, it joins the three-beam scale that's ready for use. When the apartment is absent from the family, the opportunity to break and divide the block into one-hundred-gram packets takes place. Waiting for Niko to arrive within forty-eight hours, nostalgia takes over.

Orly and I decide to check into Tel Aviv's Hotel Diplomat, where we wed twenty months prior. Passover holiday room rates are high, but cost isn't an issue. I'm flush with money from the prior run. In contact with Moshe, we agree to meet that evening at his place with one hundred grams in hand. The cash is dropped off at Niko's. Moshe telephones and speaks in code. He reserves the remainder.

He explains, "Quality material like this doesn't make it to Israel. We want it all. It isn't going into distribution. A select few well-off people will enjoy it."

Moshe is traveling to Tiberius for the holiday. Delivery in ten days doesn't sit well, but moving it all at once is more appealing than lining up multiple buyers.

Enjoying the intimacy the hotel room provides when not at the seashore across the way, we frolic and dabble with the drug. Thoughts racing through her head, Orly says she's making a phone call. Not understanding Hebrew, from her tone I surmise,

"You're taunting Avi for messing up. That was the stupidest, most idiotic thing you could have done. Not only does he now guess that I'm back in Israel with drugs, but you also threw in his face that he's a loser. He's now a danger to us."

She laughs it off.

Orly and I party with friends till the wee hours of morning. We visit the clubs and discos of Tel Aviv, dancing through the night, and walk the path to the seashore in the early afternoon. I await Moshe, who should return on Sunday. Shabbat is a busy time at the beach. I select a spot on the hot sand. Scanning the crowd is a tall, skinny man. He's standing on the esplanade facing the seashore, extending a long, bowed rod with a microphone attached at the end. The image is of him taping waves. Summoning Orly, she accompanies me to the shoreline.

The waves' roar masks our talk. "We're being taped."

She turns around to confirm this, but the figure is gone.

She laughs, "You're paranoid."

CHAPTER 15.
ALL GOOD THINGS MUST END

It's a bright sunny Sunday morning. Sun rays bathing, hair lathered, eyes closed, unexpectedly, a male voice at the doorway orders me, "You in the shower outside quickly." Fumbling a towel around a dripping wet waist, I'm ordered to sit alone on the living room sofa against the wall. A swell of plain clothes and uniformed officers converges on and dismantles the apartment. A couple of hours pass. I'm confronted with a three-beam scale, aluminum foil, plastic wrap, and a partially exposed solid block of cocaine. The police order all family members to remain in the apartment for questioning. Finally dressed, I sit observing the frenetic activity. Looking at Orly's kid sisters, I discreetly wave goodbye, the stress immobilizing us mentally and physically. Pale white and clammy, I sit frozen on the salon sofa. Orly isn't to be seen. I'm frightened. Hands cuffed behind our backs, we're kept separate and placed in different patrol cars. I haven't spoken with Orly since the night before. Police questioning takes place in heavily accented English. During the ride to the station, I construct a story designed to protect everyone in the chain. Words are a concoction that identifies no one.

Photos, fingerprints, and confiscation of travel documents completed, I'm placed in a detective's room, sitting isolated. I search my mind, wondering who the rat is and worrying about the imminent interrogation. Super alert, alone, and scared, it's clear that with every passing moment, the process targets the will to resist. With no knowledge of spoken Hebrew, to intimidate me, detectives with varying degrees of English proficiency continuously rotate a slew of accusations and questions. The two leading detectives are

Shavit and Alex. Vanunu, their boss, is the bastard. He aggressively directs them with shouts. My narrative is simple to avoid entanglement in a weave of conceit, revealing inconsistencies. Complications could jeopardize the well-being of any links in the chain. Lies require memory; the truth only requires recall.

"I'm the Assistant Dean at Ross University on the island of Dominica. My wife cannot get pregnant, and so I did this to raise the money needed to pay for her fertility treatments, which cost less in Israel than in America. Her medical file is in my luggage."

I'm quivering from head to toe. Voice crackling, I'm hesitant to speak. They insist on rapid-fire answers. This goes on for hours as I'm subjected to a rotating good cop, bad cop routine. Vanunu directs them, and I don't understand a word. Far into the night, Shavit transports me to Abu Kabir, the central detention center for this part of Israel. Orly's transported separately.

Dazed, frightened in a dream state, I'm subjected to interrogation in a foreign country and don't speak their language. Shit! Not a physically endowed person, I'm about to enter a jungle populated with danger and violence. I'll be eaten alive!

Sharing communication concerns with the detective, he says, "I have a special place in mind for you."

Being taken to an organized protective lockup keeps me away from the general population. Informers and sex offenders comprise the majority of cellmates here. Antenna up, exercising caution is the only way to survive.

Shavit and I traverse a dimly lit, narrow corridor that smells like it has never had fresh circulation. Opening a steel door off the sidewall and flicking on a switch, I see stacked to the ceiling green foam rubber mattresses stained and odorous, the woolen blankets no better. Instructed to take two blankets and one mattress, the selection is difficult. Everything stinks! The cell block is on the top floor of the building, and its population is under a twenty-four-hour lockdown. All steel cell doors are barred and key-operated. The building is antiquated and needs renovation. It's absent air conditioning, and a thick, damp smell permeates the place.

There are spots for six prisoners in the cell: two bunk beds and two singles. Detainees wear street clothes in the detention center. The orange shirts and brown pants that the indicted must wear are not provided. Sheets, pillowcases, and permissible toiletries are familial duties. A metal-framed single bed is vacant. Placing the mattress and trying to assure myself, I'm stunned and forlorn, frozen in the moment. Anxiety envelops my organs. Uncertainty fuels the angst.

"This is a bad dream, an illusion that'll pass. Right?"

Denial only heightens the intensity, realizing there's no escaping the situation. Questioning how I got here, suspicion falls on Avi as the number one suspect. If it's him, the chain is protected. Avi knows no one. The concoction should hold when the interrogation resumes the next day.

Cellmates bombard me with questions, but I don't understand anything they say or ask. Seemingly concerned about me, one fellow introduces himself, speaking elementary, heavily accented English. Speaking in whispers, David leads me to the side away from everyone. He urgently demonstrates with hand inflection that there are "ears" housed in the cell door lock casing. A microphone attached to a nylon cord lowered from above, facing the barred open-air windows, catches all sounds.

"There are no private conversations." He adds, "The telephones on the detective's desks and most electronics are also wired. Beware!"

He immediately wins trust. David elaborates.

"I'm the brother-in-law of Herzl Avitan, whose wife, Orit Arbiv, is my sister. Herzl is a member of the infamous murderous gang of lifers that includes Shmya Angel and Yaakov Shemesh."

Interrupting, attempting not to speak rapidly so I'm understood,

"I'm placed here for protection since I speak no Hebrew. I revealed nothing to the police that could hurt anyone. Why would I compromise a person's well-being when they caused me no harm? My actions are mine to own."

I'm so nervous, blabber spills out of my mouth. He's in this unit because the police suspect that while awaiting a court appearance, he's planning a hit in the general population. It's good to hear that not everyone in this section is a rat. Somehow, we manage to understand one another. David's guidance is invaluable. David Yiftach is the family's criminal defense attorney. He accepts no case if the defendant cooperates with the police. Retaining him declares to the world that Orly and I are not informers. This pronouncement is critical if I'm to remain in protective custody. Presence implies guilt by association. Orly and I consider personal honor our badge of pride. This shared value deserves total loyalty and love.

The interrogation resumes early the next morning. Shavit and Alex aggressively probe for incongruities in the description of events. Taking turns applying pressure, a deal is offered if I reveal who the others are.

I think, "I won't look behind my back the rest of my life expecting retaliation."

Defiant, I project myself as a timid pawn lost in events that overcame my ability.

Downplaying knowledge of any arrangements other than a scheduled pick up by anonymous players, the day of arrest, I implore, "If you guys had sat on me a little longer, you would have caught them. Don't pound me when you could have had them in your hands. I don't know who they are."

Shoulders downward, head bowed, and posture stooped, I appear broken. Insisting I'm cooperating, timidity disguising the truth, "I'm simply the American courier kept in the dark. I'm not to be trusted in the event I'm caught." Voice quivering, I draw a picture of daily life on Kings Highway.

"My wife and I reside in a small apartment above the Bat Yam grocery. Our windows are open to the street. Passersby hear marital strife; we scream at the top of our lungs. Money is always the issue. Overhearing our tumult provided the impetus for an approach by Israelis on the street with an offer. No identities revealed, I'm to bring a package into Israel. They will send an unnamed person to claim it. Payment happens at the same time."

If the deceit is evident, it doesn't alter my insistence, "I'm telling the truth."

The interplay with rotating detectives continues for hours.

Intimidating U.S. federal agents stand before me. The drug run commenced in Brooklyn. Their concern is, "Who are the stateside suppliers?" Painting the same picture given to the local detectives, stressing that I dealt with nameless individuals, the questioning continues. Within my hearing range, Shavit and Alex argue over permitting Orly and me to have contact for the first time since the arrest. Shavit prevails by playing the good cop. Without handcuffs, we're loaded into a civilian four-passenger sedan. Trying to comfort Orly, I'm suspicious of the setup. Nudging her side, I place fingers on her lips and point to the car radio and my ear. She immediately comprehends that this meeting is about taping our conversation. Satisfied, I release a deep sigh. Taken to a secluded concrete wharf in the Jaffa port, we're directed by Shavit to sit dangling our legs over the side and converse. Solemnly looking up, I see Shavit hovering above. I utter, "Can we have privacy, please?" He complies. I brief and direct Orly on the role she must undertake if she wants to go home. I don't believe in our good fortune.

Shavit wants to endear himself. "Is it to infiltrate or participate?"' bounces through my head.

"Orly, you know nothing about this business. I managed it without including you. Don't budge and be ignorant. Just play stupid since you weren't involved."

We're wearing the same light clothes we had on during the arrest. At the precinct, the thermostat is set to shiver. We're placed in separate offices. Discomfort is the rule. Questioning resumes. In a vacant office, Orly sits sleeveless with her torso hunched forward and arms entwined against her chest, attempting to hold onto body heat. The door is open, and the detectives are within feet of us. Pointing to the desk phone a foot distance away, placing an index finger to her ear, I brush her lips and shake my head back and forth. Message understood. Removing my shirt and throwing it over her shoulders, I touch an itch, and I'm rattled. I feel the healing crust. Shaking with fear from this realization, I grab the shirt. If the detectives see the wounds, I'll have to explain the source and implicate myself as a repeat offender. Panicking, I'm so confused. It would mean that everything said till now is a lie. That was close! Nerves frayed; I'm subjected to another round of questioning.

At the detention center, I'm moved to another cell. To communicate with David, we shout across the corridor. At the new cell, the prisoners acknowledge my entrance. On a vacant bed, staring at the ceiling and contemplating my fate, the surroundings are barren, musty, minimal, and discolored. A single incandescent bulb throws shadows on the wall. Freedom is gone. Goals to survive are what matter. Life as I lived it is gone. I can't even communicate with anyone to release the tension or ease the pain. No outlet: language and caution are the deterrents as I keep informers distant. From Assistant Dean to this hell, how far I've fallen.

Detainees are sitting opposite one another on the concrete floor, heating up a piece of hash and rubbing it with cigarette tobacco. In Hebrew slang, this mixture is referred to as "excessa." A homemade bong assembled with an empty plastic shampoo bottle, a metal toothpaste tube forming the rolled stem, and aluminum foil forming the idle bowl is waiting for the sharing to begin. Toking out of a bong is a new experience for me. It's a far change from the interrogations earlier that day. After two puffs, a cold sweat and dizziness overcome me. Tobacco is not agreeable. Spasms demand quick haste to the stained porcelain fixture that's flush with the floor, a hole placed in its center. Squatting the intended purpose, in distress, I lean backward, and relief comes. Returning from the lieu, everyone pats me on the back and jokes about me not handling the smoke. The hygienic means to freshen up consists of a small sink, and on a wall above my reach, a headless three-inch pipe sloping downward, streaming cold water aimed directly at the porcelain opening. This is how we flush. We excrete standing in the same shared spot behind a partitioned alcove where we shower. This is all so alien and gross.

The next morning, I'm ordered to gather all my possessions, of which there are none. Escorted down to the holding pen located just to the right of the building entranceway, I await transport to the courthouse. Alongside are a dozen prisoners smoking unfiltered cigarettes while imposing a garbled din that reverberates through the air; the words are meaningless to me. More Arabic than Hebrew is spoken, and I feel even more displaced. I'm a "Stranger in a Strange Land." Transport occurs in a small gray painted bare interior cage with two rows of metallic slat benches across from each other. This allows two feet of space to separate the forlorn faces. Packed inside, chained, and handcuffed, we're off in the 'Posta' to discover our fate.

Facing the judge, charged with a crime, the investigation continues without setting me free. This is the way. There is no bond or bail procedure available for felons in the Israeli legal system. Blue skies when walking in a courtyard for protective custody inmates is never available. I don't get to stand under the sky for ninety days. Any view suggesting liberty and hope during this phase of internment, the authorities deny. The environment is intimidating. I'm on guard with everyone. Police and criminal suspects are equally threatening.

At the courthouse, while in handcuffs entering the cellar holding pen, the congestion makes finding an unoccupied spot tenuous at best. There's one row of backless metal benches against the far wall that is fully occupied. I stand amongst the mob in the gloomy light, staring at a small opening. I shimmy between two Arab teenagers.

Looking about, I'm unfocused, dazed. "None of this is real! Is it really happening to me?"

Name called, chained, I'm led to the courtroom and directed to sit in the designated back row. Alongside are half a dozen charges awaiting their turn.

A female police officer brings Orly into the large hall. Her father stands up and turns. Next to him are Avraham and Pnina, my older first cousins. From the chuppah to jail, I want to die. I sob when they see me.

Situated in the rows up front, once composed, I loudly ask, "How do you know I'm here?"

"We saw it on the evening news."

Capture generates so much notoriety and harm that the Assistant Dean of a medical school smuggling a large quantity of cocaine is headline news. Shame overtakes me. I'm no longer a hero.

We're remanded for an additional seven days. Being displaced away from familiarity compounds the degree of punishment that's just commencing. Back at the detention center to assess this subject's treatment, I'm visited by a U.S. Embassy attaché. "Have you been abused?" is the primary concern. The Red Cross provides basic needs, while he has little to offer. Language is the number one problem; I beg for a Hebrew-English dictionary. Without it, I'm a lost soul set adrift without hope. One arrives days later. No distractions: monotony sets in. All I have are thoughts and memories to hold onto. The moments crawl past a worried mind.

An Arab detainee sitting on the floor in the night darkness, his back pressed against the wall, is melting a jail-issued toothbrush with a cigarette lighter. The residue is a blue-black substance. We hear the ticking sound of needle pricks and scraping skin. Mornings' light reveals him proudly showing off the linear drawing. It's a huge, ugly mess; a self-inflicted bloody wound!

The food served lacks quantity and nutrition. Its placement on cigarette-scarred plastic plates is repulsive. The barred cell door allows access below the lock for food drop-off. A hinged cover seals the opening. Served on the scarred plate, breakfast includes five tiny green shriveled olives, one teaspoon each of soft cheese spread and jelly, one oily fried egg, and a couple of stale rye bread slices. Lunch and dinner are indescribable creations or army surplus. Cauliflower in a light broth in quantity is common. No one eats it! I'm furious.

Not accepting these conditions, I rebel. Listening for keys, the sound signals that the food cart is on the way. Wristwatches are disallowed; there's no knowledge of time. The standup count and the light glowing through the window are the timepieces. Coached to speak simple Hebrew words, when hearing the rustle, facing the corridor, I shout out, "Don't receive the food. It's disgusting."

Men alongside me follow the directive. Our punishment is the loss of dignity that food quality represents. It's deserved for transgressions undertaken. I fight back.

Screaming profanities through the bars, I spit out words in uncontrollable rage. Swinging and slamming the food slot cover against the cell door creates a calamitous sound that reverberates through the corridor. I scream, "Sohare," the Hebrew word for guard, at the top of my lungs until I'm too exhausted to continue, and the insanity dissipates. This American isn't accepting deplorable treatment. Authorities ignore the commotion. I think about suicide, but my means are limited. I want to die. I don't know how. These thoughts continue throughout the day. Guilt over the pain this would cause any mother who outlives their child rules out the option. No mom should suffer their child's suicide. I think of Fay.

The authorities do not allow contact with family. The detainees, under the cover of darkness, have family members approach the outer street wall opposite the corridor's grated windows and shout to one another. Biton, who's in the cell, resides in Bat Yam and is acquainted with Moshe, my buyer. I ask him to assure everyone on the outside that they can relax. "I'm not cooperating with the police."

Accused of being despicable, labeled a Monyok, amongst criminals, this is the ultimate insult and a challenge to fight. Rumors that I'm held in protective custody nourish the assumption that I'm a rat. Responding defiantly, "Orly and I are the only ones under arrest. Yiftach, my lawyer, doesn't represent detainees who cooperate with the police."

Saying they would look into it, the taunts stop.

Attorney Yiftach visits. The embassy contacted him. His British accent makes talking easy. The synopsis I offer describing the crime emphasizes a commitment to protect associates. He agrees. We won't trade names for time off. His fee includes a ten-thousand-dollar retainer. He represents both Orly and me. Niko holds this sum since I sold one package. Smart not to locate cash and drugs together. We meet intermittently, with his workload permitting limited consultations. The visits are like a breath of fresh air. Strategizing, our prime concern is returning Orly home. I know that my fate is a lost cause. We're facing the judge. The prosecutor requests that while the investigation is underway, incarceration be extended an additional thirty days. Request granted.

Orly's hand is in a cast. Female inmates broke her pinky after she refused to share cigarettes. Orly is a Kent smoker. American-manufactured cigarettes here are more valuable than gold.

It's imperative that I learn the language. Knowing how to read Hebrew and studying word lists compiled from the dictionary is an obsession. The lack of language implicates Orly. She was Avi's translator. We must keep this simple if only I'm to serve time. It's our shot at gaining her release. Reading local newspapers when available and testing words when interacting with cellmates builds vocabulary. This reduces the isolation that holds me imprisoned in thoughts. The limited time available till trial prompts urgency. Self-talk in Hebrew hastens success. The effort helps pass the time. Achieving language fluency gives me something to wake up for each morning.

One of my attorneys agrees to discreetly mail the following:

July 27, 1986

LEON,

THANK GOD I HAVE MOM! AT LEAST SHE IS WITH ME IN HEART, AS I AM WITH HER. WITHOUT THE WISDOM AND STRENGTH SHE EMBODIED IN ME, I COULD NOT SURVIVE THIS ORDEAL, AN ORDEAL I HAVE MERCIFULLY SPARED ALL OF YOU FROM KNOWING; AN ORDEAL THAT YOUR GRACIOUS AND UNDERSTANDING LETTER HAS ONLY FUELED TO ANOTHER DEGREE WHEN I THOUGHT THAT THIS

TORMENT COULD NOT GET WORSE. THAT YOU ARE IGNORANT IS NOT YOUR RESPONSIBILITY BUT YOUR LACK OF IMAGINATION IS SHOCKING. HOW CAN A MAN OF YOUR AGE LACK THE INSIGHT TO SENSE THAT I AM IN MORE TROUBLE/DIFFICULTY THAN I AM COMMUNICATING !

I AM HOUSED IN THE EQUIVALENT OF THE "COUNTY JAIL". OVERCROWDING IN THE PRISON SYSTEM HAS KEPT ME HERE FOR THREE MONTHS, TODAY. AS A RESULT I AM NOT ALLOWED THE BASIC PRIVILEGES OFFERED IN THE PRISON SYSTEM. COMMUNICATION, (OTHER THAN A WEEKLY VISIT BY IMMEDIATE FAMILY), WITH THE OUTSIDE WORLD IS NOT ALLOWED. NO PHONE! NO LETTERS! NOTHING! TO MAKE MATTERS WORSE I AM CONFINED TO A SEGREGATED/SEPARATED SECTION OF THE JAIL AND AM ONLY ALLOWED OUT OF THE CELL FOR COURT APPEARANCES OR FOR OCCASSIONAL VISITS OF THE LAWYER. I SHARE THE CELL WITH JUNKIES THAT ARE ARRESTED AND GO THROUGH DRUG WITHDRAWAL ,ETC. (DON'T YOU GO TO THE MOVIES?) THERE IS NO FURNITURE IN THE CELL ONLY IRON BUNK BEDS WITH FOAM RUBBER MATTRESSES. ALL FUNCTIONS ARE CONDUCTED IN THE ROOM. ORLY'S FATHER DUTIFULLY BRINGS ME A WEEKLY PACKAGE CONTAINING CLEAN LAUNDRY, CIGARETTES, A NEWSPAPER AND MAGAZINE IN ENGLISH. I CHAIN SMOKE AND HAVE BEEN DOING SO FOR ABOUT ONE MONTH NOW, AFTER HATING CIGARETTES ALL MY LIFE. TO GET COUSIN ABE PERMISSION TO ENTER THE JAIL AND MEET WITH ME THROUGH AN IRON SCREEN, I HAD TO CONDUCT A ONE MAN RIOT AND THROW ALL THE PRISONERS FOOD IN THE CELL OUT ONTO THE CORRIDER THROUGH THE SMALL

OPENING IN THE CELL DOOR THROUGH WHICH FOOD IS DELIVERED. IN MY RAGE I BROKE OFF THE IRON PLATE USED TO SEAL THIS OPENING. AS A RESULT I GOT TO SEE ABRAHAM WHO ACCOMPANIED ORLY'S FATHER & SISTER ON THE WEEKLY VISIT. ONE CAPTAIN, SEEING THE HAVOC I MADE THAT STRETCHED THE LENGTH OF THE CORRIDER STATED THAT I NEEDED TO BE PLACED IN A MENTAL HOSPITAL. I WAS NOT PUNISHED FOR THIS ACT ONLY BECAUSE MY JAILORS SYMPATHIZE WITH THE HARDSHIPS I ENDURE. THE PAIN IN MY BACK & NECK IS TREATED WITH SLEEPING PILLS & MUSCLE RELAXANTS. THERE ARE NO ANTI-ARTHRITIC DRUGS TO TREAT A NECK CONDITION WHOSE PAIN CAUSES ME TO WAKE IN MY SLEEP WHEN I TURN MY HEAD IN MY SLEEP. IN FACT, THE LACK OF A CHAIR OR DESK CAUSES ME TO WRITE THIS LETTER HUNCHED OVER ON THE BOTTOM HALF OF A BUNK BED WHILE IN PAIN FROM THE POSITION I MUST ASSUME. I AM IMPRISONED IN A FOREIGN COUNTRY WHERE I AM A STRANGER, FORCED TO QUICKLY ADJUST TO THE LANGUAGE AND CULTURE. TO MAKE MATTERS WORSE I LIVE WITH THE WORST ELEMENT OF THIS SOCIETY BUT HAVE MANAGED TO UTILIZE ALL MY RESOURCES OF PERSONAL CHARACTER AND STRENGTH TO BECOME ONE OF THE MOST RESPECTED PRISONERS THIS JAIL EVER HAD. THE SITUATION WILL NOT BREAK ME BUT TAKES ALL MY CONCENTRATION TO HANDLE AS I MUST ALSO CARRY ORLY WHO IS IN JAIL AND CARRY HER FAMILY AS WELL. I CAN NEVER SHOW WEAKNESS EVEN WHEN I CRY OVER SOME REMINDER OF THE FREEDOM I ENJOYED WITH MY WIFE BEFORE MY IMPRISONMENT. YOU DON'T REALIZE THAT ALL THE LEGAL PROCEEDINGS ARE CONDUCTED IN HEBREW

AND I MUST TRANSLATE ALL THE TESTIMONY FROM HEBREW MYSELF AND ENGINEER OUR DEFENSE IN CONJUNCTION WITH OUR ATTORNEY. EVEN AS I WRITE THIS LETTER MY CELLMATES ARE SMOKING A FORM OF HEROIN THAT ONE OF THEM MANAGED TO SMUGGLE INTO THE JAIL. I AM COMPLETELY DRUG FREE & WHEN I SEE SOME SUNSHINE & BREATH FRESH AIR AGAIN IN THE PRISON, I HOPE TO BE CIGARETTE FREE.

I HAVE YET TO MENTION THE CASE AND CHOOSE NOT TO SINCE THIS LETTER WHICH I MUST SMUGGLE OUT OF THE JAIL COULD BE CONFISCATED. EVEN IN PRISON, ALL INCOMING & OUTGOING LETTERS WILL BE READ BY A CENSOR.

THIS IS NOT AMERICA !!!

I HAVE BEEN CHARGED WITH SMUGGLING ONE KILO OF COCAINE AND AM ABOUT TO BE CHARGED WITH SMUGGLING ANOTHER KILO IN JANUARY. OUR DEFENSE STRATEGY IF IT WORKS WILL PROVE THAT WE ARE BEING CHARGED WITH THE SAME CRIME TWICE. THE PRESSURE HAS BEEN CONNSTANT BUT I AM NOW CONFIDENT AFTER A MONTH OF CONSTANT DEPRESSION & APPREHENSION. THREE WEEKS AGO ORLYS' FINGER WAS BROKEN BY WOMEN PRISONERS WHO TRIED TO TAKE HER CIGARETTES FROM HER. SHE IS IMPRISONED IN ISRAELS' ONLY WOMENS PRISON. I ONLY SEE HER AT COURT APPEARANCES AND THIS MAKES COORDINATION OF OUR DEFENSE VERY DIFFICULT. I HAVE A CHANCE TO GET OUT OF THIS PROBLEM WITH A THREE YEAR SENTENCE AND WITH ORLY FREE AFTER THE TRIAL, AT BEST (ONE THIRD OF THE SENTENCE IS

SUSPENDED FOR GOOD BEHAVIOR) OR AT WORST 8-10 YEARS EACH IF MY DEFENSE IS NOT BELIEVED.

WITH SUCH PROBLEMS, YOU ARE INSULTED THAT I DID NOT MENTION YOU IN THE TWO LETTERS I MANAGED TO SEND OUT TO DATE. AFTER HELPING (I THINK, SINCE I DON'T KNOW EVEN NOW AFTER YOU KINDLY WROTE TO ME, AS IF I DON'T CARE TO KNOW) STUIE BECOMING A DOCTOR AND STAYING IN THE JOB WHEN I COULD HAVE LEFT WITH MY CAREER SOARING, KNOWING THAT HIS FINANCIAL ARRANGEMENT DEPENDED ON CONTINUING AT THE JOB I LOATHED, YOU FEEL THAT ALL I WAS EVER INTERESTED IN IS " GETTING YOU PISSED OFF".

EACH MEMBER OF MY FAMILY IS BEHAVING DURING THIS TRYING TIME TOWARDS ME IN A PREDICTABLE FASHION ALTHOUGH I AM SHOCKED BY THE INDIFFERENCE YOUR CHILDREN APPEAR TO BE DEMONSTRATING. I ASKED DAVID IF HE WOULD ASSUME THIS HEAVY RESPONSIBILITY BECAUSE I ANTICIPATED A LACK OF FULL SUPPORT FOR ALL THE "REASONS" YOU ALL HAVE AND ARE DEMONSTRATING FOR DUMPING ON ME. DO YOU FEEL BETTER NOW THAT I'VE OPENED UP TOWARDS YOU AND SHARED WITH YOU A FEW CHILLING FACTS? SHOULD I SPEND MY EFFORTS WRITING LETTERS OF THIS SORT, SHARING MY DAILY HARDSHIPS WITH ALL OF YOU, OR SHOULD I FOCUS ON HELPING MYSELF SURVIVE AND SALVAGE A LIFE THAT COULD VERY WELL BE SHATTERED BY A HARSH SENTENCE? IN YOUR LETTER YOU MADE NO MENTION OF WHAT HAPPENED TO OUR PERSONAL POSSESSIONS. GOD HELP ANYONE WHO HAS TO EXPERIENCE THE DISPLACEMENT & ALIENATION I FACE WITH THEIR WIFE ALSO IMPRISONED AND THEIR FAMILY

POINTING ACCUSATIONS IN ORDER IN ORDER TO MAINTAIN A FAÇADE OF SELF RIGHTEOUSNESS. "DO I BLAME ANY OF YOU AFTER WHAT I PULLED? AND YOU FEEL THE SAME WAY". THESE ARE YOUR WORDS AND THE TIMING COULD NOT BE MORE SELF SERVING. IF YOU THOUGHT OF ME FOR ONE MOMENT YOU WOULD NEVER SAY SUCH A THING TO ME AT THIS TIME. I DID NOT INTENTIONALLY IGNORE YOU IN THE LETTER I SENT MOM. YOU ARE SENSITIVE TO THE FACT THAT BERNARD WAS MORE INVOLVED IN SHAPING MY LIFE AFTER YOUR MARRIAGE AND THE BOND THIS CREATED BETWEEN US TO THE EXCLUSION OF YOU HAS ALWAYS HURT YOU. THE FACT IS, I HAVE NOT BEEN VERY CLOSE TO EITHER OF YOU FOR MANY YEARS, AS I TRIED TO FIND MY OWN WAY. I AM A PROUD MAN AND THAT IS SOMETHING NONE OF YOU EVER UNDERSTAND AFTER 17 YEARS OF SELF INDEPENDENCE. ALTHOUGH YOU CHOSE TO SPEAK FOR BERNARD I HAVE THINGS TO SAY I WISH TO COMMUNICATE TO HIM DIRECTLY. BUT YES I CAN BLAME HIM FOR ONLY SAYING "BYE" AT THE END OF OUR TALK IN WHICH I SPOKE AND HE NEVER REACTED.

GOD PITY MOM THAT I AM NOT THERE TO BE HER FRIEND AS SHE WAS MINE. NOW THIS PRIVILEGE, WHICH IT IS, IS LEFT TO YOU AND BERNARD. I PRAY FOR THE DAY I WILL SEE HER AGAIN. TAKE CARE OF HER AND YOURSELF.

DANNY

9/28/86

DEAR LEON,

I TELEPHONED MOM ONE WEEK AGO TODAY AND INAPPROPRIATELY VENTED ANGER AT HER THAT PERHAPS SHOULD BE DIRECTED AT YOU, STUIE,BERNARD AND EVEN JACKIE. IN THE ONE LETTER I HAVE RECEIVED IN FIVE MONTHS FROM MY FAMILY,YOU WERE HURT THAT I DID NOT INCLUDE YOU MORE IN MY REQUEST FOR HELP. IN FACT YOU FELT I OVERLOOKED YOU. CAN YOU EXPLAIN THIS DESIRE OF YOURS TO HELP ME WITH THE FACT THAT MOM WAS LEFT TO HANDLE MY LANDLORD AND MAKE CRITICAL DECISIONS REGARDING MY PERSONAL POSSESSIONS? HOW IS IT THAT THE LANDLORD KEPT TWO CARPETS WORTH $1200.00, A RUG THAT COST ME $800, A MIRROR THAT COST $350, LEVOLOR BLINDS COSTING $800, A FRONT DOOR AND LOCKS WORTH $150 AND WOOD FLOORING COSTING $1000.00 WITH INSTALLATION. TOTAL WORTH OVER $4000.00 W/O VALUING THE BLINDS IN THE KITCHEN, BATHROOM AND BATHROOM MIRROR. I OWED THE LANDLORD TWO MONTHS RENT AFTER HE KEPT THE $600 SECURITY DEPOSIT PLUS THE REPLACEMENT VALUE OF THREE DOORS. HE GAINED $3500.00 WITH THE DEAL THAT WAS STRUCK. AM I NOT WORTH YOU GUYS COLLECTIVELY SITTING TOGETHER AND DECIDING HOW TO HANDLE THE SITUATION? TO MAKE YOUR DECISIONS ABOUT MY THINGS MORE UNBELIEVABLE, THE LANDLORD GOT ANOTHER $500 OUT OF MOM. IT LOOKS LIKE MY FAMILY, GOD BLESS THEM, DID NOT GIVE A SHIT FOR ANYTHING, OTHER THAN GETTING THE PAINFUL BURDEN I IMPOSED ON THEM OVER AND DONE WITH. WHEN I ASKED MOM WHY BERNARD DOES NOT FINANCIALLY HELP MORE, SHE TOLD ME THAT

BERNARD CONTRIBUTED $1500.00 TO THE SITUATION. I THEN HEAR THAT $1000 OF THAT MONEY WENT TO YOUR SON SO THAT HE COULD MOVE MY GIFT TO UTICA, N.Y. TO MAKE THE RIDICULOUS MORE ABSURD, BERNARD SEES THE $1500.00 AS HELP HE HAS PROVIDED TO ME. I OFFER YOUR SON THE FURNITURE WITHOUT MY BED AS A GIFT AND HIS MOVING EXPENSES ARE CONSIDERED EXPENSES TO ME! FURTHERMORE, HE IS FUCKING WHENEVER HE CAN GET IT ON. ON MY AND MY WIFE'S BED USING MY LINEN, PILLOWS, BLANKET ETC. THESE ARE PERSONAL POSSESSIONS THAT COST ME $2000.00. WHEN I'LL BE FREE THESE ITEMS WILL NO LONGER BE NEW. I WANTED THE BED AND BEDDING STORED. NOW I WANT AND EXPECT MONEY FROM YOUR SON FOR THESE ITEMS. WHAT ABOUT MY T.V. AND STEREO WHICH COST ME $2000.00? AFTER YOUR SON ADDS YEARS OF USE ONTO THESE ITEMS ARE THEY JUST GOING TO BE HANDED BACK TO ME AND I WILL OWE HIM A THANK YOU FOR SAFEGUARDING THEM? IT WOULD HAVE BEEN BETTER TO SELL THESE ITEMS WHILE THEY STILL HAD VALUE AND EVEN KEEP A PERCENTAGE FOR YOUR EFFORTS THAN EXPECT ME TO BE HAPPY OR FEEL BETTER OFF WITH WHAT HAS BEEN DONE. I ASSUME YOU ARE ADDING WEAR TO MY VIDEO WHICH IS SPECIAL AND COST $800. MOM TELLS ME THAT JACKIE SAYS THE DISHES ARE HERS SINCE SHE GAVE THEM TO ME AS A WEDDING GIFT. SINCE YOU DID NOT STORE THEM IN YOUR ATTIC FOR ME, I CAN ONLY GUESS AT HOW MANY PIECES WILL NOT BE CHIPPED OR BROKEN THROUGH HER USE. WHAT MAKES ME SO DAMN BITTER IS HOW I ALWAYS TRIED TO HELP YOU, YOUR SON AND YOUR DAUGHTER.

EACH OF YOU RECEIVED MY HELP WHICH CAME THROUGH MY PERSONAL SACRIFICE, BUT WHEN YOU ALL HAD TO RETURN THE EFFORT, YOU ALL WENT THROUGH THE MOTIONS BUT YOUR HEARTS WERE NOT INTO IT. AS OF 2 WEEKS AGO, THE LETTER I ASKED OF FROM YOUR SON HAD NOT ARRIVED. MY DIPLOMAS HAVE NOT ARRIVED. MY TAX FORMS FOR 1984 & 1985 HAVE NOT ARRIVED. I HAVE NOT ASKED FOR ADDITIONAL $ OTHER THAN WHAT MOM SENT ME FROM HER MEAGER FUNDS NOR WILL I. MOM NOW TELLS ME SHE HAS HER OWN PROBLEMS PAYING THE RENT AND FACES A LARGE PROBLEM IN RENT COURT. I REALIZE I CANNOT CALL HER ANYMORE BECAUSE SHE CAN'T HANDLE THE PHONE BILL. I WILL TRY TO CHARGE FUTURE CALLS TO MY FATHER-IN LAW'S #. MOM TELLS ME THAT YOU ARE OUT OF WORK AND CAN'T HELP HER BUT WHAT ABOUT BERNARD? I AM AMAZED BY THE SELFISHNESS I SEE EVEN FROM HERE CUT OFF FROM EVERYTHING. WHY WASN'T MOM GIVEN MY T.V.WITH ITS REMOTE CONTROL FEATURE SO SHE COULD REST HER ARTHRITIC BODY WHILE WATCHING T.V.? I WANT THIS DONE IMMEDIATELY. I WANT THE VIDEO BOUGHT FROM ME OR STORED IN HER HOUSE. YOUR SON SHOULD BE MADE AWARE OF HIS FINANCIAL OBLIGATION TO BERNARD $1000 AND TO ME FOR THE BED, BEDDING AND STEREO.

I HAVE MUCH TO SETTLE WITH ALL OF YOU. HAPPY BIRTHDAY AND HAPPY NEW YEAR.

DANNY

Swaying cellmates to refuse meals is my outlet to vent anger at everyone and everything. Wound-up emotions are driving me. I'm eventually exposed. Intolerable behavior has me standing in front of Warden Touizer. We will meet his cousin later. I'm placed with the general population. Concern for my well-being has made me anxious. Agitated over the punishment, receiving a tray of grease-bathed eggplant on the food line, I brazenly react. Looking at the servings, I grab a tray and fling it skittering on a steel tabletop, its surface now covered in oil. Personal belongings I clumsily carry add to the mishap. Guards, witnessing me with their batons raised, escort me out of the dining hall and into a holding pen. Sitting isolated, I'm contemplating the consequences, accepting the inevitable. Another nightmare is about to begin.

I'm bedded down in a secured dormitory. All the beds are lined up in rows, and I find the only unoccupied one. The detainees here tonight will be commuting under guard to destinations in the morning. Startled, in the early dawn darkness, my shoulder shaken, I'm told to get up. Sleeping in day clothes, I jump to a stand. I'm surrounded by guards. Shoved along the way, I'm excommunicated from Abu Kabir.

Sitting on the holding pen metal rod assembled bench, designed to be uncomfortable, is a gruffy-looking, broken English-speaking Russian fellow traveler. He informs me, "We're waiting for a 'Posta' heading to Be'er Sheva."

"I can't go there. My physically feeble father-in-law, with his body broken from arthritis, and his daughters can't travel the distance and also visit my wife in Neva Tirtza."

He responds, "If a prisoner is bleeding from a wound requiring immediate treatment, the rules forbid transport."

It's common for prisoners to slash their forearms in protest.

Specifically, those with lengthy sentences have their arms covered with scars. It's a rite of passage to sport these markings. No knife or razor blade possessed; I'm frantically rummaging in my bag searching for a solution. A spare pair of contact lenses in two small glass vials, if broken, provides shards that should cut flesh.

He says, "Cut the moment you hear the Posta pull up at the entrance."

Three failed attempts occur. I can't draw blood. My newfound Russian assists. Extending a naked limb, my head turns away while the slashing blood gushes onto the floor. Looking at the damage, I wonder if the white reveals bone or ligaments. The troopers enter and, seeing the blood, announce that I'm in no condition to travel per regulations. It's an arduous trip.

A detention center officer responds, "He must be taken, damn the rules."

Not compromising their schedule, the guards allot minutes for the medical team to tape the wound. There's no time for stitches. The blood oozes through the gauze. Hours later, the Be'er Sheva staff challenge my presence.

"Under no circumstances are we permitted to accept a bleeding prisoner transfer."

Rejected, I'm returned.

At the Abu Kabir infirmary, an orderly examines my arm. Swelling has set in. It's too late for stitches; a thick scar will remain. Sleeping in the same dormitory with a draped hand securing belongings, I'm startled when wooden rods swat my legs, accompanied by barking orders to get up. The wound is not bleeding. It's off to the desert fortress once again. They aren't keeping me in this place for one more second.

The glaring sun and dry desert heat hit me like a sledgehammer. The speech intonation barked by the receiving officer and the rigid decorum cause shivers in spite of the rays beating down. This place is far different than the other both physically and spiritually. It's oppressive, and the sentence hasn't even begun. The majority standing alongside in a single file are of Arab descent. Struggling with spoken Hebrew and my English not being understood, we can't communicate. Being an American criminal gives me standing with the population. No way of knowing, I wonder if sequestered terrorists share the cell with me. Fighting for the opportunity to telephone family in the U.S., I'm isolated and wonder what they're thinking about the disappearance. We haven't spoken since the day before the flight. With our apartment abandoned and duties neglected at Ross, I'm a missing person. Worried about the unknown adds to the tumult. Life has turned upside down. Memories and concern are all I have to conquer monotony.

The cell houses sixteen prisoners. They're all of Arab descent. Unscreened and windowless, the grate-covered open casement welcomes the dry desert air. The nights are temperate. Withdrawing further, blaming the authorities for treating me like a foreigner, I'm classified as an American. The rationale behind placing me in this situation, isolated from contact with Jews, I'm told, is a form of protective custody. In fact, it's a punishment for rebellion. For emotional release, it's easy when available to accept the five unfiltered Omar cigarettes delivered through the door's slot soon after breakfast. Locked in the cell twenty-four, seven, I lean my head and press against the bars, anticipating this token. I've always hated cigarettes. Tobacco killed Pop. Two fingers on my right hand are stained brownish-yellow.

Obstinate, I pressure both Yiftach and the embassy through emissaries to get me moved back within striking distance of Orly's family. The back and forth from the desert to Tel Aviv court appearances wears me down. Pick up is at dawn, and there's a drop off at Ayalon. Posta from various locations unloads prisoners there. We're packed in a cell meant for ten bodies but receive over forty. No seating is available. Most stand shoulder to shoulder. Ventilation is a dream to wish for. The way station's conditions remind me of where humanity is forgotten in scenes from the movie "Midnight Express." The layover lasts a couple of hours.

Told to pack up, I'm returning to Abu Kabir. Early the following morning, I'm taken to the holding pen, where I'm trying to determine my immediate fate. I nudge past the other prisoners and wedge against the metal door. A thin slot enables a limited view of the area. I spot Shavit.

Getting his attention, he responds, "Be careful. You're going in for more questioning."

I state, "I know why."

Inquisitively lifting his eyebrow, I don't elaborate. The image of Avi appears. Anger flows. The altered explanation of construed events will fit like a glove. He's the fall guy. Ready for more interrogation, I believe I'm in control. Survival depends on it.

CHAPTER 16.
BETRAYAL

Arranging thoughts during transport that fill the gaps while not steering away from protecting others is the only course. Told that Zamir, Avi's helper brother-in-law on the beverage truck, voluntarily confessed to having knowledge of this drug business makes no sense. Where did he fit in the picture when we had no interaction? Avi has to be the rat.

Vanunu, the chief detective, says, "With the prosecution's blessing, Orly will be free and you'll serve a three-year sentence. Abandon the gang."

I respond, "You know what I know."

Hammered, I let their questions guide the answers. Since I can't speak the language and am a visitor with no known local contacts, their questioning centers around Orly being the ringleader. It turns out Avi is in love with Orly, who is thirty years his junior. The intended betrayal of his sister's marriage leads Zamir to seek revenge. He believes it is unjust to have me in prison while Avi, who's involved, walks free. Listening to Shavit sounds like a soap opera. Fury rages, but I must control it. I recall the warning I issued in Brooklyn years past.

"Orly, you'll be out of here if there's contact with this guy again." I'm convinced the phone call from the hotel caused this.

Avi, reacting, calls the detective bureau posing as Mister X. He has information that an international drug ring is smuggling coke crystal out of New York into Israel. Twenty thousand shekels is the reward he seeks. He settles for two thousand. In dollars, it's nominal. His goal is to be Orly's sugar daddy during my absence. Zamir reacts. Engaged in discovery while the police seek the truth, how ironic to learn that my way of life and freedom were sold for so little. Orly's knowledge of this nefarious activity leads to my demise. I'm stupid for not exercising discretion around her. I should've anticipated the difficulty she would endure and kept my mouth shut.

Expanding on the previous confession, coordination changed when Avi ordered the wrong product. Unable to sell it, I returned to the States. The drug remained hidden in the crawl space used for storage at the Ramat Gan apartment. The police confiscated the package that I actually smuggled months ago. The same people sent me back to Israel to hand it over. You show up on the morning of the pickup day. Avi was the original recipient.

Our not getting indicted twice doesn't work. The prosecution and police accept this confession with less than a grain of salt. Meeting with the attorneys subjected to interrogations and court appearances, I'm bouncing back and forth between Be'er Sheva and the detention center. Kept from speaking to Orly for months, after loading me on the Posta at Abu Kabir, she surprisingly appears with her thigh bandaged. We ride together, holding one another tightly in a stance, not letting go for an instant. No one else present, we compare notes. She's been in an altercation with a woman who attacked her.

When told to do chores, Orly replied, "I'm like Sue Ellen on the Dallas television show."

The prisoners responded. They drew blood by hitting her with a metal brush. The bristles pierced her skin.

Leaving the court after the arraignment, I'm on my way to Shata, located in the far north near Nazareth. The inmates are mostly of Arab lineage. I speak with no one all the while I am there. Hitting rock bottom, catatonic, I pass the time unfocused, staring out into nowhere. Months pass, and pressure from the outside relocates me to the Ayalon Prison in Ramle. There are weekly family visits now on Shabbat and regular consultations with Yiftach or his alternates. The trial is to start nine months after our arrest.

The family juggles visiting Orly and me. She is situated a long, cumbersome walk away, but they never miss the chance to bring a smile and novels that I requested. Bentzi is heartbroken seeing his son-in-law under these circumstances. Their love carries me as I battle hopelessness. I do my best to reassure them that I'm okay. We exchange laundry weekly.

Addicts look forward to Shabbat visitation as a time to reload both emotionally and physically. Adolan, like methadone, if not identical, when taken, eases withdrawal symptoms. The visiting area doesn't allow bodily contact. A worn and discolored glass window with a telephone receiver is as close as two people get. Clothing, sneakers, linen, and toiletries are allowable after undergoing inspection. Relatives or friends soak garments in Adolan, and after drying, the contraband is smuggled in. Coke Parsi is stuffed into toothpaste tubes and footwear, waiting to be shared. The cell block has drugs of all sorts available to anyone who can pay. Prisoners treat the cloth by soaking the cut strips in water until the drug dissolves and bleeds out. Curious, I try it, finding the effect disorienting and not pleasant.

Melting Coke Parsi on heated foil is the thing to do. Flicking the lighter, I look up and standing at the cell door is a Russian-accented prison guard who, shaking his head back and forth, reacts decently. Instead of confronting me, he continues on his way. He could have busted me. I instantly felt his look of disappointment. Like a child caught in the act, I am ashamed. The straw foil and straw are tossed away. Never again will I try that stuff.

Mastering conversational Hebrew, I believe, will save Orly. The first moment in detention, I realized that without language proficiency, her freedom is questionable. The trial conducted in the native tongue will enable me to divert the prosecutor's accusations that Orly was my translator. Head thrust in that paperback dictionary as if it outlined an escape plan; nothing enters consciousness to distract my concentration.

Judge Edmund Levy has the case, and Yiftach believes that's a good thing for Orly. An orthodox Jew, he rules favorably when trialing women and avoids long sentences. We're charged with two indictments each. The prosecution is asking for thirteen and seven years, respectively. Reporters from the printed media cover the trial. The American Assistant Dean of a medical school smuggling drugs to fund in vitro fertilization is a worthy news story.

The opening statements, spoken rapidly, are difficult to follow and keep up with. When there's a pause, turning towards the judge, raising my hand, I interrupt, "Could we proceed in English? It would be easier for me to understand."

As if I were mocking the bench, the retort is explicit and authoritative.

"You speak excellent Hebrew. The trial will continue as is."

Orly, sitting on the bench hunched over, her family three rows back appears like a broken reed. We've both lost weight over the months. At the Ramle infirmary, I weighed thirty pounds less than on incarceration day.

The prosecutor states that the police confiscated 860 grams of cocaine belonging to me.

"This act of smuggling causes irreparable harm to the nation and specifically young people. It affects our soldiers on active duty."

I can't help but wonder, "What happened to the missing grams? I sold a hundred, and we partied using an eight-ball worth."

Residing in New York, I viewed coke as the party drug of Club 54. Here I'm an enemy of the state. There'll be no mercy. The judge rules. There is no jury of peers determining guilt or innocence. The reading of charges and the requested sentencing completes the session. We're facing thirteen and seven years, respectively. Separation imposed; I blow a kiss to Orly. Yiftach and I meet at Abu Kabir to prepare for the court sessions.

The process drags on. In discovery, the seashore recording of waves and the garbled conversation with Orly taped during the ride to the Jaffa port confirm what I suspected. The recordings are useless for prosecutorial purposes. We're surprised to hear the judge's opening statement that he's heard enough. Calling the prosecution and defense to the bench, Orly and I are brought up to speed. The judge instructs the bailiff to clear the courtroom. We commiserate in private.

Standing before the judge, "To end the trial today, the prosecution offers to combine the two indictments. If the trial continues, a guilty verdict will result in a thirteen-year sentence for you and seven years for Orly. This is standard for a crime of this magnitude. Agreeing to plead, the prosecution acquiesces to seven and three years respectively, counted from the day of your arrest."

The attorney instructs us, "You've no better alternative than the judge messaging that he'll not exonerate either of you. You're fortunate we have a judge who is sympathetic to women. The sentence is as if we combined the indictments."

In denial, certain she's going home, it takes repeated explanations for Orly to understand her fate. Yiftach continues,

"You have no choice but to accept the judge's generosity. With time served, and one-third punishment off for good behavior, you'll be home in fifteen months."

Orly refuses to accept that she isn't being released. Self-induced hysteria takes over. She struggles to accept the inevitable. Screaming "I'm not involved," the legal team and I pound the facts into her head, until resistance slowly fades.

Returning to the courtroom, the family members are stunned by the news. Spirits break, hearing the outcome as it's read. Calculating time off for good behavior and time served, forty-seven more months of hell await me, and fifteen months await Orly before tasting freedom again. I'm sentenced as a courier. Orly's crime is knowing about these activities and protecting her husband by not cooperating with the police.

Judge Levy's final words to us are, "One day, hopefully you will have children and not experience the harm you have caused others by your actions."

Prison services transfer the accused to imprisonment once sentenced, where conditions are demanding and severe. Ayalon for me, the women's prison, Neiva Tiertza for Orly. Both are within walking distance of each other. Visitation on Shabbat continues. Lessons learned teach me to look away, keep my mouth shut, and go with the flow. Long-term residence demands adapting to the rules of the jungle.

Prisoners earn a weekend furlough every six weeks for good behavior, and after one-quarter of the total sentence is complete. Exactly twelve months more until I hold Orly in my arms. To qualify, work is mandatory, all rules are abided by, and no weapons or drugs are possessed. Drug testing never occurs. Drugs keep the inmates docile. Contraband infests the facility. Prisoners, Israeli and Arab, turn to religion for salvation. For me, this newfound faith is absolute hypocrisy; asking God's help and forgiveness when in trouble, but ignoring religious tenets when there is always free choice. This timely found faith adopted with phony intent, I reject as an option. It won't strengthen my ability to cope. My faith runs deeper than that.

CHAPTER 17.
WHITE KNIGHT

In unit Vav Shtayim, a daily routine of limited activity helps pass the time. A dozen windowless cells, barred doors accessing a dilapidated, barren stone courtyard, armed uniforms rifle ready, guard towers at every corner, and a barbed wire grid crisscrossing twenty feet above the view are a constant weight bearing down. The grid above my head imposes a poignant image that I'm caged like a bird at the zoo. In this aged hovel, spirits break. Two distractions are available: viewing Israeli or Arabic television for one hour each evening broadcast in a small community room, or walking the seventy-meter circumference of the enclosed courtyard. The inmate who selects the program is the most aggressive and threatening among the decision-makers. Like Shata, its architecture is an inherited relic of the Ottoman and British empires. Outdated Hebrew newspapers and paperback fiction published in English fill free time. I keep journals where I pour out my heart. Years later, I opened and read a page. Taken back to this place, I couldn't manage the pain. It's still too fresh. I destroyed them.

The Sony Walkman that accompanied all Ross University excursions, delivered on a Shabbat visit, never leaves my side. Favorite songs and bands help for what seems like only a moment, taking me far to a prior life. U-2 dominates. Weather permitting, I'm in the open-air courtyard sitting on a metal folding chair with these distractions. It's Shabbat. Reading the headline section of the weekend newspaper edition, Yediot Aharonot, in the lower left-hand corner of the first page, is a story and photo close to my heart. Avi's brother-in-law, Shasha, was ordered to court on a civil matter.

In the familiar crowded basement, when protesting, he draped a wool army blanket like the one I sleep with nightly over his body. Igniting the blanket with a cigarette lighter, he goes up in flames and suffers for days until dying. This is my first happy moment since the day before the arrest.

Avi is sentenced to thirty months for his involvement with me. He must have made a deal. I'm never called to his trial. His unit overlooks Vav Shtayim. It's organized protective custody where the rats and sex offenders sleep. Seeking justice, I inform the prisoners that Avi sold me and my wife out for pennies. I point them to the windows where he's housed. The criminal honor code will get to him; it's just a matter of time. One day, I'm informed he's been beaten, thrown off his upper bunk, and had a stroke. I'm elated. He was gimpy before this happened so hopefully he's miserable.

Assigned to a privately run factory on prison grounds working a seven-hour shift, Doron Layeled manufactures simple wooden puzzles for preschool children. On the assembly line, I'm cutting out five shapes that address a theme: fruit, domesticated animals, and similar subjects that will help children develop hand-eye coordination and language skills. Sitting on a tall, uncomfortable metal stool, my legs dangling in front of a jigsaw, the blade inserted through a tiny hole cuts the outline of the shapes without affecting the wooden frame. At the next station, tiny levers are attached to the shapes. The sawed frame is glued to the backing. Not calling on hands to perform since abandoning art, production is clumsy and inept. With practice, I get the hang of it. The factory is civilian-owned. Wages here are higher than at other jobs, yet in line with the prison scale. Observing how the most productive inmate at the jigsaw performs, pounding out frames at a rate no one can equal, I'm jealous. His compensation is based on productivity and not an hourly wage. His flowing movement, hands picking up speed while following the shapes, churns out puzzle after puzzle. He's a Coke Parsi addict of Yemenite lineage who often misses days.

Mohnee, the civilian manager, speaks fluent English with a Bulgarian accent. Not being a hardened criminal yet placed in a high-security prison, I'm viewed as an anomaly. Civil demeanor says it all. Our shared affinity creates a bond. We get along. I'm dependable, a trait not readily found in this place. Badgering him, seeking compensation for productivity, being the addict, is unreliable; he finally acquiesces.

Replacing the Yemenite, I'm permitted to work extended hours. Funds transferred to Orly's account motivate me to maximize earnings. Proudly supporting both Orly and my twice-monthly purchases at the cantina, the effort gives me purpose. Authorities limit aseemone purchase for telephone use to twenty per cycle. Phone calls out of the immediate area require multiple coins. This is a priority purchase. So are coffee and cigarettes. Helping Orly makes me feel special.

"We'll get through this. We'll survive. I love my wife so much!"

Dror shares a cell with five other prisoners. They're all lifers. In his early twenties, tall, abrasive, threatening violence indiscriminately, he rules the unit. He's the first Jewish person I've ever seen whose body is covered in tattoos. Everyone is a potential threat, but his presence in particular scares me. Keeping a distance to avoid any interaction that could trigger aggression, I'm on high alert, refraining from any eye contact. I observe him only from the corners of my eyes.

In the darkest of nights, we're all woken by the loud sounds of lockers crashing. We hear hushed voices emanating from a nearby cell. Legs pound metal. The tumult ends minutes later. Morning arrives. Seeing sprayed blood on the cell wall, we learn that Dror's roommates held down his head covered with a pillow while they slashed his throat and bled him out. He will no longer dictate to or dominate other prisoners. He crossed the line and paid dearly. Drugs are the culprit. Remembering serene Brooklyn, I'm facing this horrible dream, except it's reality!

Near death's door, I remind myself, "All of my life, I answered to no one. Where was I and where am I now?"

Settling in, working on acceptance to assuage any suspicion I could be a rat; smoking hashish in the cell is a communal ritual I cannot refuse. Sami, a high-strung nineteen-year-old, sports a tattoo over the entire surface of his back. It reads, "I was born to suffer." He's a drug addict who manages every week after Shabbat family visits to service his dependency. We bond. He's been in and out of reform schools since the age of fifteen. Horsing around on a Shabbat afternoon, I approach him from behind and with my index finger poke his side. The last thing I expect is a punch full force in the ribs. The family didn't show up, and little did I realize he was going through withdrawal. Seeing who he hit, a frustrated face contorts in reaction. With each breath, the pain stabs. Turning to the infirmary for relief will result in officials knowing I'm an assault victim. Choosing to suck it up and remain silent is the way to go. The worst moments are lying down and not finding a relieving position. Each breath, each movement, a dagger jabs from within. I'm miserable. This lasts the better part of a month.

Sitting on the non-padded metal high stool at the jigsaw is

affecting my lower back and legs. Shooting pain emanates from the hip and runs down the leg, causing weakness. As the months pass, the condition becomes chronic. The effects are obvious when standing. My gait is bent when walking. The infirmary physician has me taken to a health facility for a bone mapping procedure. I'm not told the result. There is no relief. Back home, I needed grass to cope. Here, I don't turn to hash for pain relief or mental distraction. Survival, not relief, is my priority. A chronic pot smoker, cigarettes are the replacement. Illicit drugs flow here.

Knowing that users have a debt to clear when returning from weekend furlough, "Don't return empty-handed if you want to remain alive."

Survival instincts keep me disciplined. No debt for me. Cough medicine dispensed by the infirmary is a knockout. I often fake symptoms.

The Assistant Warden has brought me to her office. I've been begging for permission to place a collect telephone call to my family, with whom there's been minimal contact, and inform them of the seven-year sentence. Connecting with Leon, I want to assure them that I'm okay. The familiar sound instantly triggers tears. It's difficult to speak while sobbing.

"Leon, what happened to my artwork, electronics, and other stuff?"

"Danny, we gave everything to Stuie for safekeeping. He's training away from home." It does not enter my scrambled thoughts to ask for an explanation. That it would not be secure isn't a consideration. How could it be otherwise given all the support previously received. The outcome: I no longer cherish material possessions.

"You're to let Mom know that I'm okay. I'll be in touch."

I never reunite with my artwork. When my nephew was tired of paying for storage, the facility auctioned the contents. I'm unable to forgive the slight after all the help he received from me. I question if losing one's children is this painful. I mourn the loss to this day.

The warden, before returning me to the cell, asks, "Why do you have two healing fractured ribs? How do you know?"

She replies, "Bone mapping."

Concerned that I might be in danger, she insists I reveal the perpetrator. Detailing the event without providing a name, she says, "You'll be immediately moved to the Hilton. This is a privilege."

The authorities are protecting the American to avoid embassy accountability in the event I'm harmed.

The Hilton houses two prisoners, bunk bed style, per cell. There are one hundred bodies in the unit. Occupancy is always at capacity. All are serving long sentences.

The majority are lifers convicted of murder. They serve thirty-three-year sentences, the maximum unless they're granted a President's pardon or time-off for good behavior.

Amongst the Arab prisoners, honor killings of wives and sisters are common.

The unit captain places me with Moinya, believing that since we're both American, it's a good match. He's a Russian gangster sentenced to twelve years for smuggling a large quantity of heroin into Haifa. Tattoos are on each of his fingers on both hands, symbolizing membership in the Russian criminal underworld. He's from Brighton Beach, Brooklyn, referred to by the locals as "Little Odessa." So, he says. His burly figure is menacing. He and Motie, the armed bank robber, are workout partners. Absent is exercise equipment, so they make two concrete-filled ten-gallon cans with a pole attached in between serve as weights. Moties' build resembles Tarzan and Moinya's, a professional wrestler.

Prisoners serve food in a mess hall. Showers are a shared space, and the latrine remains a hole in the floor of the cell. Moinya works in the infirmary as an orderly. The supervising doctor is also of Russian origin. The daily benefit is that we secretly eat caviar, sturgeon, smoked salmon, and similar delicacies in our cell. Moinya provides alcohol. Although he hasn't revealed the source of the treasure, I presume it's in the infirmary.

Feeling lucky, but not for long, Friday arrives. It's the day we scrub down our living space in honor of Shabbat. This is customary. Moinya orders me to scrub the floor while he supervises. Objecting, "I'm not your sanjer," he pushes me to the floor, punching and cursing in Russian. Like a good orderly, on my knees, I scrub away. Pride signals me to get out of there fast. Domination isn't acceptable. Turning to the Captain, without implicating Moinya, "We don't get along." Not surprised, familiar with his aggressiveness in response, I'm relocated to Rafi's cell.

The new cellmate is a lifer who killed his spouse with a nail gun. Mild-mannered, but having resided in these quarters for years, it's made clear that I accept his rules and idiosyncrasies. Never mentioning the crime that placed him here, the correction officer makes sure I know. Envisioning the act, playing back imaginary scenes repeatedly of killing one's wife in such a cruel fashion, is inconceivable. Violence is so foreign to me. Prisoners in the unit shun this guy. There are crimes considered worse than others, which is why a bed is available. Minimizing interaction with this monster while sharing a cell adds to solitude and loneliness. To whom do I talk?

Prisoners at the Hilton have privately owned televisions, and this is his to control. Not into local programming, books brought to me on Shabbat, and the Sony Walkman serve me well. Time stands still. On the days that I don't report to the factory, I sleep even though I'm not tired. Cough syrup helps. After twelve hours of slumber, I never wake up feeling refreshed. Inspired by Motie and Moinya, bench pressing the concrete cans in the mess hall is me trying to feel positive. Flat on my back, arms extended, a muscular, head-shaven Arab who's been eyeing me for weeks approaches. Alarmed, I place the weights on the floor, ready to protect myself. Instead of harm, he places a kiss on my cheek. "Get the fuck away," I head straight to Motie's cell. The body language of prisoners who behave like couples is, for the most part, ignored if their inclinations remain private. Concerned that this fellow would continue his advances, Motie had pledged to protect me after learning of my relationship back in Brooklyn with Shimon. He served time with Shimon's brother. Imploring Motie not to engage in violence, scared of repercussions, hushing me up, he charges out of the cell, ordering me to stay put. Animated, he returns, "This animal will never again even look at you."

I answer, "That was quick."

Often asked, "Wouldn't you be better off transferring to a prison near your family, in your country? I answer, it's safer here in Israel. No rape, AIDS or HIV to threaten me."

Considering the alternative, I'm lucky to be here.

Twenty-one months into the sentence, I earn my first weekend furlough. Completing one-fourth of the punishment and following all the rules, I'm rewarded with a Friday afternoon to Sunday morning home visit. A respite for Shabbat helps diffuse violent energy and foster assimilation back into society. After home visits, drug testing doesn't occur. We complete the last phase of incarceration in the fenced open-air camp. Orly, with only ninety days remaining until freedom visits family every weekend.

We, on the other hand, haven't touched each other since judgment day. What a time we have in her father's apartment during daylight and Tel Aviv at night. We're consumed with and can't get enough of one another. Torn away I return on Sunday morning.

Obtaining a dated Time magazine, I learn that the previous season, the New York Mets won the baseball World Series. A fan since their inception, the news brings tears instead of joy. Knowing what I've missed, it's difficult to be happy for others when feeling sorry for yourself.

There's a whisper in the air that the government is considering deportation upon completion of the sentence. Israeli law, the "Right of Return," gives every Jew in the world the opportunity to immigrate. Historically, the only Jew denied was Meyer Lansky.

"Am I categorized like him, a danger to society? Will the government forcefully separate a married Jewish couple?"

These questions linger over our heads. Logic should dissipate worry, but everything has gone wrong till now!

Incentivizing Jewish population growth is a priority. The national health care system provides IVF treatment to its citizens at no cost.

The authorities are aware of Orly's medical history. She's completed her sentence. Long-term prisoners demonstrating good behavior, but not eligible for Shabbat furlough, can request conjugal visits within the confines of the facility. The authorities deem this unnecessary since I reached the threshold to qualify for a weekend pass.

Orly resumes IVF treatments under the auspices of Dr. Atlas, a specialist affiliated with Assuta Hospital in Tel Aviv. This requires my presence. The quality of the sperm needs to be evaluated. This can only occur on weekdays. The Rabbinical council doesn't allow any work-related activities on Shabbat, the national day of rest. Confirmation that I'm required opens the way for a four-hour release without supervision.

At Assuta, a nurse provides a plastic vial, porno magazine, and directions to a closet-sized enclosure housing a toilet bowl. The tiny window above is open, the heat and sunshine streaming in, no air conditioning or fan functioning, and I sweat profusely. Hands and private parts turn clammy, not conducive to success.

"Do the IVF personnel at this hospital assume that under these conditions, a button pushed guarantees results?"

Embarrassed by failing, I worry that the authorities won't grant me another opportunity. Resigned to the absurdity of this attempt, I give up and return to the Assistant Warden's office. Elation defused, humbly sharing the experience, her reaction is gracious and comforting. I don't expect this, given the cold, stark, and violent reality I reside in.

Months later, I'm permitted another opportunity. The physician wants to assess and enhance the motility of the sperm after undergoing washing, and during ovulation, insert the liquid through a tube. To increase ovulation, hormones are administered. Knowing that with Orly in my arms, I won't fail again, I head straight to her father's apartment, where she's waiting. Once again, I've four hours to complete the mission. Coordination at this time is daunting. Tasting freedom should be exhilarating, but the pressure to return within the brief time allotted, traveling from Ramle to Ramat Gan to Tel Aviv and back to Ramle, doesn't leave time for fun. During these sparse minutes, I have to quickly perform. Joy in being together is fleeting. We flop on the bedroom carpet, the plastic vial within arm's reach.

Catching the first drops is critical, as these are the most potent.

Craving Orly's touch, stimulation comes easily, but a good time is missing.

We will pick up where we left off during a more intimate opportunity. Our interaction is clinical, and the obvious disappointment is worn on both faces. The specimen eases our shared frustration over unmet needs. It takes a month to know the outcome. We don't attain fertilization. Orly wants to give up, resigned to a childless marriage. With the passing of time, I believe she'll try again. The bloating and depression the hormone treatments cause, and my absence, coupled with failure, make these attempts more daunting. The next time we undergo treatment, I'm no longer a high-security prisoner.

Completing half the sentence and demonstrating good behavior opens the opportunity to leave the punishment phase of incarceration and start rehabilitation in Masiyahu, the adjoining open-air camp. Prisoner participation is limited to eighteen months. Noting our attempts at IVF, which in the USA are prohibitively expensive, and our insistence to remain in the country, the authorities rule I won't be deported when the sentence is complete. This allows my participation. Forty-two months behind me, I'm transferred to the camp.

For this life change to occur, there are criteria to meet and maintain. Employment outside the facility in the private sector will integrate me back into society. For the first time, random drug testing is mandatory. Orly and I have to jointly attend weekly counseling sessions with an assigned social worker who's a criminologist. The daily work schedule has to be adhered to, Sundays through Thursdays, between 7 a.m. and 7 p.m.. Fridays are early dismissal. This isn't house arrest. GPS technology has not been invented, so there's no ankle bracelet.

It's Friday, and the weekend newspaper edition has posted a front-page headline that Spiderman, when climbing up to burglarize a fifth-floor apartment, fell, breaking his back. The perpetrator was Detective Shavit. What a coincidence!

Meeting the criminologist, I challenge our mandatory presence.

"When I was younger, I attended therapy for several years and find all this unnecessary."

In response, the word recidivism previously unknown to me, is explained. Ducky, the therapist, states that three out of every four convicted ex-offenders return to prison. Intervention should alleviate this. The sessions focus on recognizing behavior that leads to detrimental outcomes.

She stresses,

"Denying need, placing yourself in harm's way by casting yourself as a 'White Knight, ' regardless of consequences, is your problem. You are always seeking recognition and acceptance."

Emotional attachment to Ducky comes naturally, admiring her charisma and intellect, we don't want to disappoint her. The sessions continue. Ducky asks if I'd be willing to attend a conference and address a large group of social workers. The topic focuses on daily life and the coping mechanisms needed to survive in the prison environment. Associating the request with past professional days, speaking before large groups, I eagerly accept. Their questions direct the meeting, which is interactive. Receiving a standing ovation when done brings me to tears.

Turning to my cousins seeking an employment lead, Avraham's next-door neighbor is a solar heating manufacturer. The factory is family-owned, employing the father and four sons. The labor force is composed of over a dozen Arabs who commute from the territories on a daily basis. Not required to provide social benefits and accepting a lower wage scale than a citizen's pay, makes this a prime resource for day labor. Other than family members, I'm the only non-Arab employee. Not choosy, I eagerly accept the opportunity. Having never seen this technology in the States, in Israel, it's found on every residential rooftop. It sounds like a good opportunity. The concept is innovative, but the technology behind it, I discover, is very basic.

Standing before a huge industrial press, I insert a heavy metal sheet one at a time and then pound it to form a large bowl. The work is manual, and no automation is available. Precise placement of the metal sheet is critical to achieving a balanced shape. The hydraulics and squeaking metal under pressure emanate a din that requires shouting when communicating with others. The bowl serves as the bottom of the boiler. Upon removal, stacking the bowls reaching chest high, I roll the stack vertically to the welder. Large metal sheets shaped into cylinders with ends welded form a container. The bowl attaches to the bottom, and a cap with piping connects to the top, resulting in a boiler. Solar panel construction consists of metal tubing partially insulated with asbestos set in a rectangular box covered in glass. This enables the sun's rays to heat the circulating water stored in the boiler. The work requires physical exertion that gradually reshapes my body.

The workday ends at 3:00 p.m.. Required to return to the camp, without the prison authority's knowledge, I spend the remaining hours at our kiosk in Ramat Gan. It's located on Bialik Street alongside a busy bus stop. Foot traffic is continuous. Open frontage enables a large heated display of nut selection to partially jut out over the sidewalk. The store offers ice cream, beverages, chocolates, liquors, and gift baskets. Bentzi, Orly, and his two young daughters staff the store from the early morning hours until 10:00 p.m.

Causing the family to suffer and wanting to again be the hero; damned the rules! Rationalizing that if caught, I'll talk my way out of repercussions, pleading mea culpa, "They need my help." Climbing a ladder, I store the excess beverage cases in the loft above the dropped ceiling. The kiosk is small, and every available inch is essential to increase the number of displayed treats. I restock the bins as needed. Never confronted by prison authorities, the detour continues until the day of my release.

Earning one-third of the time off for good behavior and released after completing fifty-six months of the seven-year sentence, I'm now able to return to the USA without restrictions. I choose to remain. No choice, Orly needs to continue IVF treatments. I don't associate Israel in any way with the consequences of my poor decisions. Taking ownership of these egregious acts, there's no desire to leave. I feel guilty for having the chutzpah to smuggle cocaine and think only of myself, everyone else be damned. Prior to imprisonment, I naively thought that Israelis lived in a civil utopia governed by religious tenets. Jews committing crimes? Impossible!

Living amongst the consequences of hard drug abuse, I now know, "I've contributed to the drug problem here. It's not any different than what's happening in America."

While incarcerated, "crack" became a scourge in the USA. Lives are destroyed everywhere, but specifically in low-income Black communities. I contributed to this by being part of the international cocaine drug trade. Back home, reputation precedes any chance of career resurrection. The crimes committed are well known in my circles. Known public servants requested pardon consideration from the President of Israel. They go unanswered. Ashamed to face everyone I know back home, I remain with accepting family and friends. At the scene of the crime, I'm not persona non grata. Israelis can be forgiving if you've paid for the crime.

Orly rents a one-bedroom apartment within walking distance of the kiosk. Her late shift coincides with the minutes stolen. I return each evening just before curfew. December 26, 1990, arrives.

Gabizon, the head of prison security, conducts an exit interview, warning me of the criminal dangers that could tempt mistakes and a return.

"Family and resuming IVF treatments stop me from doing any more illegal activities, and new adventures are behind me."

Wanting relief from the guilt of breaking the rules and now no longer in danger of exposure, I blurt out about the daily trips to the kiosk. His smiling response, "We often tailed you and looked away in compassion for your family."

The sentence is a memory as long as I don't commit a felony. Twenty-eight months hover above. Probation reporting doesn't exist. At the new home, I'm greeted with a wave of surging family and friends, surrounded with hugs and kisses. The surprise party continues throughout the night. It's difficult to handle the commotion. Solitude has been my companion. The cocktails and smoke go straight to my head. Needing quiet and rest, I persevere, not wanting to disappoint.

Opening and closing the kiosk daily is the new routine. After thirty days, changes in the product mix and displays occur. I introduce newspapers for the first time. Suppliers offer product bonuses for large orders that weren't pursued. Commencing at dusk on Friday evenings, religious law requires that all shops close on Shabbat. Violating the rules, remaining open until 10 p.m., we capture sales as the only available shop. Secular consumers thank me for flaunting the rules, and many become repeat customers. When in a jam, they count on our availability. We need the added income to support two households. Occasionally, we're warned by the municipality, but for unknown reasons, we are not issued fines. Bentzi never participates.

Within a month of my release, nationwide distribution of gas masks occurs. Iraq launches Scud missiles at Israel. Authorities instruct the public on how to secure windows to prevent gas from invading our homes. Defiant to not surrender to the fear Saddam Hussein intends to rain down on the Israeli population, I refuse to follow the dusk-to-dawn curfew imposed by the government. The only light emitted in the dark, the kiosk remains open.

Cockily, I think, "This pampered American has the balls to stand up when these Spartans are so cautious."

I refuse to believe that Saddam will inflict self-annihilation. The unconfirmed threat of chemical and biological warfare heightens the tension. A gas mask within reach, I'm the only one active on this ghost street.

Hearing air raid sirens for the first time, I hastily close the kiosk and rush home. Orly anxiously stares, frozen in the moment. I run to the bedroom window with a roll of tape in hand, a gas mask covering my face, and proceed to seal the frame and reinforce the glass. My hands shake so hard I need help.

Orly asks, "What's happening to you? Unlike Israelis, I never served in the army, and the sound of sirens is new. Just give me a minute to take this all in."

The warning is a false alarm. Open after curfew, my resolve hardens watching Bernard Shaw each night on Headline News. To minimize safety concerns, resistance is a solo act. No family allowed.

One evening, around 8 p.m., the sirens blare. Within minutes, there's a boom that rocks the ground and shakes the loft above. The proximity has me scurrying to lock up and get home, fearful that Orly and others in the neighborhood are victims.

Thoughts race, "Did the explosion hit our apartment building? In what condition will I find my wife?"

Wearing the gas mask, running up the avenue's long, steep incline to reach the building's front door, the ground floor windows of the shops are all blown out, covering the sidewalk in shattered glass.

Struggling with the gas mask on, I'm rushing up the staircase, hyperventilating. Orly is safe but scared. The missiles destroyed a row of four-story residential buildings five hundred meters from our residence.

No chemicals. No biological weapons. The threat ends within weeks after it began. Coalition forces led by the USA decimate Hussein's conquest of Kuwait. Life returns to normal.

We resume (IUI) intrauterine insemination treatments at Sheba Hospital, renowned for leadership in addressing infertility. Artificial insemination failing, we escalate to IVF, in vitro fertilization.

Undergoing this procedure five times over the next eighteen months, with each unsuccessful attempt, Orly's despair intensifies. Swinging between anger and depression, the only consolation I can offer her is that she'll definitely raise children.

"Romanian international adoptions are available if applicants come up with nineteen thousand dollars."

Time and again, this is a fallback solution I remind her of. The suggestion is meant to comfort. No physical problems are found to prevent pregnancy; stress could be the underlying cause.

"Often, soon after adoption, women become pregnant

without medical intervention. Why not us? One way or another, you'll have children," I drum in her ears.

She continuously prays to God, pleading for biological children, but isn't hopeful. She believes her fate is to be a barren woman. Bitterness masks her happy personality. Her temperament is mercurial. Outbursts of rage are frequent. Cracking a brow open with a flying plate back in Brooklyn is a reminder I wear.

There's disharmony between her and her father. In our absence, he entered a relationship with a woman who functioned as both wife and caretaker. When his wife abandoned the family for a wealthy, healthy married suitor Bentzi's physical deterioration accelerated.

A descendant of Aaron the high priest, who in the bible was Moses' elder brother, forbids Bentzi from remarrying under religious law. The newly found savior entered the home, working to break the father-daughter bond; the girls suffer from constant, unjustified accusations. Orly enters the fray, protecting her sisters, her rage a sight to avoid.

Dependent on this woman, Bentzi rationalizes explanations to mediate the confrontational dynamics. At wit's end, Orly's fury dominates her well-being. Stress, the worst enemy, guarantees failure with each IVF implant. Orly and her father are furious with one another. They aren't on speaking terms. They've always been best friends.

Bentzi, who I call Abba, and I discuss the circumstances that brought us to this state of affairs. Explaining the dynamics behind the crime, Bentzi's response holds Orly responsible: "A good wife would have stopped you."

Yomi, our closest friend, married and immigrated to Key West. Learning about the successful doubling of revenues at the kiosk, he tirelessly recruits me to return to the USA. He purchased a children's clothing store on Duval Street.

Israelis dominate tourist clothing shop ownership on this strip. Promised employment awaits. Mulling the offer over with Orly, we hesitate to accept. We love living in Israel. Orly doesn't want to distance herself from the fertility doctors. If Orly conceives, we'll remain. The family turmoil continues unabated.

CHAPTER 18.
KEY WEST

Hurricane Andrew hits South Florida. Outreach to Yomi over the months fails as telecommunication to the Keys is down. I declare that if, after twelve months, Orly doesn't conceive, we'll adopt a Romanian baby. If there's a chance of success, we must have a stress-free environment. The choice is clear. We're on our way. Ready to reach Key West, we're exuberantly insisting on joining up. Yomi tells us to delay until South Florida recovers from the devastation. We emigrate from Israel nine months later, arriving at JFK during the Spring of 1993.

I haven't seen Mom for seven years. Aging has not been kind to her. She's physically fragile and has a visiting nurse to assist with her daily needs. Lodging at the apartment where I'd spent most of my teenage years, the memories return. Associations lurk in every corner. I feel Pop's presence, but he's not here. The aged furnishings are a poignant reminder of his absence. Marrying Orly, the chronic loneliness dissipated. Chest pressure gone even while incarcerated, we're linked survivors who overcome ordeals that are self-induced. We have one another. Certainty carries us. Even when separated, thoughts constantly focus on one another. Preoccupied with her, the void is only a memory.

Mom is more than gracious in giving up her bed for my room. Favorite meals are prepared. She goes all out to be loving and accepting, even after all the grief I've caused. She's not judgmental toward us; in fact, she loves Orly. Receptive and appreciative of her efforts doesn't alleviate the flight response that wells up. Memories gnawing at me limit the visit to a ten-day stay during which we tour and dine at our favorite places.

We call on Pearl, Sharon's mom, to reacquaint ourselves and score pot. We're directed to a location opposite Sheepshead Bay. The small basement apartment is dismal, dark, and dingy. Ralph not being present, Sharon's response to questioning his absence sends shivers up my spine. Orly starts to cry. Ralph, during the stupor of a cocaine- heroin cocktail in Sharon's presence, pointed the barrel of a shotgun at his chest and blew out a hole, causing instant death. Sharon dazed describes the tragedy as if it happened yesterday. Two years have passed since that horrible day. The morbid news conflicts with Ralph's smile and cuddliness. In a state of shock, it's hard to react. After comforting her as best we could, taking our leave, Orly and I rehash fond memories of Ralph. The visit reinforces our rejection of hard substance abuse. Poor Sharon. It's all so sad, painful, and lonely.

Treating the trip as an excursion prior to settling in Key West, we fly to Los Angeles, stay at a four-star hotel, and rent a bright red Chrysler LeBaron convertible. With the roof down and the wind blowing in our faces, our spirit free of shackles, we endure a tingling sensation that runs throughout. The Passover holiday coincides with the trip. Not participating in a seder, we feel a disconnect.

Stoned, we drive with the roof down along Fairfax Avenue, a heavily populated Orthodox Jewish neighborhood. We blast a music cassette issued by the Chabad movement titled, "Moshiach Moshiach Moshiach." The sound emulates their chief rabbi as the coming of the messiah. This is our way of feeling connected. It's a holy day, and our actions are blasphemous. Cruising up and down the neighborhood, we're elated while stares of disdain eyeball our chutzpah. We compromise self-awareness. Impulsive flaunting is disrespectful and inappropriate. Its source is anger. The drug wears off. We call it a day. On the holy days that celebrate liberty, we're chained, isolated from the rituals we love. We long for Israel.

Changing venue, the trip's cut short. Arrival in Key West is uneventful. We reside at Yomi's place until we rent an apartment in the same complex. He introduces us to his inner circle of friends, all of whom own t-shirt and souvenir shops on Duval Street. New Israeli faces in this small community are enthusiastically welcome. This helps ease the uncertainty of our migration and unfamiliarity with the place.

Limited choices are available when purchasing furniture at Sears, and a new car at the Chevrolet dealership. This is our introduction to the isolated island lifestyle. The hustle and bustle of urban living is nonexistent. Serene ambiance slows us down, easing the hyperactive thought processes that rule our minds. It's the very adjustment Orly needs to address the stress that governs. We see why Ernest Hemingway considered this island to be his paradise.

Settled in, I begin employment. Adjacent to the Cuban museum on Duval Street, I'm now the manager at Spirit of Key West. Margaritaville is next door. Two sales personnel are on every shift. Store hours run from 9 a.m. to midnight, seven days a week. I average a seventy-hour shift. Placing speakers on the outer door frame, loud music blankets the immediate area. At the entrance, handing business cards to passersby stamped buy one get one free while churning to the music, similar shops line Duval Street but aren't as aggressive in capturing foot traffic.

A devious sales technique is taught, adopted, and exercised the moment I join the trade. Sales personnel strive to fatten their paychecks. Capturing tourists and foreigners, a salesperson accompanies the prospect to the t-shirt displays, where they are listed at $12.99, buy one get one free. Blank shells are stacked by size and color. Coded language informs the cashier that a SOF is in play; the customer didn't ask about pricing. Numbered decals cover the wall behind the counter. The tiny dollar sign accompanying the number is barely discernible. The consumer selects #24 for both shirts. After discerning the selection, they're asked if they want Key West added to the item. Everyone responds, of course, since this memento is a treasured token of the visit. A small sign indicating a pressing charge is set inconspicuously on the side of the heated press. Only the blank tee that costs the store owner $2.50 each is buy one, get one. #24 is actually the dollar charge for a 75-cent decal. The word Key West adds $4.99 to each one, and the pressing charge varies but could be as high as $9.99 per item, depending on the salesperson's whim and the gullibility of the buyer. The SOF pays around $45 per shirt if lucky. The cost to the store minus labor is under $4.00. Many decals are amenable to gold or silver foil coating, being heat pressed on, in which case $18 or more is added. A transaction totaling over $100 earns a 10% commission.

The commission structure incentivizes the staff to be ruthless. We see sales that surpass a thousand dollars. Foreign tourists are most vulnerable. Retail tourist vacation shops up and down the East Coast are enriching owners. Rejecting price gauging on my shift staff focus on volume. The second shirt is free, and no hidden fees are applied. The average cost of a shirt is twenty dollars. Shoppers with our business cards in hand after price shopping on Duval often return. Traffic generated by music, gyrations, and fairness makes our weekly receipts the highest of Benny's stores.

Within the Israeli community, Yomi and his circle become our extended family. Friday evenings, to celebrate Shabbat, we party until the early morning hours. Weeks after settling in, Orly receives news that Bentzi, her father, has passed away. His body and spirit gave out after all the heartache he had endured. In bereavement, booking the first available flight to Miami and then with El Al airlines to Tel Aviv goes expeditiously. Jewish custom requires burying the deceased within twenty-four hours of death. The airline is accommodating. The funeral is missed, but she manages to sit Shiva for the remaining six of the seven day mourning period.

In Orly's absence, I'm lonely. Working a one-hundred-hour per week shift, when returning home, I turn to hard liquor. Manhattan cocktails were previously introduced by Bernard. The morning hangovers are notoriously devastating. I open the shop at eight a.m. on cruise ship mornings. Reverting to old familiar social withdrawal, alcohol is my company; tequila with friends, Manhattans when alone.

The required thirty day mourning period is over. Orly returns. She commences employment at the sister store directly across the street. The shark-like Irish sales wafes stationed there squeeze tourists until they turn to city authorities, who register incidents of price gouging.

Thick, unadorned Irish accents serve them well, intimidating the objecting customers. Business is thriving at the store I manage.

Upon Orly's return, I reduce the hours. We face one another when at our respective entranceways, hustling for tourists to enter the shops. The smiles crisscrossing the thoroughfare never waver. We visit the only obstetrician-gynecologist on the island, Dr. Walker. He's a naturalist who substitutes epidurals with breathing exercises. He doesn't provide infertility treatment, but coaches couples on how to monitor and track ovulation to maximize success.

He emphasizes, "The time of day is as important as the day selected when best to copulate and accomplish gestation. Body temperature has to be just right. Make sure you have a thermometer."

After the shop's midnight closing, we ritually spend time together at the Duval Street bars. The partners and staff all gravitate to a night of drinking and laughter. Orly and I, hours later, end up in bed enjoying a tryst. This schedule is not doing the trick. An off-schedule opportunity arrives. Rosh Hashanah, the Jewish New Year, is just around the corner, and our business is closed in observance. We awake, enjoying the rays of the sun gleaming on the covers and making love. It's early afternoon. In bliss, we don't utter a word.

Weeks later, upon awakening, Orly says, "My period is due and not happening."

Pessimistic, given all the disappointments before, I instruct her to remember the dates of the last cycle. Uncertain but elated, we hastily dress and head to Walgreens on Roosevelt Avenue.

Purchasing a pregnancy kit, I discreetly follow right behind Orly into the ladies' restroom. Slipping down her garments, I hold the uncapped indicator under the yellow stream, anticipating the outcome with trepidation and excitement. Orly dresses and glancing for the answer, I see the pink lines and start shaking. I'm screaming. Orly is confused and urges me out of the store. Sitting on the bench alongside the entrance, we hug and fidget, looking at the indicator again and again. Faces over one another's shoulders staring in the distance, not a word said, we start to cry. Catching ourselves, we look at the indicator to make certain of our good fortune.

We keep saying, "I can't believe it!"

We rush to Dr. Walker seeking confirmation. He conducts a physical exam, takes a blood sample, and a urine sample, saying, "It's way too soon to see any results. If she's still late after a week passes, we'll retest, but that'll be an indicator she's pregnant."

Orly is never late. Waiting for the week to end, we oscillate between joy and despair. The next test confirms pregnancy. Announcing with wishful certainty that it'll be a boy, "God bless Key West and tequila" is my joyful mantra. Belief, tranquility, and perseverance made all the difference in achieving this miracle. With Hashem's help, we created life!

Orly conceives on the holy day of Rosh Hashanah. Just the attempt is a blessed deed in its own right. Jews call such action a mitzvah because it follows Hashem's edicts to be happy and closer to fulfillment. We are starting a family!

Over thirty-five years old, Orly has to undergo an amniocentesis. This is when aged women statistically experience an increase in the likelihood that their newborn will have congenital defects. The amniotic fluid reveals all. Down syndrome is most prevalent. Dr. Walker doesn't have the capacity to test. The solutions available are a Dade-County situated facility or the physicians we know back in Israel. Not giving it a second thought, I book a round-trip ticket to Israel, and a six-week stay is planned. The procedure target date is at sixteen weeks of pregnancy. Any delay opens the possibility of difficult choices in the event the fetus has a severe deformity. We schedule the procedure at Hasharon Hospital.

Resuming the one-hundred-hour work schedule for want of something better to do, the compensation outweighs any burden. Manhattans in solitude after midnight, lonely, I miss Orly. Three weeks following the withdrawal of fluid from her pierced belly, Orly asks about sex. We're having a healthy boy! Telephoning to inform me, I'm a proud wise ass for calling the gender.

She announces, "He'll, Hashem willing, be named Ben Tzion, my dad's name."

Bouquet of flowers in hand, the proximity of the terminal to the commuter flight enables a ground-level view of each passenger as they step onto the airfield. I stare at each face, troubled that Orly hasn't disembarked. I'm disheartened. A large black-haired woman sporting a long, flowing black cotton dress and a large medallion hanging upon her chest approaches. The bangs reaching her brow and bright red lipstick throw me off.

Startled, I shout, "Oh shit, Orly. I can't believe it. Look at you! You've tricked me."

I hug her big, round belly. She's huge, and without blonde hair, it's an unrecognizable transformation. I'm so embarrassed.

We move into a larger apartment, decorating and furnishing our soon-to-be newborn's room. Orly insists we purchase the crib, dresser, changing table, stand-up wash basin on wheels, stroller, Bjorg snuggle, bouncer, and wall and blanket decorations of stuffed harlequins at Bellini in Aventura. This is where the stars shop. Nothing is too good for our miracle baby. Bellini will deliver it all down to Key West and set it up. Family gifts defray the cost.

We locate a Chabad Moyle who is qualified to conduct the circumcision and willing to fly down from Miami to Key West. He offers to bring the pre-ordered catered kosher food on the plane after I warn him that the quantity needs to feed fifty people.

Working at the store, Orly appears comical, standing in the

entranceway, her large belly protruding like a sack of potatoes, her stamina limited by swollen feet. Her due date is approaching. We drive to Miami and order customized invitations for the Brit Milah, arrange catering, and finalize the procurement of Ben's bedroom furnishings.

I'm at the shop attending to customers. Orly telephones, confused and frantic, "Danny, I've just leaked water through my panties onto the floor. What should I do?" "I'm on my way!"

I run.

Admitted to the hospital on adjacent Stock Island, the contractions come as expected. There'll be no epidural. We rely on the breathing techniques learned at the prenatal prep course conducted by Dr. Walker. Hours drone on. The contractions intensify and occur more frequently. Moans and groans are intermittent but steady. Dilation reaches five centimeters, then refuses to budge. We're approaching twenty-three hours of labor. Urging Orly to hit me during contractions doesn't help. The baby hasn't been stressed till now, but vitals are beginning to send up a red flag. What to do? The nurses watch them both, quick to react if a beep emanates from the monitor. Approaching the twenty-fifth hour, we surrender.

Dressed in a hospital gown, shoes covered, a mask muffling speech as well, I'm directed to sit to the right at a near distance from the operating table. The staff hovers around Orly, allowing an unimpeded view of her side in a prone position. The slashed torso has a charcoal gray newborn protruding its tiny body, the umbilical cord wrapped around the neck. Nurses quickly administer to and pat the baby, and he starts to cry.

Seeing him, I blurt out, "That's not mine. Look at the color."

A pinkish flesh tone appears, and I chuckle over how stupid I can be.

Orly is in recovery. I'm permitted to accompany the baby and nurse on the elevator as he's taken to the newborn nursery. Wearing the mask, I hold him as the elevator doors open. It's early dawn. Surprise! Yomie and at least half a dozen of our friends swarm around sharing the miracle. Baby secure, seeing a crowd, the nurse asks that I hand over the neonate.

Orly, reunited with Ben, begins breastfeeding. She commits to continuing for twelve months. All that we've read states that breastfeeding provides immunity. I'm lucky to have her and satisfied with the love and intimacy I'm certain she'll share with the baby. Her mother and sisters fly in from Israel to be present at the circumcision ceremony. We don't just view this as the birth of a child, but rather a gift from Hashem. Ten years of struggle and failure to conceive behind us, a very different reality awaits.

Chabad Rabbi Schneerson, who many refer to as the messiah, passed away on June 12, the baby's Gregorian calendar birthday. Circumstance adds to our belief that Ben is earmarked for special accomplishments. Isn't this every parent's wishful fantasy? Discomfort from the Cesarean doesn't detract from efforts to organize the ceremony held on the eighth day after the male's birth. At this stage, it's believed the baby is strong enough to overcome the trauma.

We have the ceremony and party at the Holiday Inn on Roosevelt Avenue. I low-key the event and rent a party room for a nominal fee. Agreeing to clean up and vacate by midnight, of course, it doesn't happen. My elderly first cousins, Guta and Abe, drive down from Miami. Finding them very sweet and kind, I grant Abe the honor of being Ben's godfather. He'll hold the infant on a pillow placed on his lap as the Moyle performs the procedure. The droplet of soothing, sweet wine on the baby's lips doesn't prevent a loud cry. Hashem blesses the godfather for his part in performing this mitzvah. We party until 2 a.m.. The loud Israeli Middle Eastern music is foreign to the American ear, irritating the hotel staff who attempt to get us to vacate. Taking no heed, we blast the cacophony for a couple of extra hours.

Exiting, passing the entranceway, the night manager swears, "Holiday Inn Key West will never again allow Israelis to rent space here!"

We're banned! This was our signature performance. We laugh when rehashing the events of that evening over tequila shots. Orly abstains and thanks Hashem for granting her wish. Life now centers around raising our son. I also set booze aside, preventing stupor from blocking out transmitted baby monitor sounds.

Financial conflict with Benny when reassigned to Sean's Corner, absent the wafes, leads to my quitting. His good friend relocated from Branson and to fit the mix she's given the Spirit manager position. She's presentable, talented, and made welcome. I take employment with a competitor whose location is near the cruise ship dock, a prime spot. It doesn't last very long before I'm fired. The killer instinct to SOF tourists is missing.

Our marital problems escalate beyond control. Managing a budget, we don't see eye to eye. Friction increases; Benny is the target. At home, disagreements explode into hysteria. There seems to be no logical line of reasoning fueling the rage that ensues between us. It's Sunday evening, and Orly has filled a dozen baby bottles for Ben with homemade ground meals to freeze. The kitchen is in total disarray. As accustomed, I attack the mess. When complete, I allow the loaded sink strainer to drain out, resting alongside the soap bottle, and step away.

Rage emanates from the kitchen.

"How many times have I told you that leaving a mess when you're done is disgusting. Time and time again, you do what you want with no regard for me. You don't respect me, which is why you treat me this way. No matter what I ask, you choose to do the opposite. You never listen, and this is how you've destroyed my life."

Anger wells up. Loud words evolve into shoving. I threaten to rip the telephone out of the wall when Orly calls 911, declaring domestic violence and the need for immediate help. Trying to restrain her uncontrollable screaming fails. I call her a rat for turning to the police.

The uniformed officers arrive and start to interview us. Heated behavior, raised voices, and Orly hitting me over the head with the plastic dish soap bottle have us arrested for domestic violence. Handcuffed and taken away, Orly remains behind with no minutes to spare, arranging for Ben's placement with friends or family. He'll be placed with the authorities if it's not doable. Benny and Debra volunteer. It's Sunday after midnight. We're detained at the Stock Island detention center until a video conference bond hearing the next morning. We're placed on probation and sentenced to court-ordered domestic violence counseling. There is no record of foreign incarceration. Personal history doesn't surface.

I begin to realize that I don't know Orly that well. Our marriage, disrupted by incarceration, hasn't allowed enough time to realize who I'm with. Our love and anger reach extremes. The mental dynamics causing this are beyond my understanding. Focusing on conception is all-consuming, leaving no room for other thoughts. Doubts are there but readily shoved aside. Starting a family is all that I see.

There's discord between Debra, Benny's spouse, and Orly. Orly's dislike of Benny doesn't help. Sivan, her baby daughter, and Ben are classmates. An influential Key West entrepreneur, Debra's intervention with the Montessori director ends Ben's attendance. The director declares Ben a slow learner who doesn't meet the standards of the local Montessori nursery school. Debra's intent is to hurt Orly. Once friends, the chemistry between them is hostile.

At thirteen months, Ben doesn't utter a word. His alert eyes dart everywhere, absorbing everything his senses permit. A game we play when he bathes involves adhering wet vinyl alphabet letters to the tiled wall. We call for different ones out of sequence.

"Give me a P, give me a B" goes on and on. He doesn't miss a beat. He recognizes numerals one through ten. The alternate day care program available is poorly rated. Ben is a winner who doesn't belong here. We leave Key West behind. Limited choices make this the obvious decision.

CHAPTER 19.
EUTHANASIA

Professional employment, I believe, is unattainable. I'm convinced that history weighs me down. This eats away at me, killing any motivation. I'm consumed by shame. Who would touch me?

Promises are offered. An opportunity to wholesale high-end jewelry is waiting. At the behest of her cousin's brother-in-law, the new employer, we relocate. Yehudah reassures me that, in spite of my history, he has the authority to hire. I doubt if a supplier of fine diamond and gold jewelry will retain me, but Orly's aunt vouches for his word.

Awaiting additional inventory, he says, "We'll begin to show our wares at jewelry stores within weeks. Everything's good. Don't worry about a thing."

I'm worried. The delay has me frustrated and listless. Suspecting that I've been deceived by his unavailability only confirms this. Not able to ignore badgering any longer, Yehuda squeamishly reveals, "The supplier won't let you near the inventory. I'm sorry and helpless to alter the situation. It's out of my control."

I'm not surprised.

The offer never felt right, but I wanted to believe. Furious over his deception and incompetence, I blame myself. We wanted to leave Key West, but he's complicit in this ill-timed relocation. I'm lost with no direction. Bernard, feeling guilty for ignoring my existence during imprisonment, funded the move. He's not pleased.

The past follows me everywhere. Freedom is elusive. Lingering effects of the fifty-six-month imprisonment left a mark. I'm uncertain and scared. The memories are undeniable. Intermittent flashbacks of prison life hammer at any self-confidence.

"I'm floundering. Where to begin?" Health care is an option if I can bridge the ten-year resume gap.

Thanks to the Bellini shopping adventures, we developed an affinity for the Aventura neighborhood. Village-like; it's cluttered, with low-rise condominiums that cater to the over-55 crowd. The Turnberry golf course, quacking ducks, geese, and herons along the jogging path make the place special. There's a mall with a movie complex within walking distance. The shoreline is less than half a mile away. Our condominium rental community board is not child-friendly, but it approves the application.

Visiting Aventura's HCA-managed hospital, resume in hand, I'm told, "Given the employment gap, you only qualify for an entry-level management position."

It's easier to accept victimhood than resume a health career at the starting gate. The income offered at this level will not meet Orly's expectations. Discouraged and despondent, I walk away.

Unpacking and settling into our new apartment, we break away, choosing to dine at the restaurant that catered the circumcision ceremony. Sitting in the adjacent booth is a young modern orthodox couple with a child of Ben's age. The children gravitate to one another, making for easy conversation. Trust comes easily through sharing a cultural and religious connection. Mentioning the desperate search for employment, I'm directed to call their contact, who might be hiring telemarketers selling vacation packages.

Orly's manicurist, Yvonne, who lives in Key West, is visiting a friend in a neighboring community. It's Friday evening, and I drive to the Sunrise area to pick her up. Near home, driving south on U.S. Highway 1, I'm hanging a sharp left turn when a car approaches in the north lane at excessive speed. Aggressively proceeding, just clearing the other vehicle, sighing in relief, looking over my shoulder, the other vehicle stops and continues in reverse. Pulling up alongside us, the driver's window is dark-tinted, and faces aren't discernible. A rolled-down window opposite Yvonne reveals an aimed short-barreled rifle pointing at us.

Hysterically begging for our lives, Yvonne screams, "We don't want problems; we don't want problems!"

I manage to hold my pee. Cursing in Spanish, threatening, and wielding the rifle, they drive off. Facing death for those twenty seconds, we were trembling and emotionally hysterical. Yvonne and I are clearly shaken up. We share the event with Orly. Booze and smoke calm us down. In bed with Orly, comforting me, I continue to relive that evening. Passion helps release the tension, and Jake is conceived. Yvonne and I awaited our imminent murder. Instead, on this night, Hashem gives me a son. We are blessed.

The maxim that comes to mind is "Once there is a child in the home, pregnancies are more frequent."

We're in heaven, and Jake's birth is uneventful if you consider jaundice routine. I name him after Pop, whose Yiddish name is Yankel, Jack in English. With Orly postpartum, Jake daily accompanies me to Doctor Marcus. The pediatrician recalls meeting with me in Guadalajara. We're concerned that Jake's condition will delay the circumcision ceremony. Daily exposure to sunlight enables proceeding on the customary eighth day. Moyle Werde will be in attendance. Maintaining contact with Sharon, whom we love, I ask her if she'd like to be Jake's godmother. It has no religious significance but will be announced at the ceremony. She books a flight. Tikva, Orly's mom, makes the six-thousand-mile trip once again.

With two infants fulfilling her dream, Orly is struggling with depression. Routine functioning is difficult when competing with a death wish. Overwhelmed with added responsibilities, in between sobs, she screams, "I can't do this without living in help." Ben was breastfed for twelve months. Now it's Jake's turn. I recall how, as a little boy awake at dawn on Shabbat mornings and all alone, I yearned to crawl under my parents' blanket, but instead had to settle for silent cartoons. Early morning breastfeeding evolves into 'huggies', becoming the family's mandatory start to the day. Orly is fastidious. Neither child ever eats processed baby food. She cooks meals, cools, grounds, freezes, and stores them in baby bottles. The boys never suffer from diaper rash. Daily excursions to a playground or mall are frequent. Orly smothers them with nurturance but does little else.

We quarrel. Affordability is the issue, and I capitulate. I don't feel good about this. Miriam is now part of our family. The woman nicknamed me "Salvador." I'm always there, anticipating a need or when asked to help.

Vacation sales job not available, I'm referred to Trainer Nick at Telecard, a large phone room, telemarketing prepaid telephone calling cards, and dispenser vending machines. Establishing a route includes location assistance. This is a business opportunity. A novice, I'm on the 5 p.m.-10 p.m. shift. Assigned phone and cubicle, we await the inbound response to the radio or television ad. The announcer pitches the chance to land a one-time available business promising high cash returns. Providing a toll-free 800 number, we await the ring scripts in hand.

Lifting the receiver headset in place, a wave of panic ensues. My hands trembling, voice stuttering, I clumsily read the pitch. Slamming the receiver down, my instinct is to run away. Years back, I confidently spoke with physicians on the phone. This time, I was actually scared! Repetition allays trepidation; I fight to conquer. Viewing the surroundings, I rationalize, "If they can do this, so can I." The Frontor title fits me like a snug hat. Adjusting the script to reflect my morals justifies involvement. Compliance not compromised; being personable, I want the prospect to like me. Identifying and engaging in comfortable dialogue is the key to opening the sale. Guaranteeing income is illegal. We dance around that by illustrating the mathematical return of various scenarios. To guide us through the federal guidelines, Telecard retains an attorney, and a round-robin session is held periodically. All telephone conversations are monitored.

Ears pick up the greed motivating the inquiry. This determines the timed words used to set urgency. We await the live Rush Limbaugh talk show. Afternoons, it generates a stampede of inquiries, his voice and legend lending credibility to the ad. Taught that the "take away" will move a buyer forward, limited availability is the key to concluding a sale. The closers want my paper. Receptive prospects attest to the quality of my work. Presentations are informative and set the table for the close.

After eleven months, I'm promoted. The company is a three-way partnership. Gregg is the brother-in-law of one of the owners and the leading monthly closer. Two hundred thousand dollars monthly in sales is the criterion for keeping the job. These limited positions are highly competitive. His monthly numbers average three hundred and fifty thousand dollars, nearly twice the qualifying amount. My front is a good part of this success. Fulfillment of the shipment is never an issue. Due to the volume ordered, there are delays. We present the return on investment generated from the purchase of vending machine-dispensed telephone calling cards as a "not to be missed opportunity. Pressured prospects believe the availability of prime locations is going fast. The formula for the allowable number of distributors and dispensers in a geographic area is based on population density. When a prospect procrastinates, they're passed on to a "Back From The Dead" closer. This is now me.

It's "let's make a deal."

The pitch: "There are undelivered machines sitting on a palette at freight awaiting a designated destination. A buyer could not complete the transaction. I'm willing to redirect the shipment to you and add value by throwing in free machines with the inventory. This will accelerate the rate of return, more locations, more revenue. Limiting locations based on population density protects you."

The loader uses a similar pitch on buyers who pay full price.

Other pursuits have preoccupied Gregg. He channels paper to me that is not back from the dead while secretly opening up a competitive company. He doesn't have time to manage the workload. After I set up the deal, he completes the paperwork and payment pickup. We split the commission paid on top of my "back from the dead" remuneration. Income explodes! On payday, an owner in the presence of over fifty agents announces for all to see a check with my name on it for over nine thousand dollars. The hype is meant to motivate the room. What a wonderful opportunity!

Gregg says, "If we continue to work the deal and you give me a kickback on select referrals when the new company starts, you'll be my partner."

During office time, he's secretly negotiating with telecom carriers searching for competitive rates to high-volume destinations. My office door is opposite his. The back and forth is constant. He's contacting card wholesalers, private labeling our own brand to target the Mexican and American markets. The American Flag design, labeled American Prepaid, and another card, La Raza, are in print. We've access to vending machine owners who service this demographic. Orly and I attend Gregg and Sheila's church wedding and banquet dinner. They invite us to accompany them on their Disney honeymoon. Both spouses are pregnant, showing off rounded bellies and swollen calves. Billy, another closer, who's been sidling up to Gregg, is present at the ceremony. He's encroaching on the turf.

Telecard introduces a lower entry fee to start a route. The draw is voice-chipped plastic cabinets announcing the availability of phone cards. Ten units with inventory included are priced at half the vending machine offer. This replaces the wheeling and dealing pursued with the machines. I'm uncomfortable with the value received for the cost while watching returns pile up along the elevators.

Raising concern, I'm told by management, "Your continued employment is predicated on selling the offer."

Gregg is waiting in the wings. I resign. No way I'm going to be responsible for marketing this.

Liberty, after two years of pounding the telephone, allows me an opportunity to visit Mom. Mom is going to meet her grandsons for the first time. Princess Diana is killed this weekend, and the news dampens our excitement over being in Manhattan. Miriam accompanies us, and we are housed at the Doubletree alongside Times Square. I'm obligated to make this visit happen. Grandma must see the boys. Another birth with no infertility treatment occurred. We have two brothers in our home. The miracle continues.

Returning home, I learn that Billy is Gregg's new partner. I'm replaced by a ten-thousand-dollar investment that I couldn't produce if asked. Money is never mentioned; it's assumed there isn't any to spare. Facing no partnership and no readily available job opportunities that don't seem like fraud, I agree to be employed by them. No significant duties offered; they're in control. Shipping inventory is my primary duty.

The relationship sours over time. Parting ways, we agree that I'll wholesale their cards at retail establishments, opening a Miami route. They front the product as if the perk is a consolation prize.

Revenue is insufficient to cover household expenses. I borrow cash against inventory to cover bills. The housekeeper receives pay on Saturdays. This occurs before I cover the monthly rent. Without Miriam's help, nurturing two children is impossible. I see no alternative. Orly's emotional state won't allow anything else. The shortfall in the product comes back to bite me. In debt, I'm forced to sell their newly designed copycat talking plastic display. I quit unannounced and start employment with a competitor who was a closer at Telecard.

The new job offers phone card vending machines. I'll be the "Back From the Dead "man once again. Two weeks after I began, heading to my car key in hand, I'm blindsided, pummeled by a fist to the side of the head. Body falling to the ground, glasses flying off in an unknown direction, I'm stunned.

"Why are you doing this?" I scream to no avail while my torso is kicked, and my backside is stomped.

I recognize the burly guy hitting me, but can't place him while under attack. Damage done. Message delivered; the perpetrators drive away in an easily identifiable car, its paint removed, and only the gray buff undercoat remaining. Stumbling along the way, barely managing to reach my desk at the office, I try to recover and assess the damage. Everyone present is mortified. Not doing well and in pain, I drive to the hospital. Triaged in the emergency room, purple bruising from the back right shoulder to below the buttocks is an ugly sight. The CT scan rules out a concussion. It hurts!

Defiant, I won't break. I report to work the next morning, convinced that Gregg and Billie ordered the hit in retaliation for leaving. Searching memory, the attacker was previously introduced at Gregg's office. He's the guy who fills his oxygen diving tanks.

Reporting the attack to the police, I'm informed, "A lineup of outdated driver's license DMV photos is the only chance of identification. Live lineups are too costly. The department no longer offers this. This is what we got."

Only luck will get it right. These old photos were taken back when the licenses were issued. Hairstyles and body weight were different then, and neither reflect the perpetrator's current appearance. The outcome is reasonable doubt. I narrow down the selection to two choices.

The detective informs me, "One of them owns the car you've described, but we can't proceed. You didn't definitively make the ID."

I'm on an uneven playing field with Jeff, the other Back From The Dead man. His office is adjacent to mine. I hear him through the sheetrock wall, deceiving prospects, guaranteeing high returns on investment. A fraction of the commission for this paper is paid to the referring closer, and Jeff's verbal guarantees result in a high percentage of closings. Everyone makes money, so he's the favored guy. No one demonstrates any morality. His spiel is more outrageous over time. I chose to leave. It's just a matter of time before the federal government catches on.

Orly completes twelve months of breastfeeding, although Jake didn't want to let go, and she is pregnant once again. She undergoes amniocentesis for a third time. Two big brothers and a little sister, what more could we ask for? Miriam moves on, and living in housekeeping is more important than ever.

Accepting our financial reality, I self-talk, "Instead of investing in a home, prioritizing the kids is more important."

Jake is chronically ill, having fevers that run 106 degrees Fahrenheit. Ice baths have become an emergency response. Orly attends to Arielle, breastfeeding the routine, and I'm attending to Jake, who has me busy.

Dr. Marcus says, "He needs tube implants in his ears. This will end his high fevers that are caused by an inner ear infection." It amazes me how effective they are.

My reward: preoccupied with their activities, I never feel lonely.

More than money can, they bring me certainty.

Mom's placed in a nursing home across the street opposite Bernard's work location. As a Columbia University affiliate, the care couldn't be better. Being affiliated staff makes this possible. It's time Mom meets Arielle, who's nine months old. Mom is institutionalized and unable to function without assistance. The boys are older, making the visit meaningful and memorable. I feel obligated to make this happen. Visiting her bedside, the heartwarming smile and sparkling eyes when looking at the kids make the visit worthwhile. It's all about family.

In Miami, a company friend refers me to Jody, a locater who has helped me and now manages sales at a gourmet espresso distribution company.

Wanting to close deals, I'm offered a Back From The Dead position as the gateway. A fly-buy makes this seem like an easy deal. Deducting travel expense from the purchaser's cost, procrastinators foot the bill.

Proprietary espresso machines manufactured in Italy, requiring specifically designed coffee capsules, were the forerunners of today's coffee solutions.

The units can be placed in restaurants and fast food/convenience stores. Advertised on the internet as a business opportunity, prospects tour the manufacturer's service center at the Comobar warehouse in Miami.

Machines are placed free of charge; the capsules supplied

cost seventy-five cents per serving. The distributor earns a fifty-cent profit per transaction. The proprietor charges whatever the market will bear for the finished product. The machine brews espresso and cappuccino using Arabica beans. The distributor is responsible for locating the machine. We're compliant with all equipment delivered on time. Cash on delivery is not acceptable. All purchases must be prepaid. Business opportunity companies typically have a five-year life span. Investor complaints accumulate. Unhappy buyers, no matter what the product, will blame the source for their displeasure rather than be introspective about the cause of failure. Oftentimes, it's just the wrong fit and not a fraudulent enticement. Over a two-year period, I annually average two and a half million dollars in sales. I have no reason not to feel moral working at this.

Bernard phones. I don't remember the last time we spoke.

"Mom is dead. The arthritic pain in her shoulder wasn't responding to the steroid injections, and she cried for relief. Danny, she'd call all hours of the workday driving me crazy, and I couldn't see any other way."

"Bernard, was her heart good?"

"She had no other health issues. As a professional courtesy, the attending physician gave Mom a heavy dose of morphine, putting her peacefully to sleep. Danny, I'm sorry."

"Why didn't you let me know beforehand so I could have seen Mom one last time?"

The tears don't stop. Bernard euthanized Mom. Didn't see that coming. No one would believe it if they knew! I don't say a word.

At the funeral, I'm identifying the body before it's buried alongside Pop. This is a private moment I have with Mom. Saying goodbye is unreal. The stiff and waxen face forces a quick glance, and I look away. I think about how Mom suffered physically to rationalize away my pain. I'm emotionally detached from the attendees. I miss you, Mom.

CHAPTER 20.
CHOICES AND CONSEQUENCES

Orly and I are financially sinking. The mortgage industry is robust, but we have no chance of obtaining a loan. Half a dozen rental properties since our return to America have evicted us. If we managed the household budget within realistic parameters, the income would prevent these mishaps. On Fridays, no matter what the earnings, while bill payments are juggled by the end of the weekend, no money remains.

Over the years, we have attended court-ordered weekly marriage counseling therapy at the Jewish Community Services. Bonding with the social worker comes easily. We are eager to attend. Believing that I have a handle on my behavior thanks to the knowledge gained when visiting Dr. Korn at Bellevue Hospital, I eventually decide to discontinue. The years spent there evolved into a sounding board of complaints orchestrated by both of us. Each of us blames the other for words spoken; a couple need not regret.

Confidently, I announce, "My presence is a distraction. It's deflecting attention away from Orly's problems. I'm not participating any longer."

At the five-year mark, hurricane season freezing sales, it's time to leave coffee and move on when hearing of Daniel Touizer. The name rings a bell when announced at the annual Chabad Aventura dinner. His cousin, it turns out, was the Abu Kabir warden. He pledges a charitable donation of one hundred thousand dollars. It'll assist in the construction of a new school. Daniel is not present. Paul, an acquaintance, tells me that they're friends, and

Daniel owns a telemarketing business opportunity offering revenue-generating internet terminals. The end-user pays a fee. I want to meet this guy who's connected to and a major contributor here. I might entice him to listen. Soliciting contact information, then calling the next day, excited, invited to his Aventura residence, a friendship begins, or so I surmise. My goal is to have Daniel fund Cafe Gourmet 2 Go, a spinoff of the now-defunct Espresso Italia. I gained thirty months of knowledge that's ready to be profitable.

He's launching his creation, Palm Health, a discount card health subscription. Its network is accepted and marketed directly to the public. The pitch describing coffee and its profitability as a business opportunity investment is hard to ignore. The markup for a machine is six hundred percent. We meet the manufacturer who maintains a warehouse and service center in Miami, happily cutting a deal as their new wholesalers. Daniel waffles between joining me in a second venture or devoting time to building Palm Health.

The marquee lettering above the entrance of the Aventura Chabad synagogue reads "In honor of Eliyahu Ezagui, the builder." We make acquaintances at the synagogue, and I accept an invitation to sit in his Sukkah, a holiday tradition. Presenting himself as a highly successful Brooklyn real estate developer and venture capitalist, he's animated, jolly, stout, and bearded. Quizzically, we sit together throughout the evening eating, drinking spirits, and laughing freely under the stars along an open buffet. We joyfully identify with the Yiddish word "bondeet," describing our characters. A friendship commences, and he steadily gains interest in the business plan. He envisions kosher gourmet coffee as an attractive investment possibility. Playing Eliyahu off against Daniel and vice versa, I'm certain one of them will fund the business. Eliyahu steps forward, and I launch Café Gourmet 2 Go. John, a former manager at the internet terminal deal, is my assistant. Without John and his graphic designer girlfriend, our brochures wouldn't be a first-class presentation. Office space build-out occurs rapidly, and I find a wholesale cookie and biscotti kosher baker who privately labels the treats with our logo.

The credit markets are in decline when we launch. A Google pay-per-lead campaign and promotional banners are on the internet search engines, keywords generating inquiries. Compared to the lead response generated over the previous ten years, the results are meek, lacking energy. The mortgage crisis is underway. Credit, which drives investors, has dried up. I couldn't foresee this before the launch. Frustrated over our performance, we're in the dark.

Pressure is mounting. With no background in marketing, Eliyahu takes control of all daily decisions. It's his money. We have buyers, but we don't cover expenses even with the huge profit. With each funding infusion he alludes to, "better unspoken problems" that weigh on him. Eliyahu's forte is to take a dilapidated building and convert it.

The renovated residential apartments were sold to Orthodox community members. Eliyahu and his family hold the titles. He takes out second mortgages, refinancing against the collateral without the dwelling owners' knowledge. The properties are in the Crown Heights neighborhood.

Wanting to expand his portfolio, Eliyahu asks if it's possible to leverage a raw residential zoned forty lot parcel he owns outright in the Catskills. I suggest the Costa Rica land deal model. It's a fly-by. The buyer who visits the location selects a parcel, and the deal concludes with a signed contract. Placing down a significant deposit in escrow secures the parcel. It's forfeited if, at a preset date, a call for additional payment is missed. Build as you pay doesn't sit well with me.

It's a cold winter. We head up to the site, walking the barren woods, surveying the terrain. Eliyahu meets with a licensed civil engineer, addressing new sewage and water line costs that are compliant with local code. During the return drive, Eliyahu asks me to develop a business plan that will market forty lots following the Costa Rica approach. Not a beautiful jungle, the Catskills Mountains have their own appeal.

Eliyahu claims to own property on Sterling Place near the Brooklyn Museum and Grand Army Plaza. He wants me to develop a prospectus for constructing an apartment condominium building on the empty lot. The coffee business isn't succeeding. Refusing Eliyahu's demands on time, explaining that the distractions will inevitably cause the business opportunity to fail, he can, for assistance, turn to John or Chris, our comptroller. He's not swayed from retaliating by halving my remuneration. Choosing to leave: Daniel's solicited advice is to empty the bank account as compensation for creating the company. The friction between Eliyahu and me leaves no alternative but to go.

Gathering personal belongings, carrying a loaded carton to my car, shoved under the windshield, is a flier. It describes Eliyahu's nefarious activities, accusing him of ripping off his own Hasidic community members in Brooklyn to the tune of millions. Was he hoping to raise funds with these new offerings to pay the previous investors, who only recently learned of their mortgage delinquencies? I escape just when his secret is revealed. What a satisfying coincidence! The independence that comes with entrepreneurship ends. Taking five thousand dollars, abandoning the dream of business ownership for the sake of survival, I move on.

Visiting Daniel at his home is pleasant as our friendship grows. He bounces around entrepreneurial ideas, seeking validation, rejecting contrary reasoning. He raises money from private investors to fund the promised company and maintain a lifestyle befitting an accomplished entrepreneur. Unemployed, I'm open to his suggestion,

"You can front prospects, qualify their accreditation as the gateway to learning more about this can't lose opportunity."

Questioning licensure requirements,

"You're only qualifying their accreditation and interest, and not knowing details exempts you from any government statutes. My attorney confirmed this. Private placement of limited shares is available. I've registered the offering with the Securities and Exchange Commission as a REG D. It's limited to qualified investors."

A threshold of personal wealth that can absorb monetary loss while not being subjected to unmanageable harm determines accreditation. The shares available are on a first-come, first-served basis. A discussion with the CEO to learn more can be arranged. If there's mutual interest, the company at its own expense sends a FedEx package with all required documentation,

My remuneration is lucrative but intermittent. It is based on goodwill. I have no knowledge of shares sold, who purchased, or the dollar amount. This fosters dependency I've yet to recognize. I have no mentor and sure could use one. I don't hold onto names by choice, handing over the notes on each individual. Since the Schumer days, I've never removed information from a work setting. The vehicle promising investors high returns is stock ownership. This health insurance telemarketing agency will grow to employ over one hundred agents and reach two thousand policies sold weekly.

Homelife is a struggle. Orly and I do not get along. Arguments occur over the simplest uttered words. Always raising her voice, my reflex is to respond in kind. We're out of control, and it's become a pattern. Leaving Eliyahu behind, we're evicted from our residence of four years. There is no household income. I'm desperate. Need work. No way does compensation reflect the monetary gain Daniel realizes. Daniel's in control. This opportunity is a shortcut to earning more than I could otherwise. All appearances seem legal. Daniel and I spend time smoking dope that he supplies, watching sports, and reviewing how we could improve Cinergy's enrollment rate. Offer accepted.

Dreams of Bernard unexpectedly intruding, I decided to call after years of no contact. Joe answers the phone, but Bernard broke up with him a while back.

"Danny, how come you're calling now after so much time has passed?"

"Joe, I've been dreaming of Bernard and want to speak with him."

"Danny, your brother died six weeks ago from lung cancer. Bernard was cremated. I respected his wishes not to tell his family he was dying. One morning, he woke up coughing blood, at which point it was too late to save him. We spent his last two months together. He left all property and assets to me. There are old family photos if you want them."

Bernard's relationship with me deteriorated when Joe

entered his life years earlier. If I saw him, I wouldn't be able to restrain my anger towards him and the pain I'd feel. I forego the mementos.

Bernard didn't like Orly, and he didn't like me. The slight is not a surprise. I am hurt by him once again. He was always insensitive towards me. He didn't love me. The outreach took place in Daniel's conference room. There was no privacy. Knocking on Daniel's door, crushed by the news, I barely make it to a chair. The loss hurts. I choke back tears. Daniel assures me, "Everything will be okay now that we've found one another."

Days before the sheriff is to enforce the eviction, I find a three-bedroom home to rent in Sunny Isles Beach. The landlady, seeing the cash I'm about to hand over, doesn't bother to invoke a background check. Unaffordable unless Daniel's promises come true, I proceed anyway. Arielle must continue to have a bedroom of her own. Short on funds, Daniel makes up the difference. Instability reinforces Orly's depression. We've been through several housekeepers over the years. Compensation has been erratic. I lament that this expense is costing us the chance to own a home. This festering thought is ready to burst out each time Orly mentions new expenditures that I deem superfluous. She is my excuse for caving in and making compromising decisions that only deepen the malaise. I'm playing the hero. I want to escape this loop repeated daily while taking no responsibility. It's convenient to blame Orly. I'm a phony myself!

Participation in the "raise" is over. Daniel stopped marketing discount plans. Limited health insurance plans are an upgrade. American Medical and Life Insurance out of New York is the underwriter. The call center functions like a well-oiled engine. A top-five agent out of over one hundred, I'm also salaried to teach rebuttals and how to close the sale. Having earned a health, life, and annuity license, I spend eighty hours weekly selling health insurance. These inbound callers are responding to television commercials. The combined income from both efforts ties me to Daniel. I receive a car allowance as compensation for being listed as the on-site State-licensed manager. Hanging out and getting stoned reinforces the relationship. I think of him as the big brother I've been seeking and believe his pronunciations offer financial stability. Thoughts of Bernard sometimes flash before me in Daniel's presence.

AMLI approves a television commercial promising nonexistent health benefits. The inference: limited benefit plans are not so restrictive. New York State sues. For false advertising, AMLI receives a cease and desist, and Cinergy is out of an underwriter. Cinergy is fined hundreds of thousands of dollars. No readily available product in the wings, Daniel places everyone on paid sabbatical. Training and experience are commodities worth retaining in spite of the cost. Obamacare is now the law. Limited medical benefit plans don't meet the federal mandate for catastrophic coverage. Recovering from the loss of our underwriter during the uncertainty of new federal legislation is a challenge we struggle with and never overcome. The paid sabbatical continues for almost one year. The kids are getting a lot of attention.

Restarting, Cinergy offers short-term major medical plans that are an acceptable bridge for coverage, but still not Obamacare. Companion Life Insurance provides limited medical plans. Unsuccessful, Cinergy ceases marketing, and enrollment comes to a standstill. We've achieved fifty-three thousand policies sold and active.

Searching for direction, Daniel launches unsuccessful businesses with funding from private placement. The cookie-cutter approach succeeds since the story always weaves a venture that is dynamic and promising. The formula supports a 1% lifestyle. Those who trust incur loss. The overall success of Cinergy keeps me believing that Daniel's genius will prevail with one of these ventures. I weigh the continuation of employment. I rationalize referencing the Forbes-published article: self-made millionaires endure bankruptcy repeatedly before life experience brings success. Repetition best describes Daniel as a serial actor. Each new undertaking requires fronting to cull accredited investors from the lists purchased.

He turns to me and others. At his office, Daniel schedules all accredited prospects for appointment. The pitch occurs behind closed doors. We don't sit around and plot how to bilk investors. Bouncing back and forth between organization and product concepts, building a plan that will raise capital and be profitable, we enjoy smoking pot during the exercise. Hours pass until we call it a night while zonked on weed. Daniel always has the best stuff. To placate and ease Orly's hostility for all the broken promises, he sends me home with whatever remains.

A new idea comes up. The glamor of fancy-colored diamonds seems an easy sell. Infinity Diamonds, offering GIA-certified stones with accompanying paperwork, will target collectors and new investors. Daniel is convinced that, with the contacts he has in the industry, he'll be able to purchase at wholesale prices, a private buyer can't accquire. Infinity Diamonds, in turn, via telemarketing and the internet, will retail to investors. Daniel believes his experience, knowledge, and genius at working the phone guarantee success. He decides it's essential the company has a certified gemologist on staff. I push for the position. After mulling over alternatives, Daniel decides to sponsor me for training at the Gemology Institute of America.

Mandatory lab attendance at the Manhattan or Carlsbad locations and successful on-site completion of a practicum exam are required. Precious stones requiring identification are received with each lesson. I complete the sections sequentially. Developing skills to identify and map imperfections: grading diamonds, rubies, emeralds, and sapphires with dexterity a problem and an eye loupe unmanageable, my fingers don't respond to the effort. Infinity provides a Nikon microscope. The stones ship from Carlsbad, where a proctor is on call to assist.

I'll be the Infinity Diamond gemologist on staff. No longer a telemarketer, earnings will be a salary and not commission-based. Weekly generosity is no longer in play. Earning a salary while gaining a new trade is a dream come true. What an unpredictable, crazy, winding path life has taken. The joy is fleeting. Receiving the first paycheck, income is again reliant on munificence. It's a personal and not a company check. Promising much, he's unreliable. Barely managing to maintain the status quo week to week, the stress at home between Orly and me is explosive. Turning to hard liquor intoxication, released rage only makes home life more turbulent.

Daniel manages to allay concerns with what ends up always proving to be false assurances. Often on late Friday afternoons, the promised weekly check under his doormat is not there. Shabbat dinner is in jeopardy. I turn to friends who come through.

Convincing myself that in telemarketing I won't find better,

"He's charming and persuasive, but is this dependent programming arising from the past? Reliant on him is this a big brother substitute? I can't break away! I'm in his control."

Trapped between the demands at home and Daniel's promises, I don't see an escape route.

Summoning me to his office and shutting the door, Daniel animatedly waving hands in the air says,

"I'm in desperate need of your help. Would you just this one time confirm, and reference previous success having invested in my companies? You'll pose as a past investor for a prospect who'll contact you and is on the edge of committing. The company cannot begin without this money."

Hangover clouding my judgment, I hesitantly agree. Personal experience demands otherwise, but I'm blinded by dependency and constant financial pressure. Acquiescing, blaming myself to this day for knowingly engaging in deception, I've evolved into the very phony character I disdain.

The cell phone sounds, and the prospect is confirming my name, not allowing me a moment to reconsider. Not volunteering, I'm uncomfortably verifying what's been shared. We review Cinergy's successful history.

Chatty and personally wanting to project credibility, "I didn't earn a profit but recovered the investment."

Unable to alleviate the uneasiness, I inquire repeatedly about her satisfaction, only to hear, "She's been taken care of and is happy."

I managed to stay clean when I was in so many immoral workplaces. Now I'm compromised and scared!

The diamonds are stunning, but the business is not. It's a

difficult sell. Preoccupied with coursework, the goal is to complete the gemologist licensing curriculum post haste. Sitting in a windowless, tiny office that only allows for a desk and small bookcase, I'm poised over the microscope from 9 a.m. to 6 p.m. Monday to Friday. The coursework without classroom guidance is a challenge. The proctor and I speak daily. Eyesight doesn't help matters; the acid used to highlight diamond imperfections is causing ocular rosacea. Irritated red eyelids constantly fog my vision. Work is tedious, trudging through the packets and fighting to identify their contents.

The precious stones under magnification take me to another world where I imagine how the cosmos appears in a microcosm. The depth of the field with no surrounding distractions in the darkness energizes the effort. The images are captivating. It's been a long time since coming, but butterflies are back. Crazy as it seems, I'm going to be a gemologist! Ready to take the final exam after ten months of full-time study, the Carlsbad proctor is praising my intensity and speed in preparing for it.

There's an internet outage in the building. Unable to complete the exam in the allotted time, the proctor, who is present, permits resumption the next day. Completing all the questions, the answers are recorded on worksheets that I need to transpose onto the computer app. Reporting to work, my clicker disabled, I'm told via intercom to wait. Confusion and apprehension take over. Permitted entry, I'm escorted to the unoccupied conference room.

Daniel and two members of senior management enter wearing downcast faces and inform me, "Infinity Diamonds is shutting down the venture as a failure, and your employment is terminated."

I'm in disbelief.

Begging to complete the final exam on the clock, the proctor, upon entering the room, states, "GIA disqualified submission of the exam because copying answers off worksheets is a violation of their policies."

Demeanors adversarial, a nondisclosure form rests on the table, prohibiting future employment in the industry. Daniel offers five thousand dollars in termination pay if I comply. They want my signature. In shock, walking through the storm, I surrender. Previously, researching the starting incomes of gemologists ruled out this career. Sales are what I know, earning the greatest return for the effort. I'm distraught, lost again.

I hold Daniel accountable for not relenting, withholding completion of the final exam, and having the proctor, our employee, call GIA to sabotage the effort. "You're now obligated to take on responsibility for my family's well-being."

Daniel, on due dates, promises to pay the landlady, only to default. He swears, "I've taken care of the landlady."

After four years of occupancy, the police and movers are at the door. We're ordered to leave. Our possessions are piled on the driveway and front lawn, and it begins to rain. We are a household of five with a lifetime of possessions and memories discarded outdoors as if valueless. Standing in the street, desperate, finally connecting, Daniel speaks with the landlady, offering to immediately pay the arrears and more if she'd relent. She refuses, tired of the chronic instability. Daniel's secretary finds movers who arrive within two hours. She arranges a unit at Cube Smart. Our damp possessions go there. Mildew grows. The police won't allow entry under any condition. Items don't join the evacuation. The landlady confiscates what's momentarily forgotten or ruined by rain and left behind. The fiasco, which Daniel's conscience cannot run from, costs thousands of dollars more than if he had just kept his word. He has a love-hate relationship with me. He won't let go. I won't allow it.

We find lodging in a condo-hotel on the beach. The location is no consolation. It's a distance to school. We are emotionally wiped out and unexpectedly homeless. Three teenagers undergoing this event is traumatic. Offspring shouldn't go through this! I feel guilty for letting them down. The one certainty I can offer them is me.

Over the years since leaving Key West, I've been unemployed for lengthy periods, often lasting months. I've had time to be active in the daily lives of the children. Simultaneously attending Little League games a mile apart was a challenge. Weekly ballet sessions were easier to manage, but swim lessons were more difficult. At dawn each morning during the school year, starting in early childhood, I transported them to the attended drop-off point, or if missed, then to school. Being kosher, they had fresh homemade food to start their day. No school buses for them, even during high school. Helping with homework, I tell them that what matters is that they give it their best try. No pressure to achieve goals is applied. My presence anchors the family. Daily, we share the intensity of our lives. We are open and honest with one another. It makes the kids mature quickly. I think of Pop and the love I want the kids to have. Waking each morning in their early years to a session of hugs in our bed was an integral part of this. Uncertainties have me stressing to the kids that our strength as a family comes from functioning as a team, helping one another if it's called for. It's working. The kids maintain focus on both their academics, sports, and social life. They enjoy one another's company. I'm secure telling them to police themselves and not rat on each other. Two brothers and a younger sister are the ideal combination.

Renting a four-bedroom house on my behalf, a pool included, eases Daniels' guilt for manipulating my destiny to his advantage. I'm an asset he won't release, included in his dreams but in practice omitted. Rent is always paid late, and the landlord is haunting us for his due. He withholds repairs, citing past due payment as the reason for retribution.

Daniel keeps me unemployed again, dependent on his handouts, stating, "You're on hold to be part of a new commercial real estate venture."

I'm in bad mental shape. Economic stress and idleness have me catatonic. Vegetating around the house thinking, "Daniel is supporting me to not work for someone else." It never enters my mind to do otherwise. I'm depressed and have no energy. Nightly, I rely on hard liquor to soothe away the anxiety. Orly and I quarrel daily. She hates Daniel and curses at me for my dependency. I'm trapped, held by Orly's demands that I deliver what she holds to be necessities. She blames me for not delivering more. Hysteria rules the day. How ironic when I'm trying to be the hero. The only way out of this is to leave, but I'm afraid to break up the family and be alone.

Ben makes staying easier when he asks me, "Who will take care of Mom if you leave?"

I think, "Who will take care of you?"

Daniel's charm and promises convince me that he is my only salvation. Diamonds forgotten, idle, and depressed for an additional nine months, once again, life takes an unexpected twist.

Wheat Capital is set in motion. After the long sales hiatus, I'm uncomfortable. The company will develop commercial real estate properties, the first strip malls, and later storage facilities. There are two offerings in play. Daniel determines which of the two he'll offer the accredited prospect. We're in a room of five frontiers that receive a draw against commissions. Daniel, the closer, functions with his door shut. The manager has his own office.

There is a compliance officer taping all telephone conversations. Participation in developing a strip mall within two miles of Las Vegas gambling is the pitch. Daniel claims that he is under contract on a property and needs funds to finalize the land purchase.

Traffic is congested on the adjacent roadway. Owning a stake in the commercial strip will see earnings from rentals. Land appreciation is promising. Wheat Capital's intent is to flip the property at the earliest opportunity and distribute profits. The quality of the printed prospectus is Madison Avenue. A commercial real estate developer with a history in the area is on board. The quality is meant to impress; a standard Daniel will not compromise, as it supports the storyline. The excitement of cashing out and walking away with a profit attracts the "mooch." This is a person whose pursuit makes him want to believe in easy money. The Mooch is a repeat player. Find the mooch!

Private placement is also in play. Shares in the parent holding company, Wheat Capital Management, are available. The investor will share cumulative profits from all projects. Two projects have been scheduled. Capturing accredited transfers is slow going. I'm not helping. I'm perplexed. Is it lead quality or ambivalence caused by more broken promises that make me ineffective, bitter, and indifferent? It doesn't take long before I'm let go. Daniel says that he's changing the sales approach, and the crew is no longer employed. We're evicted from our home. We're not having a repeat performance. Seeing it coming, we are able to evacuate and avoid a repeat disaster. Airbnb, thanks to Ben and his credit cards, puts a roof over our heads.

Over the years, when trying to rationalize away our financial problems, I've apologetically told the children, "One day the anomaly of why a learned guy who pushes education is stuck in telemarketing will be explained."

Ben's attending university away from home. His maturity requires an explanation. Visiting for the holiday, we sit together side by side, and only Orly is with us when I open up.

His first words, "How did I fucking not feel it all my life? Dad is an international drug smuggler imprisoned in Israel. HOLY SHIT!"

I elaborate, "My employment possibilities are limited. Because of this, here we are. Life hasn't been easy. This knowledge will help you understand. Keep in mind that if you think with different parents, things might have turned out better; in fact, if that were the case, you wouldn't exist. Parents give their kids the gift of life. Think about it."

The secret off my chest relieves the hypocrisy I feel having not been truthful all these years.

Reaching out to insurance agent colleagues, I'm directed to a telemarketing insurance agency that is offering limited benefit health plans. Availability is a government exception to the Affordable Care

Act mandate requiring plans to cover preventive and comprehensive care without pre-existing condition discrimination.

Giant corporations with substantial numbers of low-salaried personnel lobbied government officials for an exemption. Limited health plans cost less. Again, I'm selling an item that challenges fairness. Federal and state health regulators permit the sale. When needed, the consumer rarely receives coverage that justifies the value of premiums paid. Consumers gain more power from their buck if the premium were squirreled away in a bank account.

The call room employs over sixty agents. The sales volume doesn't come close to what we achieved at Cinergy. ACA-approved plans decrease the number of prospects who find limited plans an acceptable alternative. Competitive pricing is what keeps them attractive. A top-five writer, conversation on the inbound call comes easily when I reference in a funny way the upcoming presidential election. Eliciting laughter, not reading but following the structure of the required script, and quick bonding make the sale easier. I remained compliant and continued with Simple Health for twenty months.

Learning about an agency that works from home and writing ACA-approved insurance coverage draws me to attempt it. Anxious, not believing that I can handle independence, worried thoughts slow me down. It's been so long since doubt arose like this. Selling insurance on a simple computer application, I'm now required to simultaneously navigate several portals. I lack technical savvy. I'm intimidated. Taking on the challenge, I leave limited health insurance plans behind.

Months prior, I reached out to Daniel to offer my condolences when a mutual acquaintance told me his father had passed away.

Now turning to him, "Can you help with mothballed Cinergy Health equipment? I need a computer and two monitors."

Two years passed between contact, and yet he's amenable. Picking up the equipment, it's revealed that the FBI recently raided Wheat Capital Management and confiscated all the computers and files.

Daniel insists, "There is nothing to find. It's all harassment."

He doesn't act like he has a worry in the world. Foolishly, I believe him. I leave with the cache.

Unseemly emotional outbursts continue at home. There is no rhyme or reason that could rationally justify either of us participating. Words intended to comfort Orly are heard as judgmental criticism. I unwittingly feed into a pattern of discourse. Driving Orly to the gym, she insists that I turn on the windshield wipers to clean the windows. I comply.

Asked to do it again, I respond, "It will only smear the dirt."

Screaming that I never listen to her, she shoves me while I'm driving in heavy traffic.

The words that follow are,

"This is an example of how you've destroyed my life. No matter what I ask you to do, you make sure to do the opposite. This just shows me how you are worthless."

The rage just keeps on coming. I feel responsible for not being more selective in choosing my words. I wish the cacophony would stop.

CHAPTER 21.
FINDING CERTAINTY

At home, unable to overcome all the uncertainties, panic attacks when callers are on the other end leave me ineffective. I need the security provided working out of a structured setting. Having people around is settling. Lacking confidence, struggling, I share this with Daniel. He offers me a partnership in a recently licensed telemarketing insurance agency. Cinergy was not an operational failure, generating tens of millions in monthly premiums. Insurance is what he knows best, and he is drawn to it once again. I'll be a ten percent owner. I'm hopeful. I convince Daniel that, in leaving behind a pipeline of sales, the price for joining him is to bring the apartment rent up to date before eviction. If raising children is the number one challenge in marriage, in our home, it's replaced with living within one's means. To avoid dependency, in lieu of a verbal promise, this time the arrangement has to be set down on paper, and a stock certificate handed over. We agree. We're feeling good. Daniel delays the signing of documents for a couple of days. I'm not concerned, and this time I am company-salaried.

There is an unexpected knock on the door. Security doesn't prevent this. It's mid-afternoon and I'm home. Standing there are two gentlemen who hold up FBI photo IDs, asking for me. Acknowledging my presence, they wish to speak. Intimidated, passivity takes over, knees ready to buckle under at any moment. Assured the focus is not on me; questions are centered around Daniel and his investment activities. Cooperation is voluntary; however, if I refuse to participate or request the presence of an attorney, we'll proceed in their office. Rattled, we all sit down at the dinner table.

The thought flashes, "I've been through this before."

It's Deja Vu time. Spread before me is an organization chart showing players they're interested in. One by one, I'm questioned about each one's role and told that cooperation is in my best interest.

I wonder, "If I'm not a target, why is answering in my best interest?"

Offering little, the probing begins to reveal their concerns. Moving on to investors, I'm confronted with a specific name that is not recognized. Learning that this person is a female physician jogs my memory.

Referencing and taking copious notes, questions, and answers about the lady I lied to ensue. Asked, "Have you ever invested in any of Daniel's companies?"

Answering, "No."

I'm confronted with the lie. Pounding me about commissions, "I functioned, bending to Daniel's pressure, and didn't earn any commission."

The interview ends. A broken reed, shaken up, muttering under my breath, "I'm now going to prison."

They thank me for cooperating and for my time. My first thought is, "Why wasn't I prepared for this? No heads up? Irresponsibility, not retaining legal advice, will result in my demise."

Guilt over recalling the deception negates mustering any resistance. Facing this brings cognitive surrender. No fight left; I'm resigned to just rolling with the punches.

The Director of Finance quits. There's no one to issue or sign our weekly paychecks. Daniel is under arrest! He was about to fly off to Israel and spend the Jewish New Year meeting his newborn daughter when he was stopped as a flight risk. Bond denied!

Reaching out to fellow insurance agents, I find employment selling predominantly term life. It's early Monday morning after the Thanksgiving holiday. Ben is with us, taking a respite after a series of undergraduate exams. Recently, I returned to hitting the bottle. Any wonder? Last night was no exception.

In the dead of sleep, a distant sound breaks through the stupor. The metal door is undergoing a pounding with what sounds like a battering ram.

Stumbling in the dark wearing only briefs, the shouting behind the door is telling me, "This is the FBI. Open up!"

It's 5 a.m.. Taken into the hallway by a young agent carrying a sledgehammer, his abrasive words stated, "Face the wall with hands over your head."

Moments later, Ben and Orly are in the same predicament. We're all in sleep mode, wearing undergarments while attempting to focus on what's happening.

Searching the apartment, marijuana is found on the night table, and an agent tells my wife, "We're not here for this."

An arrest warrant is produced, and we're all scared to death. Allowed to dress, cuffed hands behind my back, I'm escorted to their vehicle.

Processing at FBI headquarters, prints and mugshot complete, I'm transported to the federal courthouse. The weight of the authorities when subjected to their edicts smothers any resistance. Breathing is difficult and shallow. Marching through the dimly lit basement corridors, chained to other defendants, gloom envelops us. Walking is clumsy. Shackles removed before I stand facing the Judge, I'm grateful. The court appoints a public defender. I'm charged with conspiracy to commit wire and mail fraud. Judge Bloom grants release on a quarter of a million dollars' bail. Family liability if you don't return, the judge makes clear, will destroy their economic future. That's all the guarantee required.

She declares, "From this moment henceforth, telemarketing is forever forbidden."

She explains that I can continue selling insurance to inbound callers. I'm aware that State law prevents continuance. Family present, the look on their faces contorts in anguish; their pain increases mine. We leave the courtroom together. The next day, the public defender and I meet. Charged with two counts of deception, I only recall one. Did alcohol affect my memory? At a jury trial, contesting the accusations and losing could mean never again enjoying freedom. Most white- collar crime defendants take a plea deal under duress. Sentencing guidelines established by elected officials require the degree of punishment to be commensurate with the monetary loss. In a jury trial, the plaintiff's personal circumstances play a role in the verdict and sentencing. The public defender is pressing me to immediately confess and cooperate with the prosecution. The first defendant to assist receives the most consideration. Jonathan is a codefendant.

Justice in most jurisdictions is not what the system is all about. Hearing the charges, I'm portrayed as an evil, plotting, selfish individual with no conscience for my actions. Charged with a series of activities that I never participated in, the crime falls into the rubric of conspiracy. That's not me! Conspiracy implies scheming behavior. The crime was episodic and not part of a serial activity. Before the doctor, I had never lied to bring about a sale. This is the playing field dictated by the justice system. It's not about fairness, it's about the prosecutor winning. Are sporting events any different? A plea deal is a check on their resume the fate of the convicted be damned.

Daniel, incarcerated, reaches out with a collect telephone call. He's pleading with me not to remove my name from the paperwork filed with the Florida Office of Insurance Regulation. I'm listed on record as the agency manager. Maintaining innocence, saying that the new insurance deal will reopen, he adds that his brother will arrange my legal representation.

Suspicious that hiring an attorney on my behalf might only serve Daniel's best interest, the candidate, in fact, is a pleasant surprise. After our initial meeting, I endorse his hiring. Discovery provides video, voice, and records of all activities undertaken by the companies that Daniel controls. He was under surveillance and set up by an old acquaintance wearing a wire to entrap him, enticing him with a promised list of accredited investors. Daniel's greed got the better of him. An internet search would have shown that this double agent is, in fact, serving a federal sentence while taping him. To compound matters, the other co-defendant turns state's witness upon arrest in return for a reduced sentence. He fabricates stories about me so that his testimony is valuable. Jonathan, who is federally incarcerated, knows the rules of the game. The government is using a repeat offender to get me. This isn't about guilt or innocence, it's about conquest and oppression. We call this justice. An eye for an eye.

No choice, I plead to one count of wire and mail fraud. The

Proffer lists the names of Daniel's companies that I'm accused of representing. Arguing the guilty plea is for one occurrence only, I'm defrauding myself by agreeing to sign. They've referenced companies where activity was marginal.

Going to trial with the intent of explaining how I'm also a victim deserving mercy and leniency; punishment can be the maximum. Those present insist the punishment is for one act.

"Let's get this done instead of starting over."

The record will show that I'm a conspirator, implying a serial offender who schemed and plotted the way.

They impatiently insist, "It's imperative to accept the deal before it changes. Daniel's about to plead guilty, making you his accomplice."

Looking back, the outcome would have been the same if I had retained the public defender.

Standing sworn in once again before Judge Bloom, I have to acknowledge the plea deal. Tears flowing, I'm unable to maintain control of my sad state. In a hoarse voice, I plead guilty.

Stating to the court, "I was raised under fatherless circumstances and underwent psychiatric counseling when much younger."

The judge reduces the guideline-recommended sentence to three years. Her kindness saves six months. I'm sentenced to thirty months and one year of supervised probation. Restitution for three hundred and nineteen thousand dollars is on the tab. Failing a drug test on the day I was arrested, I'm an eligible drug user qualified to participate in RDAP, a drug treatment program. The sentence reduction is six months if completed. With time off for good behavior, incarceration will last twenty months. Orly's birthday is in two days. These are tough days for us.

Once again, we face eviction. We sell or abandon the remaining furniture. We can't afford storage space. Orly's girlfriend has to leave Miami to attend to a family emergency. She needs us to dog sit. We squat at her condo. This buys time to relocate. Homeless, Ben finds and charges Airbnb, where we remain. Arielle takes a sabbatical from the University of Florida and rents a one-bedroom apartment.

She concludes, "Mom should not be left alone while you're in prison."

Without friends' financial help, we can't purchase groceries. The free community shuttle bus to the kosher supermarket is a lifesaver. The Jewish-sponsored food bank is another resource.

The family undergoes punishment far worse than the criminally infected, enduring pain while innocent of any wrongdoing. Orly's unwillingness to forgive the stubborn alliance with Daniel exacerbates the self-deprecation that has overcome me. Lying around useless for months, counting the days before surrender, liquor and pot are always present, but Marvel superheroes on Netflix are the favorite.

It's August 24, 2018. In front of the prison entrance, with Orly and her sister, I'm having a final cigarette before surrendering, a habit that began in Be er Sheva. The prison and camp are smoke-free environments. The authorities enforcing zero tolerance must be looking after our health. The rolled barbed wire along the base and top of the fencing is a formidable reminder of memories to draw on when coping gets rough. Recalling Israeli high-security confinement, this is manageable. The authorities know nothing about events in Israel. Paperwork and security intake complete, the physical exam consists of a stethoscope and blood pressure reading. Questions are asked about my medical history, and I'm dismissed. The medium-security prison where intake is completed is a short walk across the road to the adjacent camp.

Entering the world of RDAP, we are a closed community unto ourselves. Cognitive behavioral therapy deployed prevents recidivism. We learn to weigh our thoughts, actions, and consequences before behavior takes place. Concerned about the family's well-being, it's my responsibility every other day to stay in touch with a member. In my absence, it gives us a modicum of certainty. At the phone bank, finally with a receiver in hand, you hope that someone will answer so as not to lose your turn in the queue. Familiar voices soothe away the remorse brought on by the loss of freedoms.

Speaking with Orly, she updates me on how the kids are managing life in my absence. Switching gears, she says,

"We need to talk. I know you can't wait for us to be together, but things need to change. We can't be together any longer except as friends. Danny, you need to change your behavior. Everything that's no good is because of you. You don't listen to what I say and make all the wrong decisions. We can be the best of friends."

Shocked by the timing and lack of consideration, her words cut sharply. How can my wife be saying this after calling me Salvador for so many years? I'm in fucking prison.

"Orly, just relax. Thanks to RDAP, I've learned about myself and have changed. You'll see when I come home."

It's September 2018. The camp dentist treats my abscessed tooth with Amoxicillin. The alternate option is to extract the tooth. It's the only dental treatment available. Weeks later, the infection returns. I elect to have the tooth removed.

I'm on sick call. I'm urinating four to five times nightly. The amounts aren't significant, but the urgency can't be delayed. Given my age, maybe it's a prostate problem. I'm ignored when requesting lab work to measure PSA, an indicator of prostate disease. Prescribed Doxazosin 2mg by the physician who is a foreign-trained general practitioner; no medical exam takes place. His intervention is based on my suggestion. On separate occasions, I insistently ask for blood work. Request denied. No tests are ever ordered by the Bureau of Prisons.

With swollen legs and ankles, my feet always hurt. This might have nothing to do with my prostate. Charcot-Marie-Tooth, a hereditary muscular dystrophy disease, runs in the family on the maternal side. This was confirmed when DNA testing became available. It explains my struggles in sports since boyhood. Mobility limited; my step is deteriorating daily, bit by bit. My ankles barely support my legs. Each step is a slap on the ground without bounce. Stance shaky, the doctor prescribes form-fitted orthopedic sneakers. They're sized on swollen feet. Still no blood exam, I continue ingesting prostate medicine.

Submitting a BP8 form that seeks administrative action for proper medical care, I wait. No response.

Leg swelling worsens. The painful, repetitive urges to urinate throughout the night won't permit sleep. The medicine is ineffective.

The urine color is brown, and so are the pills. Enquiring about the possibility that the medicine is causing this, another doctor says this is not possible. Still no blood work or urine sample taken. My requests are ignored. I'm told, "We're not obligated to have your blood checked regardless of age."

Prostate treatment continues. I have a loss of appetite. All foods taste awful. Tomorrow there's a mail call at 7 am. I hope to make it.

Looking back, reckoning how this bed became my companion presents the challenge not to be phony.

The process, it turns out, is therapeutic. Taking responsibility for my behavior without blaming my spouse for it is a revelation. We've lived off one another. She is difficult but my decisions and actions are mine to own. Compelled to be the hero, coupled with her need for this in a companion, made it appear a perfect match. Now the anger I've held towards her for years is no longer in play. Understanding brings catharsis.

Forty-three days spent in bed means I've to relearn how to walk.

I'm ordered to only practice small steps with a walker when an attendant is holding the back of the leather belt around my waist. Disobeying, I topple and fly. Lifted off the ground, reaching the bed with assistance, it's good to know the fight is still there.

Three weeks of recovery at Larkin Community Hospital have come to an end. I'll miss the peace and quiet but not the isolation. Snoring is no more. No explanation available. A physician resident asks me if I've had a gum or staph infection. Lab tests found it in my blood. It's caused endocarditis, which blood analysis could have prevented. Was all this for nothing?

At the camp, coping physically is a struggle. With small assisted steps, the walker is a friend. Prisoners are startled to see me. Absent information, they believed the Bureau of Prisons sent me off somewhere to die. The reception brings me to tears. Having bonded with the group, reuniting is uplifting. I missed them. All the prisoners show kindness, acknowledging the shimmy, stepping aside so there's adequate room to slowly move down the paths.

Their shouts, "Hey RAPPER, how ya doin'?" bring me a smile.

On the food line, prisoners permit me to step up front, minimizing my struggle to stand in place and wait for a turn. Resting the food tray on the upper crossbar of the walker, Detroit confronts me from behind. He's new to RDAP.

"What the fuck ya doin cutting the line? What's wrong with you, man?"

I rip my shirt over my head and point to the ten-inch wound running down the center of my chest. The picture speaks for me. The wrong words chosen could escalate things. I manage to reach an unoccupied spot.

Time lost results in a rollback and repetition of the RDAP completed coursework. Deferred graduation is in four months. The date coincides with the completion of the sentence. Incident reports and shots issued for transgressions never happen.

Daniel has arrived at the camp and is in RDAP. He's in the unit, but two therapeutic cycles behind me. Bureau of Prisons rules forbid the placement of co-defendants in the same location. Out of revenge, I could file a complaint that his presence threatens my safety, gambling that I arrived here before him and should be given preference. I chose to remain silent. We share the same pain. His intentions were not to place us here. A quarrel between us would result in sending one of us to an alternate facility far from Miami. That's not going to happen.

Jewish prayer services take place in the chapel every morning. Mondays and Thursdays require the attendance of ten Jewish men, allowing the reading of that week's Torah portion. If in attendance, a Cohen and Levite tribe member is called to the podium. The only Levi available I'm asked to participate. I can't refuse. The service lasts forty minutes.

During Monday morning prayer, an announcement over the loudspeakers states, "RDAP will commence this morning in the chapel instead of the regular location." In prayer, wearing our tallit and tefillin, a stampede of RDAP attendees bursts in. Taking no heed of our presence, out of joint, we hastily complete the service.

Anger overwhelms me. Reasoning goes to hell. Fidgeting in the seat, my face bright red, I'm about to explode. The morning meeting begins, and I demand to speak at the podium. "You people have no respect."

Before I can complete the words, "The chapel at this hour is designated for prayer," the heckling drowns me out.

I'm irate, and not hesitating to confront the crowd. "Christian prayer would not be interrupted in such a disrespectful manner," only incites a louder uproar. No longer heard the minority community wants to get at my throat. Hearing the words "You People" is received as exclusionary, racist incitement.

The words targeted everyone present. It's useless to explain. RDAP teaches us how not to be phony with ourselves, recognizing and examining our self-talk and motivation. Before acting out, we weigh the consequences of our choices. Neglecting to pause and take a moment is a violation of the therapeutic model. I face the music. The program director takes control of the chaos. She orders me to leave the room and return to the dorm. The counselors, following a hearing with me, decide a formal warning is warranted. My sentence is for thirty days. I'm to complete two daily reports in RDAP format and maintain a log describing conflict management. This is in addition to completing the workbook assignments. Another inappropriate event of any kind will result in expulsion, loss of time off for good behavior, and a six-month reduction of the sentence no longer in play. It's time to keep my mouth shut. Only months remain until eligibility for a halfway house assignment. Caring minority members in the unit remind me, "If not for fear of losing camp privilege, this behavior would be physically dealt with. Suster, think before you talk."

Familiarity with me in the community brings acceptance. With a smile and knowing nod, YOU PEOPLE is freely tossed about. Insults and teasing between prisoners are constant. There's a nightly cacophony after the lights are out. A Jewish acquaintance is singled out. It's excessive. The offenders remain anonymous voices shouting in the dark. From behind the shower curtains, it intensifies. Each night in the dark, listening to the derogatory remarks thrown his way, his silence pains me; not responding and accepting victimization, I see him as a brother. This hazing turns my stomach.

Freaking out, I'm in a full voice for all to hear, "No one here has the right to put down this man. He has so far completed ten years in these shit holes without ever ratting out anyone: minding his business, never messing with anyone, sleeping in a corner at the end of the aisle. His group graduated. The teasing belongs with the guys who know him. Whoever is the wise guy, stand up with lights on and be a man. If there's something to say about this guy, say it now."

Walking up and down the dorm, men shout back, "Suster, settle down."

He has three more years to go here. Not pleading- bargaining for five, maintaining his innocence, he was sentenced to fifteen years for a white-collar crime. Murderers serve less time.

Program completed; the assigned halfway house is located about ten miles from our home. Prisoners spend weekends at home if we maintain employment and pay half-way house rent, but must wear the mandatory electronic ankle monitor. Depending on the length of stay, when eligibility requirements are complete, it leads to home confinement, the final stage of incarceration. Once home, returning for random drug testing is mandatory. A landline home phone with no call forwarding feature is a condition for acceptance. It can ring multiple times at any hour, day, or night. GPS confirmation of location is not sufficient. The early a.m. calls serve as a constant reminder that we deserve what we've reaped. Big brother is watching! Home confinement offers comfort, but is still imprisonment. Netflix serves its purpose.

Lights out, I'm drifting off to sleep. The monitor and charger are connected to an extension cord. In the distance, a house phone chirps the check-in confirming my presence. Tripping over wires in the dark, my ankles unsupportive, I land on a stone tile. Instantly, I know there's trouble. Waiting out the impact of the shock, forty minutes later, trying to lift upright but to no avail, I don't wake Orly, knowing she can't help. I dial 911.

EMS transports me to the hospital, where it's confirmed I've fractured my femur. The orthopedic surgeon attaches a bracket. He prescribes Oxycodone. The stay continues for four days. Prior to imprisonment, since the incubator, there's never been an overnight stay in a hospital. Now I'm a regular. Near-death wouldn't have come if not for incarceration. All I needed was blood work to avoid this. Wow! I'm really punished one way or another.

Home confinement reveals that Orly has mentally split from our marriage. When telephoning from the camp, her suggestion, "We can only be friends," indicated that Salvador for thirty years is now persona non grata.

Each incident, emotionally charged, leads to me asking,

"Orly, what happened to Salvador? From admiration to disdain, it's okay that you don't love me anymore, but you're constantly yelling at me."

"Danny, you never listened to me, and that's how you destroyed my life."

The words are now her mantra. How ironic that after being the White Knight, any good that transpired is devalued, negated, or forgotten. The tall glass of freshly squeezed grapefruit juice that waited for her every morning is now readily dismissed. I'm a stranger. I'm looking forward to life's next chapter. Mentally, I've never been in a better place. The near-death experience and subsequent hospital stay gave me the opportunity to reflect on who I am and how I got here. Self-awareness is our best friend. I'm returning to the Danny I once was. If my hands allow it, I plan to once again paint with oils. I'm certain!

COVID-19 is the new reality. In quarantine, home

confinement rules tighten up. I'm no longer allowed to take medically advised, daily thirty-minute strolls, nor walk the apartment building hallway to the patio pool area. Writing is a pastime, a venture, and therapeutic. This story could be anyone's. Sharing it might help others. Home confinement is complete, and quarantine continues with no end in sight. Probation ends in eighty days.

Leon dies from COVID-19 complications after testing positive. Missing him, I cry when his image appears. He always loved me. Death is inevitable, but now the dying are all alone. The nursing home where he resided wouldn't allow me to visit him. What a sad time.

Arielle graduated from the University of Florida, and the boys graduated from the University of Central Florida. All three offspring are higher-ed graduates. Orly and I never suggested a career direction or applied pressure to perform.

Smothered with love from both parents since birth, all three have made it a point to domicile within a minute's distance of us. We have Shabbat dinner regularly. Completing the blessings over Orly's handmade challah and kiddush wine, her cooking is always the best. Having almost lost me, they're sticking close.

Their eyes and smiles radiate even when they witness their parents' discourse. Scars are not evident, yet growing up in our home was a challenge. The lack of phoniness makes coping necessary. I often say to Ben, "You kids are our creation, and raising you is how I channeled my creativity."

Everywhere life has taken me, I've faced phonies. My early instincts were correct. Channeling creativity by raising a wonderful family is fulfilling, but I should've stayed true to myself. Painting pictures far away from the phonies offered certainty. None of this would have transpired, but without the kids, I would be very lonely. They've given me purpose and the certainty love requires. The two are inseparable. When certainty was absent, the resulting anxiety led to bad decisions. It's always been like that. Happiness, it turns out, is all about having kids who are good people. Familial love will decide to what degree it's achieved.

EPILOGUE

The Thanksgiving RDAP talent show is announced, and prizes are available. It's early Sunday morning. I have no visitors planned, so I started to compose. With rehearsals complete and percussion accompaniment, I'm good to go. Microphone in hand, drums behind me, the crowd's cacophony pulsates the air. After each stanza, the accompanying audience shouts: MISTER SUSTER, MISTER SUSTER. I look at the program director, who is standing alone behind everyone, and smile.

Being in RDAP means joining a brotherhood.

It will wrap itself around you, and you'll feel its motherhood.

At first, the unknown will cause you to fear.

But after a while, it will become clear.

Joining RDAP is taking responsibility.

Now I approach this with objectivity.

That it is available to me, I feel gratitude.

Up until now, I've had an attitude.

I thought I knew it all.

This made me feel very tall.

Then I experienced a great fall.

Now, what comes into play is humility.

As I come to realize my past stupidity.

I go and telephone my son.

He says we need to talk, and this won't be fun.

Dad, the family has been talking as a team.

Don't forget for a moment that it's your dream.

Dad, Mom has always been an excuse,

As she sat home every day, a recluse.

Since you've left, she's put it together

Is handling life as smoothly as a feather.

Dad, you can't come home and be as before.

Stubborn as a mule and a know-it-all.

That will lead you and Mom to a fall.

Dad, you must learn open-mindedness.

Accept other opinions, and we'll follow as your minions.

The key for you, Dad, is humility!

Achieve this, and coming home will be serendipity.

I ask myself, do I have the willingness?

Or will I continue like before to pursue resistance?

It's all a matter of reviewing my thoughts.

As I learn to reprogram much of what I've been taught

As we dream and think of our families

This incarceration doesn't have to be a tragedy

If I just learn how to truly care.

I can get through this with a flair.

My advice to all of you is just don't despair.

Being in RDAP means joining a brotherhood.

It will wrap itself around you and feel like motherhood.

www.ingramcontent.com/pod-product-compliance
Lightning Source LLC
Chambersburg PA
CBHW051134120626
46547CB00012B/798